SEVEN MASTERS:
THEIR PAST LIVES AND KEYS
TO OUR FUTURE

Lords
of the
Seven
Rays

Mark L. Prophet
Elizabeth Clare Prophet

SUMMIT UNIVERSITY ❧ PRESS®

Gardiner, Montana

To the students
of the Lords of the
Seven Rays worldwide
I dedicate this tome
of wisdom with all the
love of the Holy Spirit.

THE MAHA CHOHAN

LORDS OF THE SEVEN RAYS
Seven Masters: Their Past Lives and Keys to Our Future
by Mark L. Prophet and Elizabeth Clare Prophet
Copyright © 1986 The Summit Lighthouse, Inc.
All rights reserved

For information, contact Summit University Press,
63 Summit Way, Gardiner, MT 59030 USA
Tel: 1-800-245-5445 or 406-848-9550
info@SummitUniversityPress.com
www.SummitUniversityPress.com

Library of Congress Control Number: 86-63284
ISBN: 978-0-916766-75-7
ISBN: 978-1-60988-300-3 (eBook)

Cover: Keeper of the Flame (Nicholas Roerich's *Lumen Coeli*)
For information on the magnificent art of Nicholas Roerich, write to
Nicholas Roerich Museum, 319 W. 107th St., New York, NY 10025.

SUMMIT UNIVERSITY ❦ PRESS®

Summit University Press, ❦, Keepers of the Flame, *Pearls of Wisdom*,
The Summit Lighthouse, and Summit University are trademarks registered
in the U.S. Patent and Trademark Office and in other countries.
All rights to their use are reserved.

23   22   21   20   7   8   9   10

Contents

BOOK ONE

MIRROR OF CONSCIOUSNESS

Lords of the
Seven Rays:
Past Lives and
Performances

*The whirling of the mind
must be stilled.*

*The thoughts that arrange
the molecules of the
mirror of consciousness
need the calmness
of a still pool—*

*that we may be able
to see clearly.*

*F*or centuries mankind have had dangled before them the baubles and trinkets of life. Swinging before our gaze, their hypnotic effect has confused and diffused our sense of direction so that the meaning of Love is lost in the strange phantasmagoria of the world whirl.

Let us, then, still our minds, the mirror in which God is reflected.

Though we had never seen before—if this were our first day on earth and we had come in with the full-blown consciousness of our present moment—in order to see the face of God, we would still require a clear mirror. For it is we, the individual, who must perceive God.

It is not enough that his Spirit is omnipresent in the world. He is everywhere. But we do not necessarily perceive him in the wind that blows nor in the temperature changes that affect the weather. Nor do we see God in the faces of those whom we meet, for our attention goes to the outer appearance, the overlay of error that requires transmutation.

> *Come,*
> *let us still the mind*
> *for a more perfect vision.*

INTRODUCTION

On the Mystery of Christ's Universal Body

There are many hearts hungering and thirsting after righteousness. And it is the will of Christ that they should be filled. Who will fill them? Where are the shepherds who will feed the sheep?—shepherds who see themselves as the LORD's instruments, through whom he will answer the soul longings of his children.

Yes, the command "Feed my sheep" tells us that God expects us to do that which he, by the divine Law and the divine Will, has reserved for his servant-Sons and their disciples.

"Feed my sheep." The very words and the imploring of the Master tell us we are needed by the LORD above to care for his own here below. Because we are so loved, we are sparked with the desire to serve as mediators of the Word, to be positioned in an orderly hierarchy of offices ordained for the performance of specific duties and responsibilities within the Body of God that are vital to the Holy Spirit's intercession.

Listen, now, to the apostle Paul as he recounts Jesus' teaching to him on the mystery of Christ's Universal Body:

For as the body is one and hath many members and all the members of that one body, being many, are one body: so also is Christ.

For by one Spirit are we all baptized into one body, whether we be Jews or Gentiles, whether we be bond or free, and have been all made to drink into one Spirit....

And whether one member suffer, all the members suffer with it; or one member be honoured, all the members rejoice with it.

Now ye are the Body of Christ, and members in particular.

And God hath set some in the church, first apostles, secondarily prophets, thirdly teachers, after that miracles, then gifts of healings, helps, governments, diversities of tongues.

Are all apostles? are all prophets? are all teachers? are all workers of miracles?

Have all the gifts of healing? do all speak with tongues? do all interpret?

But covet earnestly the best gifts: and yet shew I unto you a more excellent way.

And that "more excellent way" is Charity—the Self-givingness of Love itself. Therefore in Charity's flame we see the disciples as intermediaries between Christ and the sweet children of the Light who hunger and thirst after righteousness and must be filled day by day by the co-workers and co-servants of the Brotherhood.

And Charity herself, the beloved complement of

Archangel Chamuel, is the heavenly handmaid of our labor of Love. Through her compassionate, all-knowing eyes we perceive that as man hungers for his daily bread, so his soul thirsts for the one thing that can quench his thirst: the spiritual graces that are here and everywhere reflected in and beyond the world order.

We see them hiding in the sunbeams and just behind the rainbow in the sky. In the play of light and shadow in the clouds. In the dancing of wind and wave upon the sea and in the rolling of the waters undulating with the earth currents. Through the golden wheat and the blue-green grasses, as they bow to the dominion of the hierarchs of the elements.

We also glimpse the spiritual graces through the alternate manifestations of sickness and health and the ups and downs of the economy that so affect our world— and sadly. For here, man—by reason of his artificiality, his fickleness, his shams and hypocrisies (all masks of his pseudo-self)—has created the illusions of life that make him think that God plays hide-and-seek with him. And we ourselves have set up the obstacles to the crystal mirror and the clear seeing of the Divine Image all around us.

"For now we see through a glass darkly..."

Let us invoke the Dispeller of Obstacles! Let us seek and find the true Teacher of our path and our spirit's calling!

For we would see him face to face. We would know him even as we are known of him.

Lords of the Seven Rays
and the Great Lord
Hierarchs of the Spirit

The manifestations of God in Nature are woven in and through the Spirit-Matter cosmos by the Holy Spirit, whose Sons—known as the Lords of the Seven Rays and the Great Lord,* their hierarch—tutor our souls for receptivity midst the all-pervasive spiritual graces. To these servant-Sons in heaven, graduates of earth's schoolroom, Jesus introduced us many years ago.

The Master pointed to this teaching on Christ's Universal Body which he gave to Paul to explain to us that in heaven the same Body which we all share with light-bearers† on earth consists of angels and masterful beings, great spirits akin to our own, ensouling and directing the cosmic forces, all of whom 'embody'[1] some special office and function of the universal activity of the Mind of God.

---

*called in the East the Seven "Chohans" and the "Maha Chohan," which translates Seven Lords and Great Lord

†Lightbearer: The word means Christbearer, one who bears the light which is Christ, one who bears the responsibility for Christhood in himself and others by defending the Truth and Honor of God; one who is anointed with the Christ consciousness and bears this enlightenment to all. The light-bearer is the Keeper of the Flame whose motto must be "I AM my brother's keeper—I AM the keeper of the light who is Christ in my brother."

The Lord showed us his emissaries who teach the godly on earth the path of individual Christhood on the seven rays and the seven chakras (spiritual centers in the body of man)—each ray being a light-emanation of the Universal Christ concentrating particular gifts and graces and principles of self-awareness in the Logos that can be developed by the disciple through his life's calling.

He explained with perfect logic that the work of the Great White Brotherhood and all heavenly hosts associated with it, including those whom they sponsor on earth, was and is to nurture the nascent divinity of every child of God while teaching him self-discipline and love for his sacred labor, which love kindles the soul to be in love with her Lord and to desire to glorify the full complement of his light (Christ consciousness) in all her members.

He showed us that in this cycle of our cosmic history, earth's evolutions transiting from the Piscean to the Aquarian ages are scheduled to balance the three-fold flame of the heart and to expand the attributes of the Trinity—Power, Wisdom and Love—through each of the seven rays as these rays are consciously focused in the seven chakras.

This work of the soul—and it is indeed *our* work, even as we are His handiwork—is the preparation that is necessary prior to receiving the very special spiritual and physical assignment with one's twin flame—a mission drawn from the higher spheres of their divine plan (causal bodies) which must be fulfilled ere they are allowed to graduate (i.e., ascend) from earth's schoolroom.

Yes, we can learn, and we would do well to take the opportunity, from the Lords of the Seven Rays, our mentors of the Spirit who lead us on the paths of righteousness for His name's sake—I AM THAT I AM—toward our soul's receptivity to the gifts of the Holy Spirit.

In divine order, they are:

I. El Morya, Chief of the Darjeeling Council of the Great White Brotherhood, statesman, poet, economist and saint, founder of The Summit Lighthouse and beloved Guru of the Messengers and chelas: *"Not my will but thine be done!"*

II. Lord Lanto, sponsor of the Royal Teton Retreat and Council overseeing all systems of education and institutions of higher learning, exponent of the ancient wisdom made practical for the Western mind, facilitator of the new age path to Eastern traditionalists: *"Wisdom is the principal thing; therefore get wisdom and with all thy getting, get understanding!"*

III. Paul the Venetian, divine artist conferring by the excellence of works the image of Christ unique to every soul, preparing lifestreams by Love's disciplines for the initiations of the Sacred Heart and the Tree of Life: *"Learn to love to do well and you shall!"*

IV. Serapis Bey, hierarch of Luxor, initiator of the ascending ones in the applications of the sacred fire, architect of holy orders, the inner life, and golden-age cities, military disciplinarian of the forces of Light, Peace, and Cosmic Freedom:

"I AM the Guard!"

V. Hilarion, teacher of immortal Truth, Divine Science, all physical and metaphysical branches of science and the healing arts; the eternal empiricist who brings the seeker to the initiatic path of the apostle Paul:

"And ye shall know the Truth, and the Truth shall make you free!"

VI. Lady Master Nada, the soul's advocate before the bar of divine justice, unifier of families and twin flames, qualifier of Love as ministration and service to every part of Life—a path of deeds prerequisite to self-mastery on the Ruby Ray:

"The servant is not greater than his Lord."

VII. Saint Germain, sponsor of the United States of America, Lord of the Seventh Ray and Age, alchemist of the sacred fire who comes bearing the gift of the violet flame of freedom for world transmutation:

"The light of God never fails, and the Beloved Mighty I AM Presence is that light!"

On September 23, 1962, a most unusual event took place which was recounted by Lord Lanto in his dictation delivered that day in Washington, D.C. These Lords of the Seven Rays led by Archangel Michael materialized tangibly and walked in physical forms upon the hillsides of Mount Shasta in northern California. At sunrise their figures could be perceived and the print of their feet upon the mountaintop would have been

LORDS OF THE SEVEN RAYS

RAY	MASTER	RETREAT	GIFT
I	El Morya	Darjeeling, India	Faith in God's Will Word of Wisdom
II	Lord Lanto	Grand Teton, Wyoming	Word of Wisdom Word of Knowledge
III	Paul the Venetian	Southern France Temple of the Sun, New York	Discerning of Spirits
IV	Serapis Bey	Luxor, Egypt	Working of Miracles
V	Hilarion	Crete, Greece	Healing
VI	Nada	Saudi Arabia	Diverse Kinds of Tongues Interpretation of Tongues
VII	Saint Germain	Transylvania, Romania Table Mountain, Wyoming	Prophecy Working of Miracles
IX All Rays Law of the One	Maha Chohan	Ceylon (Sri Lanka)	Free Will, Threefold Flame Initiation of the Chakras All Power in Heaven and in Earth

To facilitate the student's progressive perception of the rays, the Chohans, their retreats, and their initiatic path in the acquiring and mastery of the gifts of the Holy Spirit, we offer this chart for easy reference.

visible to anyone there to see it.

Addressing the group of chelas gathered in the nation's capital, Lanto said, "Beloved ones, this is a most precious and gracious occurrence of Light—a manifestation of Hierarchy's concern for the peril of the times and the need for the immediate intercession by those of us who are of the octaves of light. Therefore, this beauteous and wonderful materialization took place and the Lords of the Seven Rays gave their benediction to the world from the heights of Shasta."

Tutoring the souls of humanity in the internalization of the Word and the Work of the LORD on each of the seven rays, these Ascended Masters are selected to hold their offices in the spiritual hierarchy of the planet by the "Great Lord" (in the East he is called the "Maha Chohan"), whose official title is Representative of the Holy Spirit. Also involved in the selection proceedings are the World Teachers Jesus Christ and Kuthumi, Lord Maitreya, representative of the Cosmic Christ, and the eight-member Karmic Board. And the Lord of the World, Gautama Buddha, seals their appointments with the blessing of the Seven Holy Kumaras, who ensoul the seven rays of the seven spheres.

Each of the Seven Lords teaches the balance of the threefold flame, the harmony of the four lower bodies and the transmutation of personal and planetary karma through the qualities of his ray. Their function includes meeting the needs of humanity's ascent to God by means of the rainbow rays, which culminate in the white light and the Law of the One.

Thus, through these Seven "Chohans" and the entire Spirit of the Great White Brotherhood we find fulfilled the prophecy of the LORD through his scribe Mary Baker Eddy: "Divine Love always has met and always will meet every human need." Truly the heavenly hosts are the hands of God in action gaining Victory for human life every day.

For the seeker following in the footsteps of these representatives of Christ Truth, each step of self-mastery secured on one ray is gain on the other six rays, for the shaft of white light in the center of each ray is the uni-fier of them all. This shaft *is* the Law of the One in manifestation, even as the white-fire core of the seven flames and seven spheres corresponding to the seven rays is also their sun center—the unifying Holy Spirit of these light-emanations of Cosmos itself.

The Lord of the Ray is therefore one who embodies the consciousness of the LORD—the I AM THAT I AM—who is the Lawgiver of the ray. The Word and Work of the Chohan, i.e., his 'Path', are the expressions of the authority he holds in the interpretation of the Law of the ray.

Thus we know this 'YAHWEH' of the ray, this indi-vidualization of the God flame, by his outpicturing of the ray in the outplaying of events. And when we ask the beloved Chohan, "Who art thou? What is thy name?" the answer comes back—"I WILL BE WHO I WILL BE: Know the LORD, and you will know me as I AM one in Him in the stream of history and in the cosmic cycles: WHAT I HAVE SPOKEN, I HAVE SPOKEN. I Will Be Who I Will Be."

The Lord of the Ray is also the authority of the path of Christic initiation leading the children of the light who are joint-heirs with Christ to their full Sonship through the incarnation of God's Word "on" (in the frequency of) the ray. In this role the Chohan bears the veneration "Guru" to the chelas advancing on his Path. He is fully the Dispeller of Darkness on behalf of his chelas by his light-incarnation of the ray. Always he is the glorifier of the Divine Mother and the Trinity through the ray, even as he is the God flame of the ray personified in his service as Judge and Advocate before, and on behalf of, the people.

Truly, the authority of the Lord of the Ray vested in his mantle derives from his attainment of the Cosmic Christ consciousness in the light frequency of his ray of service *and* from the grace of God who is "a rewarder of them that diligently seek him."

As the Representative of the Holy Spirit, the Maha Chohan embodies the white light of all the rays and teaches the sevenfold balance of the rays of the Seven Mighty Elohim, which in turn manifest upon the brow of the initiate as a crown of crystal light when that God-mastery of the seven rays is reached.

The Maha Chohan is a very present help to all who call to him. Because of his pledge to all mankind "I am keeping the flame for you until you are able," this truly

Great Lord is called the Keeper of the Flame. He is the endower of Christ-mastery through the disciplines of right choice and right action—patterned after the eight-fold path of Lord Gautama Buddha, which parallels the path taught and demonstrated by Jesus Christ.

These disciplines are accomplished through the mastery of free will, of the desires and the desire body, and of the path of the Sacred Heart and the Ruby Ray as the initiate balances the threefold flame and attains equilibrium in the white light of the seven rays in his chakras. Engaging in service to Community—the world body of lightbearers—by the engagement of one's forces, body, mind and soul, is the means to accomplish this goal.

Finally, the Maha Chohan prepares the Christed one for the empowerment by the LORD, the Mighty I AM Presence, of "the all power in heaven and in earth." Conferred through Maitreya, this initiation was acclaimed by our Lord and Saviour when he gave the great commission to his disciples:

> All power is given unto me in heaven and in earth.
>
> Go ye therefore, and teach all nations, baptizing them in the name of the Father, and of the Son, and of the Holy Ghost:
>
> Teaching them to observe all things whatsoever I have commanded you: and, lo, I AM with you alway, even unto the end of the world.

Truly, the key to Christhood through loving obedience to Father and Son is fulfilled in the disciple's acceptance of Jesus' calling to be a mediator of the Word and Work of the LORD. Mirroring His consciousness that all might see His reflected image, the disciple is readying himself to receive the chakra initiations of the Holy Spirit given by the hand of the Maha Chohan through the Seven Chohans according to the degrees of the seven rays.

These initiations are the measured steps and stages of the soul's preparation to receive and put on the graces of the nine gifts—first as a bridal veil, her pure conception of the quality, virtue, and vibration of each gift, and then as the wedding garment, the full awareness and infilling of the flame of the gift and its application in her ministrations to life.

The Seven Chohans acquaint her with the powers, principalities and angelic hosts of the nine gifts of the Holy Spirit as she diligently applies herself to the putting on of the graces, even as each gift bestowed is beautified by her special qualification of the rays.

While this training is taking place, the Maha Chohan strengthens the fibers of the spirit in his role as counselor, comforter and enlightener, laying firm foundations for the rainbow spheres to descend in concentric rings of light, coalescing the aura of the causal body around the central sun of the heart chakra here below, as Above. Tenderly the Great Lord shows each bride of Christ how to fill in the rough places and make them plain for the mirroring of the Holy Spirit's healing presence to all life.

And for those who have the understanding of the Inner Light (to use a Quaker term), we will say that the bestowal of the nine gifts is, by definition, the transfer of the initial matrix of *the power of the three-times-three* which the disciple must learn to wield, enhancing it through the balanced threefold flame and the Science of the Spoken Word.

As Paul would not have his converts to Christ ignorant of the spiritual gifts *(pneumatika)* conferred by the Holy Ghost, so we would not have you who would study the Lost Teachings of Jesus that are being brought to the fore by all the Ascended Masters remain in ignorance of the law involving the conveyance of spiritual gifts. Listen again to the Christ-anointed apostle:

> Now concerning spiritual gifts, brethren, I would not have you ignorant.
>
> Ye know that ye were Gentiles [aliens to the Spirit of Christ], carried away unto these dumb idols [Nephilim gods and their mechanization (robotic) man[2]], even as ye were led.
>
> Wherefore I give you to understand that no man speaking by the Spirit of God calleth Jesus accursed: and that no man can say that Jesus is the Lord, but by the Holy Ghost.
>
> Now there are diversities of gifts, but the same Spirit. And there are differences of administrations, but the same Lord. And there are

diversities of operations, but it is the same God which worketh all in all.

But the manifestation of the Spirit is given to every man to profit withal.

For to one is given by the Spirit the *word of wisdom*; to another the *word of knowledge* by the same Spirit; to another *faith* by the same Spirit; to another the gifts of *healing* by the same Spirit.

To another the *working of miracles*; to another *prophecy*; to another *discerning of spirits*; to another *divers kinds of tongues*; to another the *interpretation of tongues*:

But all these worketh that one and the selfsame Spirit, dividing to every man severally as he will.

And so, we come to the Chohans, who are also mirrors reflecting to us from the ascended state, as well as from their past lives, the image of Christ made clear through their accomplishments on each of the seven rays, or paths, to God. For theirs are the gifts of the Holy Spirit. Heart to heart we would learn of them and their transfer of the spiritual graces by which our souls should also be adorned. For the Beloved said: "My grace is sufficient for thee…"

Let us embark, then, upon a journey of discovery through the causal bodies of the Seven Chohans. As our vessel ventures forth upon the stream of their consciousness, we will pull the charts of their missions, examining their karmic circumstance in the recurrent cycles where they have been the lights of history.

We will enter into vignettes of their lives taken from forgotten ages on legendary continents and civilizations buried in the sands of time or beneath the seas. For we would understand the making of a Chohan, why they were chosen to administer the gifts and graces of the LORD's Spirit, and learn of them the path of our soul's preparation to be the bride of Christ.

From this introduction to the heart and spirit of the Noble Seven we move on to an inner knowing and love of the best of Friends earth's experience has allowed us.

Eastward ho! The Mahatma of the Himavat awaits.

1

EL MORYA
the Statesman

Gifts of Faith in God's Will and the Word of Wisdom

Morya has served in numerous embodiments as a ruler of men, monarchs and nations, becoming thereby an expert in economics and the affairs of state, in the psychology of power in the human psyche, hence in its outworking in the politics of personal and international relations.

Through the initiations of his individual path of Christhood, this beloved Master of the Himalayas has acquired a quintessential devotion to the will of God—a virtue for which he is supremely adored and trusted by his chelas and for which he was twice canonized by the Roman Church. All of this and more has qualified him preeminently to hold the office of Lord of the First Ray.

Come! Let us trace the image of this soul in his life as Akbar, greatest of the Mogul[1] emperors. This will

The Emperor Akbar, Bichitr, c. 1630

provide us with a study in the correct use and mastery of the blue ray of power as it was focused through the blueprint of his life.

Akbar established an empire that spanned a large part of India, Afghanistan, and modern Pakistan and made him the richest and most powerful monarch on earth. Born in 1542 in Sind, he ruled wisely for fifty years, exercising a tolerance and an enlightenment astounding in one descended from the line of Tamerlane and Genghis Khan. (But then we already know that more than human genes make up our true self—indeed more than human genes could ever convey.) Distinctly apart from his ancestors, Akbar has been described by a leading historian as "one of the few successful examples of Plato's philosopher-king."[2]

A Portuguese priest described him as being of "a stature and of a type of countenance well-fitted to his royal dignity so that one could easily recognise even at the first glance, that he is the King.... His forehead is broad and open, his eyes so bright and flashing that they seem like a sea shimmering in the sunlight.... His expression is tranquil, serene and open, full also of dignity, and when he is angry, of awful majesty."[3] He was of middle height, powerfully built, having a love for sports and much bravery and prowess in the hunt.

Despite his great wealth, power, and the pomp and splendour in which he lived, he was a man of simple habits, eating little and forgoing meat at least six months out of the year. He did not even like it, saying he found meat dishes tasteless. The only reason he did not give it up entirely, he said, was because "many others might willingly forgo it likewise and be thus cast into despondency."[4] However, he did go as far as forbidding the slaughter of animals in his realm for six months out of the year.

Akbar's genius was apparent in military, religious, and social affairs as well as in his ability to rule once he had established his empire—a quality lacking in his forebears. Instead of crushing the conquered Hindus, he brought them into positions of government; he even took Hindu princesses as wives. He abolished the practice of enslaving prisoners of war and of prejudicial acts against Hindus and set up an efficient and fair system of administration, tax collection, and justice.

This friend of the common people bade them come to him as a father with their grievances. "He was pleased to accept their presents, taking them into his hands and holding them to his breast (which he never did with the rich gifts brought to him by his nobles)," an observer wrote.[5]

All of this Akbar did because he believed he was the divinely appointed ruler of all the peoples of his realm and that he must deal with them equitably, regardless of their religion or race. Thus he is known as the father of religious tolerance in India and his legacy persists to this day.

However, to bring to his people peace and prosperity was not enough: Akbar would bring them to a higher spirituality. According to court historian Abul Fazl, Akbar's entire life was a search after the Truth. He looked upon the performance of his duties as an act of divine worship.[6]

The Mogul ruler was tolerant of all religions, for he saw the insufficiencies of Islam. Thus, Portuguese priests who came to convert him to Christianity were well received. After discoursing with them for hours, he commissioned a Persian translation of the Gospels. He showed reverence toward the images of Jesus, his Mother and the holy twelve, and when he was presented with the sacred Scriptures, he placed them upon his head as a sign of respect.

But it was never his to fully embrace Christianity, for Akbar could not reconcile himself to the doctrine of the divinity of Christ apart from the divinity inherent in every son of the Solar Flame. What's more, the idea that Jesus was born of a virgin thus excluding the instrumental role of earthly father/mother (through whom even the Hebrews believed the divine nature of offspring was conveyed) or that this son of man was the only son in whom the Word had or would ever incarnate was impossible for him to accept—given the exclusivity in which Jesus' life and mission was presented to him. But he did see Christ Truth behind Christianity. As a matter of fact, Akbar saw God in all religions and wanted the best of God, hence the best of religion for his people.

Once there was brought to him from Mecca a stone upon which there was said to be an impression of Mohammed's foot. "His Majesty went out four kos [about 8 miles] to receive this stone with every mark of honour. An order was passed that all the Amirs in turn should carry it on their backs a few steps. So each one carried it a little way and brought it into the city."[7]

But Akbar saw that it was impossible to rule the country well while adhering strictly to Moslem principles. For example, an orthodox interpretation of the Koran required Mohammedan supremacy over unbelievers, but Akbar saw that tolerance was the need of the hour—the basis of brotherly love essential to society's cohesion.

After deep meditation upon the will of God, he decided to unify the country's religious life. Accordingly, he took upon himself a seven-year study of the world's religions, meditating "on the various aspects of their teachings, customs, and ceremonies, and their effect on the life and thought of their respective followers,"[8] whereupon he concluded that all of them contained limitations, prejudice, and superstition.

His solution was to call a council of the learned of all faiths to establish a universal religion for which he sought to gain their support. He began by pointing out that the Hindus, Moslems, Zoroastrians, Jews and Christians are all different, and all think their religion best, and that if an infidel will not be converted, they declare him their enemy. After addressing the shortcomings of each belief system, the wise one proposed that *they* should decide which was the best religion.

Predictably, each pundit in turn pointed out the flaws in all sects save his own. In their pride of person each "attacked and endeavoured to refute the statements of their antagonists,"[9] losing sight, in their blind spots, on the universal theme of adoration of the pure Person of the Godhead.

At the end of this debate, Akbar stood up and said that since it had now become obvious that there were flaws in every religion, "we ought, therefore, to bring them all into one, but in such fashion that they should be both 'one' and 'all,' with the great advantage of not losing what is good in any one religion, while gaining

Akbar Presiding over Discussions in the Ibadatkhana,
Nar Singh, c. 1604

Questing the truth in all religions, embodying a true spirit of
ecumenism, Akbar caused to be erected at the side of his great
palace at Fatehpur Sikri a building called the Ibadat Khana, meaning "house of worship." He decreed that on Thursday nights, "all
orders and sects of mankind, those who searched after spiritual and
physical truth and those of the common public who sought for an
awakening, and the inquirers of every sect, should assemble in the
precincts of the holy edifice and bring forward their spiritual experiences, and their degrees of knowledge of the Truth in various and
contradictory forms in the bridal chamber of manifestation."

Here is depicted a scene in which Father Acquaviva, a Jesuit
missionary, argues with Mohammedan exponents over whether
the Bible or the Koran constitutes the true word of God.

whatever is better in another. In that way, honour would be rendered to God, peace would be given to the people, and security to the empire."[10]

Whereas they could not agree, Akbar presented his synthesis of Truth:

He called his new religion *Din-i-Ilahi*, "divine faith," or *Tauhid-i-Ilahi*, "divine monotheism." In assembling the tenets, Akbar had "seized upon whatever was good in any religion," comments Abul Fazl. "He is truly a man who makes Justice his leader in the path of inquiry, and who culls from every sect whatever Reason approves of. Perchance in this way that lock whose key has been lost may be opened."[11]

But as for his doctrine-bound subjects, Akbar's innovation placed his person too close to the divinity—too close for comfort. Members of Din-i-Ilahi would greet one another with the words *"Allāhu Akbar,"* meaning "God is great," and the reply was *"Jalla Jalāluhu,"* meaning "resplendent is his splendor." But *Allāhu Akbar* could also mean "Akbar is God," and the response would then apply to Akbar himself. This was insupportable!

He had opened the door for his people and bidden them enter, but they would not.

It was not the emperor's way to force adherence to his new religion, consequently few joined it. Opposed from many quarters, most forcibly by his Moslem brothers, Akbar found himself at the center of a circle of devotees at court who accepted him as their spiritual as well as political guru. Although the nation basked in the glory of his reign, after his passing the empire declined. The light of Akbar was no longer the light of India, for neither his sons nor his followers nor his people had captured the spark of God's will that burned in the heart of their leader.

What is this will of God that in the presence of this high initiate of the Order of Sirius becomes the backbone of any civilization he enters? What is the mystery of this Order and the all-consuming love of its adepts for the diamond of God's will whose emblem taken from the God Star is the mighty blue rose?

Just ask the Master (he thought you never would) and he'll recite for you one of a thousand poems or chapters of a thousand books he has written—all on his passion for the crystal of the Mind of God that is His Will. But first he'll tell you the story of Christ in Gethsemane, of his prayer the night before his trial and crucifixion, "Father, if thou be willing, remove this cup from me: nevertheless not my will, but thine, be done."

And then he'll tell you the mantra of Guru and chela on the First Ray of God's Will—"Not my will, not my will, not my will but thine be done!"—that binds their hearts in service to this one, Christ Jesus, whose life, every hour of it, is the greatest exposition of God's will there is. Having so said, he, the truly humble servant of God, recites this offering which, if you will allow him, he will place as his blue rose upon the altar of your heart:

"Down through the centuries men have discussed the will of God as though it were a thing apart from the will of man, bearing no resemblance to an offering that affords the best gifts to man. Contrary to human opinion, the will of God seeks to vest man with his immortal birthright and never to deprive him of his freedom.

"The enigma of life is hidden within the will of God. When properly understood, it provides a stimulus for every worthy purpose and re-creates a passion for living that many have lost. What you call zest or sparkle, when imbued with the Holy Spirit, is no chimera but a flash of joy that ripples across the belly of the world, that sways the tallest pines and moves all things toward cosmic usefulness and cosmic purpose.

"The will of God is the flawless diamond, it is the shining of the Divine Mind, it is the rushing of the wind of the Spirit, and it is the strength and laughter of real identity.

"'How can I know the will of God?' This is the cry of millions. Man presupposes that the divine will is hiding from him, as though it were a part of the plan for the Eternal God to play hide-and-seek with him.

"Not so! The will of God is inherent within life and merely awaits the signal of release from man's will in order to ray forth the power of dominion to the world of the individual. There is a sovereign link between the mortal will and the Immortal. In the statement of Jesus, 'It is the Father's good pleasure to give you the kingdom,' men can be aware of the eternal will as the fullest measure of eternal love.

"Release, then, your feelings of possessiveness

over your own life! Surrender the mean sense of sin and rebellion, the pitiful will to self-privilege which engenders bondage. See the will of God as omnipresent and complete, the holy beat of the Sacred Heart throbbing within your own. Know and understand that surrender is not oblivion but a point of beginning and of greater joy.

"Knowing the longing and the hunger of the souls of men for the Real, I am diligently evoking the symbols of his will to manifest in you as alertness of mind, willingness to change, and the courage to offer the self of mortality to the lovely designs of the Father's purpose.

"Create unto yourself the new sense of the ownership of God's will! You have long thought of God's will as a thing apart from yourself. Now, new longings and a fresh perspective can re-create the best gift you have ever had. The memory of his grace can come alive within you as you accept the infinite care of the Eternal One for you. His blessed consideration of your lifestream must be contemplated and made a living, vital part of your whole consciousness.

"Why do men set up a counterfeit will and call it their own? Why do they engage in a continual struggle between the will of God and 'their own' will? In the answers to these questions is to be found the key to happiness for every part of life. When man understands that there is no need to struggle for a personal existence outside of God (because he is complete in God) and that, in actuality, there are not two wills—the will of man and the will of God—but only the will of truth and freedom, inherent within the very Spirit of Life which is the Spirit of God, then he will enter into the new sense of harmony and grace.

"The will of God is the sole source of man's freedom.

"There are so many forms of subtlety in use upon earth today that the process of knowing the will of God is at times difficult. For example, some conceive of poverty as being the will of God; these make their lives an example of total simplicity. Others see opulence and abundant supply as the will of God.

"In reality, neither state can guarantee victory to the soul but rather the gift of nonattachment, which can either use the empire of the universe in all its fullness or be content in any environment. The truly illumined are able to rise above states of mind or expression to the place where they identify with the allness of God.

"The will of God is everything. For it provides the spark that pushes back the darkness of sense consciousness, of ignorance and despair while holding forth the torch of true illumination to the seeking soul, enabling each individual to find himself, lost in the passion of God's will!

"The fiat 'Not my will but thine be done' was not intended as a statement of sacrifice but one of heavenly inspired wisdom. In the higher schools, this mantram of the Spirit is intoned invocatively so as to create the needed liaison between man and God. Whereas it is God's will that man intune with him, it is incumbent upon man to recognize that his responsibility demands search, willingness, and an understanding of the self-created barriers that must be taken down so that the clarity of the will of God can come through.

"Be ready mentally, spiritually, and emotionally by an act of simple devotion or a feeling of awe to accept the will of God as a gladiator would a laurel wreath. Eras of achievement lie ahead—the planning of great cities, civilizations, and humanitarian doings. But until the will of God becomes acceptable to men, until they can put aside their double-mindedness, they will remain unstable and fluctuating in their aims.

"The will of God assures man that he will survive, for it is the will of God that those whom he has created should inherit his kingdom—but the rules of the game must be followed, for the law of God is inexorable in its demands for perfection.

"It is just as easy to serve the will of God—in fact it is far easier—than it is to serve the decaying will of man with its varying standards. The human will propels men to false aspirations at a dizzying rate of ascent and leaves them stranded without spiritual knowledge to plummet to their destruction.

"Realize that the will of God can best be known by a spiritual experience. Desire then that experience. Desire to reach outwardly toward the Godhead in the Great Central Sun galaxy.

"The will of God is a sacred adventure. I have said it thusly for a reason, for the average individual considers an encounter with the will of God a remote possibility. He prays to have the will of God made known to him, but he does not understand that he can have an a priori glimpse of that will while yet in mortal form. He does not realize that the will that sees can also be seized, in part, as a treasure-house of consciousness and carried back into the domain of the life within. There the great lodestone of truth acts as a divine revelator to reveal to each man from deep within his own heart what the will of God really is.

"Above all, let him understand always that, complex and all-embracing though it may be, the will of God can always be reduced to the common denominator of Love, Life and Light.

"Forward we go together."

Tracing his footsteps back through the desert sands and oases to the advanced civilization of Sumer c. 2100 B.C., we discover the keystone in the arch of El Morya's past lives: Abraham, great 'prince' of the Chaldees and father of the Hebrew nation to whom the LORD said, "I AM the Almighty God; walk before me, and be thou perfect. And I will make my covenant between me and thee, and will multiply thee exceedingly.... And thou shalt be a father of many nations."

And so the seed of the lightbearers descended through him and the twelve tribes, now Christed ones reborn, are his spiritual progeny—a lineage continuous by the Guru-chela relationship they share with the God Presence of Abraham, Isaac and Jacob—for flesh and blood alone could not contain it.

As Melchior, this Master Morya, who pens his initial "M" with three dots, came with the wise men of the East, Balthazar and Caspar (known today as the Masters

One of the Three Angels Assures Abraham That within the Year a Son Will Be Born to Him, Julius Schnorr, 1860

Yahweh appeared to him at the Oak of Mamre while he was sitting by the entrance of the tent during the hottest part of the day. He looked up, and there he saw three men standing near him. As soon as he saw them he ran from the entrance of the tent to meet them, and bowed to the ground. "My lord," he said, "I beg you, if I find favor with you, kindly do not pass your servant by. A little water shall be brought; you shall wash your feet and lie down under the tree. Let me fetch a little bread and you shall refresh yourselves before going further. That is why you have come in your servant's direction." They replied, "Do as you say." (Genesis 18:1–5, Jerusalem Bible)

Adoration of the Magi, Heinrich Hofmann

The "three Kings of Orient" probably were not kings at all but dubbed that by later tradition to fit the prophecy in Psalm 72:11, "All kings will do him homage." Rather, the "wise men from the East" were Magi, the priest class of Persia who were the "keepers of the sacred things, the learned of the people, the philosophers and servants of God," who also practiced the art of divination, sooth-saying and astrology. During the Persian empire, they were advisers of kings, educators of princes, and were held in highest reverence.

The names of the three wise men are not mentioned in the Bible but appear to have arisen or been passed down through tradition. Eighth-century British historian Bede was the first to record their names as we know them today. Melchior signifies "king of light"; Caspar may come from the name of the Indian king Gondophares whom the apostle Thomas converted; Balthazar is the Chaldean name for Daniel.

Kuthumi and Djwal Kul), following the signs of the stars and the inner calling of the Christ all the way (historically speaking) from Ur of the Chaldees to Bethlehem.

Reappearing in the fifth century as Arthur, King of the Britons, warrior and guru of the mystery school at Camelot, he guarded the flame of the inner teachings, instilling the quest for the Holy Grail by triumph over tyrants and the greatest tyrant of them all: that idolatrous carnal mind. His lessons in "might for right" were an exercise in the qualified use of the power of the will of God by the standard-bearers of Christ's mission, for and on behalf of the people—always.

Thus, under King Arthur the chivalry of knighthood, side by side with fair maidenhood to Motherhood, portrayed the ideals of twin flames united in Love for the defense of Truth. Endued with piety and a genuine concern for those of lowly estate, these keepers of the flame of Camelot endured tasks and tests which included exorcising dragons, giants and demons and battling wicked kings, bastards and female enchantresses.

Throughout their quest these initiates were balancing karma on a path foreknown—of individual excellence in Christhood leading to the inner unfoldment of the mysteries of the Holy Grail and true self-knowledge: "I AM the Grail."

In the end as the shadows fell upon the once and future mystery school, the wounded Arthur, having fought his last, was heard (as recalled by Tennyson) to

The Wedding of Arthur and Guinevere, Lancelot Speed

> Then Arthur charged his warrior whom he loved
> And honour'd most, Sir Lancelot, to ride forth
> And bring the Queen....
> To whom arrived, by Dubric the high saint,
> Chief of the church in Britain, and before
> The stateliest of her altar-shrines, the King
> That morn was married, while in stainless white,
> The fair beginners of a nobler time,
> And glorying in their vows and him, his knights
> Stood round him, and rejoicing in his joy....
> And holy Dubric spread his hands and spake:
> "Reign ye, and live and love, and make the world
> Other, and may thy Queen be one with thee,
> And all this Order of thy Table Round
> Fulfil the boundless purpose of their King!"

Alfred Lord Tennyson, "The Coming of Arthur," *Idylls of the King* breathe these words to Sir Bedivere from the barge where he lay dying:

The old order changeth, yielding place to new,
And God fulfils himself in many ways,
Lest one good custom should corrupt the world.
Comfort thyself; what comfort is
    in me?
I have lived my life, and that
    which I have done
May He within himself
    make pure! but thou,
If thou shouldst never
    see my face again,
Pray for my soul. More
    things are wrought by
    prayer
Than this world dreams of.
    Wherefore, let thy voice

The loyal Sir Bedivere tends
the wounded King Arthur

Rise like a fountain for me night and day.
For what are men better than sheep or goats
That nourish a blind life within the brain,
If, knowing God, they lift not hands of prayer
Both for themselves and those who call them friend?
For so the whole round earth is every way
Bound by gold chains about the feet of God.
But now farewell. I am going a long way
With these thou seest—if indeed I go—
For all my mind is clouded with a doubt—
To the island-valley of Avilion;

Where falls not hail, or rain, or any snow,
Nor ever wind blows loudly; but it lies
Deep-meadow'd, happy, fair with orchard lawns
And bowery hollows crown'd with summer sea,
Where I will heal me of my grievous wound.[12]

Sic transit gloria mundi. Thus passes the glory of this world. Enter the glory of the next.

Reentering the familiar lists in the twelfth and sixteenth centuries, the soul of Arthur, who with tender words and gifts of love so touched the heart of a world forever, served as chief adviser and conscience of English kings Henry II and Henry VIII in the persons of Thomas Becket and Thomas More. The twice-born Henry twice elevated him to the role of Lord Chancellor and twice martyred him for obstructing his ambitions.

The parallel of lives did not escape the authors who annotated Thomas More's path to sainthood:

"Twice in the history of England there appears the figure of a great martyr who was also chancellor of the realm. Thomas Becket… gave his life to keep the English Church safe from royal aggression; Thomas More gave his in a vain effort to preserve it from further aggression. Each was a royal favorite who loved God more than his king. The coincidence is striking.

"St. Thomas More was born at London in 1478. After a thorough grounding in religion and the classics, he entered Oxford to study law. Upon leaving the university he embarked on a legal career which took him to Parlia-

Sir Thomas More, Hans Holbein the Younger, 1527

Omnium horarum homo, the Dutch humanist Erasmus labeled him. Later the phrase was rendered in English "a man for all seasons." Lawyer, judge, statesman, man of letters, author, poet, farmer, lover of pastoral life, ascetic, husband and father, champion of women's education, humanist and saint, Thomas More was outstanding among the avant-garde of the English Renaissance.

ment. In 1505, he married his beloved Jane Colt who bore him four children, and when she died at a young age he married a widow, Alice Middleton, to be a mother for his young children.

"His charity was without bounds, as is proved by the frequent and abundant alms he poured without distinction among all unfortunate persons. He used himself to go through the back lanes and inquire into the state of poor families.... He often invited to his table his poorer neighbors, receiving them... familiarly and joyously; he rarely invited the rich, and scarcely ever the nobility.

"A wit and a reformer, this learned man numbered bishops and scholars among his friends, and by 1516 he wrote his world-famous book *Utopia*.

"Erasmus gives us a picture of More at this period: 'In serious matters no man's advice is more prized, while if the king wishes to recreate himself, no man's conversation is gayer. Often there are deep and intricate matters that demand a grave and prudent judge. More unravels them in such a way that he satisfies both sides. No one, however, has ever prevailed on him to receive a gift for his decision. Happy the commonwealth where kings appoint such officials! His elevation has brought with it no pride.... You would say that he had been appointed public guardian of those in need.'

"Another tribute from More's confessor speaks of his remarkable purity and devotion. But in spite of his many honors and achievements, the public esteem

Sir Thomas More, L. Cubitt Bevis, 1969, London

Humanists and Christians around the world worked together to commission this statue. It is based on the spirit of Holbein's portrait of the chancellor.

Thomas More's talents attracted the attention of King Henry VIII. In 1529 Henry appointed him chancellor of England, a post he fulfilled faithfully until the king determined to divorce Catherine of Aragon, who had failed to produce a male heir, and marry Anne Boleyn. He resigned his chancellorship in 1532 rather than openly oppose the king, but Henry would not allow his foremost servant to withdraw from the controversy. When Thomas' opposition extended to refusal to sign the Act of Succession, as it implied rejection of the pope's supremacy, he was thrown in the Tower and later charged with treason. The jury convicted him based on the perjured testimony of the solicitor general Richard Rich. The sentence directed he be drawn, hanged and quartered, but the king changed it to beheading. Thomas was executed July 6, 1535, affirming himself "the king's good servant, but God's first."

which he enjoyed, and the many tokens of the royal regard, More knew well that there was no security in his position.

"He resigned in 1532 at the height of his career and reputation when Henry persisted in holding his own opinions regarding marriage and the supremacy of the Pope.

"The rest of his life was spent in writing mostly a defense of the Church. In 1534, with his close friend, St. John Fisher, he refused to render allegiance to the King as the head of the Church of England and was confined to the Tower. The fifteen months that he spent in prison were borne with a serene spirit; the tender love of his wife and children, especially that of his daughter Margaret, comforted him. He rejected all efforts of wife and friends to induce him to take the oath and so pacify Henry. Visitors were forbidden towards the end, and in his solitude he wrote the noblest of his religious works, the *Dialogue of Comfort against Tribulation.*

"Fifteen months later, and nine days after Saint John Fisher's execution, he was tried and convicted of treason. He told the court that he could not go against his conscience and wished his judges that 'we may yet hereafter in heaven merrily all meet together to everlasting salvation.' And on the scaffold he told the crowd of spectators that he was dying as the 'King's good servant—but God's first.' He was beheaded on July 6, 1535.

"More was beatified by Pope Leo XIII in 1886, along with other English martyrs, and canonized in

1935. Had he never met death for the faith he still would have been a candidate for canonization as a confessor. From first to last his life was singularly pure, lived in the spirit of his own prayer:

> Give me, good Lord, a longing to be with Thee; not for the avoiding of the calamities of this wicked world, nor so much for the avoiding of the pains of purgatory, nor the pains of Hell neither, nor so much for the attaining of the joys of Heaven in respect of mine own commodity, as even for a very love of Thee."

The following excerpt from the *Dialogue of Comfort against Tribulation* is staunch and true advice for the chela of the will of God who has a heart for any fate: because he loves God, the Great Guru, whose presence he has known intimately in the beloved—El Morya. This comfort for the hour of our tribulation, if taken as a cup we drink—as the Saviour said, "Drink ye all of it" —will spare us from the perfidy of the liar's cowardice and inescapable hypocrisy (that liar who has sworn to lie and cheat and steal and kill to save his skin) who would have us do the same and lose our souls:

"The devil it is therefore that, if we for fear of men will fall, is ready to run upon us and devour us.... Therefore when he roareth out upon us in the threats of mortal men, let us tell him that with our inward eye we see him well enough and intend to stand and fight with him, even hand to hand. If he threaten us that we be too weak, let us tell him that our captain Christ is with us and that we shall fight with his strength which hath vanquished him already. And let us fence us in with faith and comfort us with hope and smite the devil in the face with a firebrand of charity. For surely if we be of the tender loving mind that our master was and do not hate them that kill us, but pity them and pray for them, with sorrow for the peril that they make for themselves, that fire of charity, thrown in his face, striketh the devil suddenly so blind that he cannot see where to fasten a stroke on us.

"When we feel us too bold, remember our own feebleness. When we feel us too faint, remember Christ's strength. In our fear, let us remember Christ's painful agony that himself would for our comfort suffer before his passion to the intent that no fear should make us despair. And ever call for his help such as himself wills to send us. And then need we never to doubt but that either he shall keep us from the painful death, or shall not fail so to strengthen us in it that he shall joyously bring us to heaven by it. And then doeth he much more for us than if he kept us from it."[13]

The last rose of Morya's summertime in Britain was a bittersweet romance of popularity and personal tragedy lived out as Ireland's poet laureate Thomas Moore— until he plucked himself from this karmic soil and stepped into the form of a nineteenth-century Rajput prince of India. This poet/prince seems also to have once occupied time and space as Prince Mori Wong of

Thomas Moore

Capturer of the soul not only of the Irish but of all freedom-loving peoples, Thomas Moore belongs in the pantheon of the world's great poets. A poet distills the essence of a people's longing, and that is precisely what his *Irish Melodies* did. While his celebrity in Ireland, England and America during the early nineteenth century is well known, his popularity in Eastern Europe, especially Poland and Russia, is not. Many peoples have since caught the fire of his poetry that sang already in their blood. His haunting songs with words that pull the heartstrings, such as "Believe Me, If All Those Endearing Young Charms" and "The Harp That Once through Tara's Halls," still evoke tender memories of bygone days.

This Thomas who had survived two Henrys awakened his people through more than music and poetry. His political satire and parodies were in the same vein as today's political cartoons. His aim in recording the *History of Ireland* was to interest his people in their past and to awaken the British to their errors in governing the nation.

Koko Nor, having alluded to this unchronicled Chinese figure without a hint of an historical context.

In these and other lives the diamond heart of Morya was being fashioned by his Guru for his future role as Lord of the First Ray. Thanks be to God that all who anticipate his return as the once and future king—Jew and Christian, Moslem, Hindu and Buddhist alike, calling Abraham! Arthur! Akbar!—have today the opportunity to know him as the Master Teacher of devotees in pursuit of the holy will of the Father.

And what better way to know him and to love him than through his own musings on life as this tutor of our souls parts the veil and allows us studied glimpses of the secrets of his heart. Of that episode of ignominy put to book and film, dramatized in T. S. Eliot's *Murder in the Cathedral* and Jean Anouilh's *Becket,* he startled us with these words:

"Four murderers came. They were determined to put out the Light of myself. But I could only mock the evil in their eye and behold the risen Christ who gave to me and my heart such grace as to be able to continue to minister to the people of Canterbury and the world even after my passing.

"Thus, I did not die in vain, as you have never died in vain. For life moves on, outwits and outsmarts the evildoer. And they themselves (who have repeatedly murdered the heirs of Christ) return to the scene of life so blank and charred and hollowed out, with scarce an identity to continue their folly.

St Thomas and the Men of Strood, by Meister Francke

Serving two masters proved impossible for Thomas Becket. As friend and lord chancellor to King Henry II of England, he warned him he could not also serve as archbishop. "Should God permit me to be the archbishop of Canterbury," he said, "I would soon lose your Majesty's favor, and the affection with which you honor me would be changed into hatred." Upon becoming archbishop, therefore, he resigned his post as chancellor. Having been assigned the highest office of the Roman Church in Britain, answerable to the pope alone, he fulfilled it meticulously. When Henry's wishes clashed with the interests of the Church, Thomas refused to grant them. He was later forced to flee to France where he entered a monastery. But after the French king arranged a reconciliation between Thomas and his king, the archbishop returned home, remarking to the bishop of Paris, "I am going to England to die."

Murder of St. Thomas Becket, Michael Pacher

After a tumultuous welcome by the British people after his exile
in France, Becket returned to Canterbury. But the inevitable clash
with Henry took place when he refused to rescind his excommuni-
cation of three rebellious bishops. Upon hearing of this the king
went into a rage and is said to have demanded, "Will no one rid me
of this traitor Beckett!" Whereupon, Dec. 29, 1170, four of his
knights journeyed to Canterbury, where they brutally murdered
the defenseless archbishop as he prayed in the cathedral. Within
three years of his death, Becket was canonized, miracles abounded
and pilgrims came from far and wide until his tomb was destroyed
and his veneration interdicted in 1538 by Henry VIII.

"They are to be pitied, beloved ones, but never to be despised. Evil itself may be despised for a moment as the Ruby Ray from the Sacred Heart of Jesus utterly consumes and dissolves it. For the Ruby Ray of the Blood of Christ is always a laser beam that goes forth to devour the unreality of all hate and hate creations by the intense Love of the disciple who is, therefore, *in Christ* perfectly able to meet the adversary of His little ones in the way.

"Our God is a consuming fire. And this consuming fire is indeed Love. Love fulfills her purpose in many, many ways. Love, of course, is the most creative and ingenious element of God's heart, for Love seeks and finds many ways to comfort, to uplift, to instruct, and to rebuke....

"You *are* ascending, beloved. This is my message to you this day because this was my realization when as Thomas Becket I stood on December the 29th at the altar of Canterbury Cathedral. I said to myself in the face of these whose darkness was so great as to be equally unreal—I said to myself, beholding His glory as truly Saint Stephen did, 'I am ascending. I am ascending to the heart of God. This is the meaning of it all. This is the meaning of it all.'

"Beloved, at least it was action. After all, I had wasted away in France for a number of years. And as for them, they had had good opportunity to rally to the cause of Christ. Thus the karmic law descended. God called me home and allowed their drama to be outplayed with a particular contrast of light and darkness so typical of winter solstice.

"You see, they were left to face the tyrant king. And Henry must live with himself and his image and the world. Karma decrees therefore, and karmic law, that when individuals reject the representative of the Christ —which for that moment I was before pope and king and France and England, and soon all the world—when that messenger of the Son of God is rejected, then the light is withdrawn and they must then overcome the darkness by their own devices, else be swallowed up by it.

"When they reject the messenger of light, they must go their way until they become surfeited in the very wall of darkness he, the shield of the Lord, had held back from breaking upon them, that finally, perchance, they might come to the point of that same love of the honor of God the Lord's servant bore, whereby that honor is preferred beyond a paltry existence in cowardice, dumbness, ignorance and silent or violent infamy.

"Some have come around since that hour in the twelfth century. Today the hour is late. And I can tell you that some of them have not changed a whit.

"Take it from my heart, beloved ones—take it from me. Let God save whom he will through you. Be nonattached concerning the conversion of those who will not be converted and whom the Lord himself desires not to convert. Do not be stubborn in determining who shall be saved by you. Save no man. Give God that grace, for he will do it better than all of your contrivances."

Enfired by his zeal as Becket and his ever-present goodwill—his attention to detail in the affairs of Church and State with a piety and learning ignited from the sacred fire burning in the secret chamber of his heart— Morya's chelas know that they must rise to emulate his example in assuming responsibility for leadership roles in all fields. In his presence they are able once again to capture the vision and make the sacrifices crucial to the survival of a viable existence for mankind on planet Earth.

If this world has a dearth of knights, heroes, statesmen, saints and poets, it does not have a dearth of Teachers. Among them standing tall is the chiefest of them all, whose title is Chief of the Darjeeling Council of the Great White Brotherhood: El Morya Khan, our most beloved Guru who faithfully brought us to the diamond heart of God's will in Christ, in Buddha, in the Mother and in all the holy luminaries of history.

Devoted friend of lightbearers in every religion, race and creed, formidable enemy of serpents who have inveigled themselves into the governments, economies, and religious orders of East and West, champion of the people, inspiration and verve of kings, rulers, advocates and presidents, he is indisputably the chela's "man for all seasons."

Without Morya's godly person and presence the universe would suffer a cruel vacancy, our hearts a void unspeakable, and the earth should have missed the sparkle of one so initiated by the star sapphire of God's holy will: *"Allāhu Akbar… Jalla Jalāluhu!"*

Appropriately and to the great blessing of devotees of all faiths, El Morya initiates souls in the stepping-stones of the path that leads to the Holy Spirit's bestowal of the gifts of *faith in God's will* and the *word of wisdom.* He is ever the instrument of the Father and the fearsome Comforter. Sharper than a two-edged sword, his word is the extension of the Lawgiver who sent forth his First Ray in the beginning as His will to be in manifest form—the crystallization of the God flame—by faith…

> And by faith Abraham, when he was called to go out into a place which he should after receive for an inheritance, obeyed; and he went out, not knowing whither he went.
>
> By faith he sojourned in the land of promise, as in a strange country, dwelling in tabernacles with Isaac and Jacob, the heirs with him of the same promise:
>
> For he looked for a city which hath foundations, whose builder and maker is God.
>
> Through faith also Sara herself received strength to conceive seed, and was delivered of a child when she was past age, because she judged him faithful who had promised.
>
> Therefore sprang there even of one, and him as good as dead, so many as the stars of the sky in multitude, and as the sand which is by the sea shore innumerable.

As Akbar, this original model of First Ray achievers was convinced that the course he set for his nation was the will of God. With single one-pointedness, he acquired the penetrating wisdom to strip the layers of misinterpretation from the ecclesiasticism of the times and to bring forth the wisdom of the Word, as God—he was certain—had intended it to be. He was thorough and exacting both of himself and others as he endeavored to deal wisely and judiciously in the affairs of state.

And so it was in each of his embodiments: increasing in the power of these gifts as he exercised them, he grew in grace and evolved to a masterful understanding of the dynamics of the First Ray.

Morya's sensitivity to the individual, his respect, honor and deference to the God flame of the One within the one, was and is the key to his love for the will of God expressed individually in all of His handiwork. His profound understanding of the soul on the path of God-realization drawn from many a round in earth's schoolroom is brought out in his dictations and fond notes to his chelas which extol the word of wisdom perceived through faith in God's will.

These have been published in *The Sacred Adventure, The Chela and the Path, Morya: The Darjeeling Master Speaks to His Chelas on the Quest for the Holy Grail,* his *Encyclical on World Good Will* and bound volumes of *Pearls of Wisdom,* weekly letters from the Ascended Masters to their chelas dictated to the Messengers and published by The Summit Lighthouse since 1958.

Morya is the singular Friend for whom everyone he has befriended (excepting evildoers) has felt a special loyalty and commitment. As Abraham he was counted the Friend of God, who placed such stock in his chelaship and the purity of his heart that the LORD did not impute his sins to him. He was the best friend Henry II and VIII ever had and lost, and to this day he is the friend of every Briton and of generations who have continued to benefit from his policies on the Indian subcontinent.

And his enemies? They too were bound to respect him—even to admire if not himself, then his sense of justice and fair play.

Above all, he is the staunchest of friends at court a chela could ever have. No one loves us more. As a brother he has picked us up in our soul's nakedness and properly clothed us in robes of disciplined whiteness, presentable and acceptable to meet our God and our Saviour Jesus Christ.

By 1898, Morya had fulfilled the requirements for his ascension and then some. As an unascended Master, known as the Master M. of the Himalayas, he had sponsored the Theosophical Society—H. P. Blavatsky, Col. H. S. Olcott and early heralds of the new age—with Koot Hoomi, Serapis Bey, the Master R., Saint Germain, the Maha Chohan and others of the mahatmas.

Never letting go of his dream to free the earth, El Morya, dictating to his amanuensis Mark (whom he had prepared since childhood for his later training as the Messenger of the Great White Brotherhood), the Master wrote on March 13, 1964, "Every blessed soul can arrive at the very summit of his own existence, which is God."

Throughout his many embodiments to the present hour, beloved El Morya has held this goal in heart for all who love the will of God. Whether as one of the sons of Enoch, progenitor of the seed of the Universal Christ who "walked with God and was not, for God took him" in the ritual of the ascension, as a seer who penetrated into the highest octaves of light in the ancient land of Ur of the Chaldees, or as a native of Persia who worshiped the one God through the Great One, Ahura Mazda (Sanat Kumara)—through these and many other embodiments apart from those touched upon in this chapter Morya experimented with "divine electricities," becoming increasingly aware of the spiritual power flowing through man.

Later he became accomplished in the constructive use of fohat—the mysterious electric power of Cosmic Consciousness (quiescent or active)—that impelling vital force which, when called into action by divine fiat, moves the evolutions of a universe, a galactic or solar system, or a single human being from the beginning to the completion of a mission.

From a treasure-house of wisdom, gleaned from such active participation in the affairs of God and man as we have briefly reviewed, the Master recognized what a great spiritual potential could be drawn forth and

utilized for the salvation of the planet if and when the
sum of all of mankind's energies were focused in the
worship of the one God. What a house of light this
would be!

His dream was first to gather lifestreams from many
spiritual endeavors and to offer them the opportunity to
channel divinely bestowed resources, their own Christ
consciousness, into a fountain of light—a veritable lighthouse whose wide powerful beams would sweep over
the darkened sea of humanity as a beacon light of eternal hope until unity replaced diversity, and the transcendent, all-inclusive understanding of the one LORD and
the one God who is all Love would be known throughout the earth—until the golden age would blossom with
God-happiness and the ascended ones would walk and
talk with mankind as in bygone ages.

This dream, endorsed by the Darjeeling Council
of the Great White Brotherhood, has come to pass. In
August 1958, The Summit Lighthouse was founded by
El Morya. On August 14, the first *Pearl of Wisdom* was
sent to a small student body in the United States, Great
Britain and Canada.

In his letter of August 8, 1958, El Morya wrote,
"Our ideas are born within the flaming heart of Truth
itself and fortunate is every one of you who can share in
the glorious karma of producing the perfection which
we shall externalize through you—if you care willingly
and lovingly to serve this cause in the name and by the
authority of Divine Love itself."

In his letter dated January 31, 1961, beloved El Morya stated, "I am therefore authorizing the formation of a specially dedicated group within The Summit Lighthouse, to be made up of actual members in good standing.... This is to be called 'The Keepers of the Flame.'... To this end class lessons are to be offered to the members of the Keepers of the Flame group. Regardless of one's station, all those interested in both basic and advanced instruction ought to enroll in this dedicated group of servers for many reasons. A word to the wise is sufficient."

It was Saint Germain as the Knight Commander who sponsored the organization of this inner circle. It is called the Keepers of the Flame Fraternity because it is a fraternal, outer order of the Great White Brotherhood whose members have vowed to keep the flame of Life blazing upon the hearts' altars of all mankind, to be their brothers' keepers and to keep constantly in mind and heart all that the Father, the Mighty I AM Presence, has already given into mind, heart and hand for his glory and the speedy externalization of his kingdom upon earth.

In May of 1961 beloved Lanto stated, "Because this activity is builded so solidly upon the Rock, I, Lanto, declare in Wisdom's name, it shall stand to fulfill El Morya's dream." And in his letter dated November 10, 1959, El Morya further elucidated the purpose of The Summit:

"The true Lighthouse is but a dream of spiritual unity yet to be externalized to its fullness here!...

Knowing that faith and harmony are ever a part of the light and that The Summit Lighthouse asks no special fealty or allegiance other than your love for deeper contact with us, I trust that all of you who love the Truth of which I speak will continue to enjoy the *Pearls of Wisdom* for a long time to come until in God's memory-record of light you become illustrious and in manifestation self-luminous. Then as one of us you will need no other 'thread of contact,' having attained the glory of full reunion for which you ever and always seek.

"The continuing support you give to the physical activity of The Summit Lighthouse in the future will, as it did in the past, make possible my continuing allotment of spiritual energy in the weekly releases of the *Pearls of Wisdom.* You see, we cannot give it all—the Cosmic Law decrees that part must come from your side of the veil. Whatever you do, do in goodwill, for in God one is indeed never alone, but all One!"

Archangel Jophiel, on October 14, 1967, gave the reason for the founding of this outer organization of the Lord of the First Ray from the standpoint of the evolution of spiritual understanding on the planet:

"The great cosmic reality of the wisdom teachers is not yet in full bloom before the eyes of mankind because there are many people on this planetary body who have never even heard of the Ascended Master Jesus the Christ.… How, then, can men who are concerned with the link to Cosmic Hierarchy expect for one moment that mankind, who know not the reality of Jesus the

Christ, will know about the Archangels or about the angelic host or about the Ascended Masters? Today, only a few in America, by a relative sense, are able to have a composite picture of the Great White Brotherhood.

"When Madame Helena Petrovna Blavatsky in 1875 revealed the Ascended Masters of Wisdom through the Theosophical Order, it was a nova bursting upon the metaphysical sky.... The founders continued to work for world enlightenment and to pour out an increasing measure of teachings and techniques blessed by the Hierarchy of light. As a countermeasure the brothers of the shadow released other information as a sham manifestation, a pseudoactivity designed to pull men away from the great Mother lodestone manifest in the Divine Theosophia....

"The Ascended Masters have found it expedient through the years to create new activities of light and to endow them with specific functions in the name of holy progress. I shall explain:

"On the planetary body individuals of a very devout nature, when they become attached to a specific segment of holy instruction from 'on high' are often concerned with the enormous responsibility involved in keeping pure the teachings that are vouchsafed to them. Therefore, in their desire to do just that they close themselves off and they deny to their followers the right to alter or to change the power structure, the revelatory structure and the messianic message in any way from its original dispensation.

"The Brothers of Wisdom are of the opinion that there is much wisdom in this action. However, because of the rigid (i.e., orthodox) stand that is taken by the followers of a specific movement, from time to time it becomes expedient, in order to break the old matrices of thought and feeling, that a new activity of light should be launched so that the Ascended Masters may take by the hand those avant-garde individuals who are willing to be God-taught in every age, who are willing to behold the great onrush of Cosmic Reality as it parades across the sky of their minds, infusing them with ever-new flashes of intuitive intelligence and teaching them spiritual techniques destined in the future to give the children of the coming race a new glimpse of Divine Reality.

"This, then, is the reason why in 1958 The Summit Lighthouse activity was endowed by the Cosmic Hierarchy with the right to function, ordained by God, so that Messengers, two in number, should go forth and proclaim to the world (because of their previous training in connection with the great temple at Tel el Amarna) the manifestation of the monotheistic technique of the Ascended Masters under the rule of the cosmic panoply, or Hierarchy of Ascended Masters, teaching both the Law of the One and its corollary in the law of the many manifestations emanating from the One.

"For it must always be remembered that as God is One, this God that is One has seen fit in his greater holy wisdom to extend himself forth in a manifestation of the many, and therefore to mankind is given the opportunity to be brought into captivity to Divine Love whereby the love they bear within themselves for the Divine does capture their whole hearts and cause them to welcome with open arms the ministering love and service, the holy wisdom that descends from on high.

"Thus are men drawn out of the mass sea of miasma and human emotion and raised up to a place where they can clasp to their hearts and minds holy Truth and understand its role in freeing them from the shadow of the present age."

Pursuant to these goals and his well-documented "programs of assistance to mankind" and his "plan to free the earth," El Morya holds classes in God-government and the path of personal Christhood through the soul's blueprint in the will of God in his etheric retreat over Darjeeling, India. Called the Temple of Good Will, it is situated among the pines on the slopes of the Himalayas. Let us go, then, to El Morya's retreat and sit in on one of his famous fireside chats...

Traveling in our etheric bodies, we enter the library and take our seats in cushioned chairs before a crackling pine-log fire. We look up and the Master is seated in his favorite chair before us.

He begins to weave the story of the Brotherhood's work on earth, of battles fought for the sake of nations— or of one single soul. Of the triumphs and failures of our lifestreams and earth's evolutions.

He tells of the aims of the Brotherhood at Darjeeling whose credo is "I will," their desire only to see men free from self-limitation, narrow-mindedness, and the ego-centered consciousness of the synthetic self. And he challenges us to become chelas of the will of God.

"The Darjeeling Council is a unit of hierarchy. I am its chief. Numbered among those who deliberate in our chambers are Saint Germain, Mary the Mother, Jesus the Christ and the Master Kuthumi.... Assisted by many unascended chelas, we serve the cause of the will of God among humanity, in the governments of the nations, in the economic councils, in the social strata, in the institutions of learning, and above all, in the diamond hearts of the devotees....

"Here at Darjeeling we offer a crash program in chelaship and initiation on the Path for those who are willing to follow implicitly the demands of their own Christ Self and to respond with a flame that leaps and with eyes that sparkle with the kindling fires of soul discernment."

Many have passed through the doors of Darjeeling. "We have entertained the world's statesmen in our retreat and we have received the humble chela. We have received all whose love for the will of God has been greater than the love for the will of the lesser self." He speaks of those who come to the retreat for counsel— souls "who serve in the governments of the nations, who serve as teachers and scientists and musicians, and those who control the flow of the will of God that is power, that is the abundance of supply.

"The will of God is applied in all levels of human

endeavor, for the will of God is the blueprint of every project. It is the foundation of every task. It is the skeleton of your body. It is physical energy. It is the etheric fire. The will of God is the fiery diamond in your heart."

And he confides to us his soul lessons drawn from his life and death as Thomas More:

"Here in Darjeeling, we are the followers of the path of Christ and the Buddha which are one. And we follow the byword 'nonattachment to the fruit of action.' This means that we strive for the excellence of Divine Love in all things and leave the rest to God.

"Therefore, we inform you that it is the ritual of effectively challenging the liar and the lie whereby you will earn your ascension. And when you stand before the Lords of Karma (who are so very real) at the conclusion of this life and you must give answer whether or not you have defended these little ones, the Lords of Karma will not judge you according to whether or not you have accomplished the goal of wiping out planetary Evil— nay, you will be judged by the effectiveness of your effort, by the strength of ritual of your having engaged your energies to counteract the fallen ones.

"Witness my own embodiment as Thomas More.

"I was well aware of the fact that I would not undo the edicts of the king, nor the separation of the Church of England from the Church of our Lord Jesus Christ. I was well aware that my voice would simply be the testimony of righteousness—not of a righteous man but of a righteous God. For, I do not count myself a righteous man but the instrument of the One who is Eternal Righteousness.

"And so, beloved ones, the infamy of the decisions of Henry VIII have continued, multiplied and spawned, as error is wont to do in a corruptible milieu; but the voice of one who chose to be the voice of God remains as the clarion call of a trumpet.

"And the moral of the story is that whereas by and by I entered into the ritual of the ascension at the conclusion of the Divine Plan for my incarnations on earth, those who valued their lives, their paltry positions, even their flesh, are yet evolving; and I might say that whether or not they indeed are evolving Godward is questionable.

"Beloved ones, I am here—here in Darjeeling, here at Camelot—in the fullness of the light* of the will of God; though others determine to remove that light, it is invincible in heaven and on earth. And so you see, physical light, physical righteousness or beauty, or flesh and blood will come and go but your eternal Sonship hid with Christ in God is a light that cannot be dimmed.

"Blessed hearts, let us not count worthiness as an accrual of good deeds, for if it be so, then unworthiness will become an accrual of wicked deeds. This is a mystery, for at a certain level it is so and at a certain level of life evolving life this becomes the measure and the mark of the judgment of the Lords of Karma; but to be in the center of good deeds, one must be in the center of the

---

*Christ consciousness

awareness that God himself is the doer and the deed. And therefore, one does not make too much, neither of human achievement nor of the little human mistakes, for to do so can cause that insanity which is born of pride and that division in one's members, the schism in consciousness which comes on the heels of failure.

"If one is to acknowledge error or ego as supremely real, then there is no hope for salvation. For the fulcrum of salvation is not good and bad deeds per se, but it is the forsaking of error and the erroneous consciousness that produced the human ego in the first place and the realization that it is the soul's centering in the will of God, that it is the soul's realignment with that will, that makes all the difference.

"It is not that you are right or wrong but that you are nonattached to your rights and to your wrongs. And with that nonattachment the resolution of your life will be that all that proceeds from you will result in right action, right consciousness, right goals, right mindedness— *rightness that is God's Rightness!*

"Therefore, shun Evil not because it is real but shun it because it is unreal and *no part of God!*"

Now we hear the sound of an ancient bell intoning, and the Master explains, "It is a call to the humble the world around, to the servants of the will of God, and to the avant-garde who would carry civilization forward into a new age. Morya summons chelas of the sacred fire who would become adepts, followers who would become friends of Christ, exponents of the word of living Truth, imitators of the Master Jesus, and finally the heart, head, and hand of our cosmic retinue....

"The path that offers much requires much. As you say in the world, you get what you pay for. The price is high, but then you are purchasing the ultimate reality.

"To ascend into the plane of reality..., you must garner within your soul the thrust of Power, Wisdom, and Love. To transcend planes of consciousness, to make the giant leap into the arms of God—this requires thrust. Therefore from the wellspring of Life, out of the fount of living flame which Almighty God has anchored within your heart, draw forth the thrust of Faith, Hope, and Charity.

"Whether Christian or Jew, Moslem or Zen Buddhist, or none of these, know, O seeker after higher reality, that the path of initiation can be trod wherever you are. But *you* must take the first step. My responsibility is to guide and guard: yours is to follow."

He pauses, then begins to speak more forcefully, cautioning: "Let it be made clear at the beginning that all who read the words of the Ascended Masters and all who hear our word are not necessarily counted as chelas of our will. Let it be quite clear that there are requirements. As the chips of wood fly when the pines in the forest are cleared, so the winds of Darjeeling blow. Let the unworthy chela be cleared from our path. We clear for a noble purpose—the ennoblement of a cause and a race. Hierarchy has also said, 'Let the chips fall where they may.'"

He speaks of the problems burdening the world, and of the dire need for dedicated hearts to assist it. "The weight of world karma has never been greater. The Divine Mother intercedes before the Court of the Sacred Fire on behalf of the children of God that the descent of their own karma might not destroy the very platform of their evolution. As Thoreau said, 'What is the use of a house if you haven't got a tolerable planet to put it on?' So we say, what is the use of the path of initiation if the planetary platform can no longer sustain its evolutions?"

With this unsettling thought, Morya bids us farewell.

"I thank you for your attention, I thank you for your love for the light, I thank you for your presence here, and I ask you to remember that I am a cosmic being, that I am an Ascended Master, that I am your friend so long as you adore that will. For there is no other power in the universe that can act except the will of God, which goodness surrounds you now....

"May the angelic hosts and the ascended hosts surround you always and keep your goings and comings until you enter that state of consciousness equal to my own. And I care not if you surpass it; for in adoration to my own I AM Presence I give all that I am to the service of the light—to the service that raises, that lifts, that transmutes, and makes hearts reverent, happy, and God-free.

"Thank you, and good night."

El Morya reminds us in parting that he waits for the

knock of the chela upon his door. Angelic hosts now arrive to escort us back to our physical bodies after our sojourn in the etheric realm.

As to the strains of the retreat keynote (*Pomp and Circumstance*, by Elgar) brothers of the diamond heart file to their early morning duties, we contemplate with grateful hearts the mystery of God's will: What a privilege to know such a one as this!

To become worthy of him as the Guru of our soul, to extol his virtues, to serve his mission, to combine our forces with his own for a planetary revolution in Higher Consciousness—to this, to all of this his presence has inspired us. Our spirits need no other ennobling than to know him as he is.

In the strength of his vision of the future we discover the will to be Godlike.

─────────────

As the days pass, the memories of Darjeeling do not fade but "grow and bloom" like Edelweiss "forever." The forget-me-not's tiny blue face reminds us she is his favorite, her smile and color his own. Fondly we remember.

How can one presence, one being so set the heart on fire?

Like the new love of springtime or the blaze of winter, such a burning desire has this tall, fierce, turbaned Master kindled in us to do the will of God! Surely, the zeal of this Lord—like Abram's "burning lamp"—has opened our breast to the all of heaven and God's covenanted Love. Through him the Divine Lover of our souls appears and we greet the All-in-all with the ancient chant:

> O unifying Spirit of the Great White Brotherhood,
> Opalescent mother-of-pearl,
> Milk and honey of Resurrection's happiness,
> Drink me, while I AM drinking Thee!

Morya's own words tell of his love for us in whatever state he finds us. And they tell of ours for him, the one who taught us of holy chastisement and strong arms of all-enfolding charity—of Love that never gives up, never turns back, but bears its flame in honor.

Had the Irish bard written but these lines, we should have known him anywhere in any guise or gait, that we might fly to him when our souls would cry out or rejoice with nowhere else to turn. In life's saddest, most solemn or exalted moments—in setback or triumph or beautiful bliss or any endurance test—it is with Morya we must be.

'Tis then we would hear him sing to us the ballad he sang to his stricken wife as Thomas Moore:

> Believe me, if all those endearing young charms
> Which I gaze on so fondly to-day
> Were to change by to-morrow and fleet in my arms
> Like fairy-gifts fading away
> Thou wouldst still be adored as this moment thou art
> Let thy loveliness fade as it will
> And around the dear ruin each wish of my heart
> Would entwine itself verdantly still.

It is not while beauty and youth are thine own
And thy cheeks unprofaned by a tear
That the fervour and faith of a soul can be known
To which time will but make thee more dear.
No, the heart that has truly loved never forgets
But as truly loves on to the close
As the sun-flower turns on her God when he sets
The same look which she turn'd when he rose.

True Love is the flame of El Morya. This love awaits the waiting bride—the chela-to-be of the Lord of the First Ray.

Now if you lend an ear and listen, you can hear the love song of this Guru as he sings it to your soul.

2

LORD LANTO
the Sage

Gifts of the Word of Wisdom
and the Word of Knowledge

L ord Lanto, great light of ancient China, now serves
as one of America's foremost savants. The devotion
to the *word of wisdom* and the *word of knowledge* of this
quietly-wise sage and fiery-eyed bodhisattva has truly
qualified him to initiate the evolutions of earth in both
gifts of the Holy Spirit.

Lord of the Second Ray, he is an Ascended Master
in whose presence the sublimity of the Mind of God
can be touched and known, by portion, as he teaches
the path of Americans—Yes! a Chinese master teaching
Americans the ancient way of universal Christhood that
made the golden age of China great, that comes down
from Maitreya, the Coming Buddha who has come, and
is brought to the fore by the hierarch of the Royal Teton
Retreat—another Chinese master, more famous than

The Grand Teton, Wyoming

his Guru, the Ascended Master Lord Confucius himself!

Lanto conducts classes at the Royal Teton Retreat,
congruent with the Grand Teton in Wyoming, for it is
here in this ancient focus of great light that the paths of
all the Seven Chohans are taught and the seven rays of
the Elohim and Archangels are enshrined. The Lords
of Karma, Gautama Buddha, and all members of the
Great White Brotherhood frequent this gathering place
of the Ascended Masters and their disciples while also
maintaining the specialized functions of their own pri-
vate retreats.

A master of sages and philosophers, Lord Lanto
teaches us the path of attainment through enlightenment, definition, and dominion in the crown chakra.
He gained his mastery while studying under Lord Himalaya, Manu of the Fourth Root Race, whose Retreat of

the Blue Lotus is hidden in the mountains that bear his name.

Electing to use the yellow ray to enfold the hearts of all mankind, Lanto dedicated himself to the perfectionment of the evolutions of this planet through the golden flame of Cosmic Christ illumination he bears, charged with his momentum of God-victory for the youth of the world.

We can trace his evolution as a high priest in the temple of the Divine Mother on the lost continent of Lemuria, which occupied a large area of the Pacific Ocean, as well as subsequent embodiments on Atlantis. Following the sinking of "Mu," as the Motherland of the Pacific was called, and the later disappearance of Poseidonis beneath the Atlantic, the last of Atla (Atlantis) which went down in stages, many adepts and priests of the sacred fire bore the flames they had guarded to other parts of the earth, a most necessary ritual as the flames that focus certain qualities of God's consciousness for a planet and its people require sustaining by a highly evolved body of initiates.

Lanto was and is a Master of the power of precipitation—an alchemical process of drawing forth cosmic light and substance from the Universal and coalescing it into physical form (a predetermined matter matrix) by the Science of the Spoken Word. Therefore, appropriately he was chosen to bear the flame of precipitation—a Chinese green tinged with gold—to the stronghold of the Grand Teton, where the Brotherhood had established the magnificent physical focus known as the Royal Teton Retreat.

Lanto later embodied as a ruler in China and as a contemporary of Confucius (551–479 B.C.). Following his ascension, he accepted the office of presiding Master

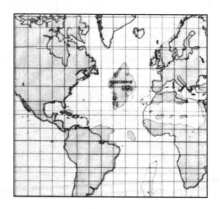

Map of Poseidonis
(Atlantis before the final cataclysm which destroyed it 11,570 years ago)

Astral clairvoyance, says A. P. Sinnett in the foreword to W. Scott-Elliot's *Story of Atlantis*, revealed the records of its civilization. Scott-Elliot's book is a compilation of the discoveries of a number of students who, Sinnett says, were "allowed access to some maps and other records...from the remote periods concerned" to promote the success of their work. These maps, he says, had been physically preserved by those other than the races presently occupying Europe—presumably by the Adepts who tutored students of Theosophy, although Sinnett does not specify. Scott-Elliot writes that the continent was destroyed in stages, with cataclysm occurring 800,000, 200,000 and 80,000 years ago. The last remnant of Atlantis was the continent-island Poseidonis, located near the Azores, which in 9564 B.C. was submerged in a catastrophe referred to in many ancient writings, including those of Plato, he says.

of the Council of the Royal Teton and of the retreat itself in order to bring to the Western world the flame of science, technology, the culture of the Mother and reverence for Life which he and Confucius had sponsored in the Far East.

Master of the fiery core of excellence at the heart of Wisdom's Ray, hence devotee par excellence of the Divine Mother's white fire lilies, Lanto remains the Guru of gurus not only of the Chinese, whom he desires to assist in once again raising up the flame of illumination, but also of all souls who share his love for the golden Sunward path of the Buddhas and bodhisattvas under Sanat Kumara.

Knowing his love and mastery of the arts and music, we are not surprised to learn from his own lips as he recalls the journey from Hesperus and the building of

Confucius,
Jack Fang, 1973, Chinese Cultural Garden, San Jose, California

Wisdom's Smile: The people of the Republic of China on Taiwan dedicated a cultural garden in the Overfelt Botanical Garden in San Jose in 1984. It contains memorials to Sun Yat-sen and Chiang Kai-shek, founders of the Republic, as well as a gateway modeled after one at Confucius' birthplace and this 15-foot bronze statue of the immortal Chinese Master of Wisdom. The statue was constructed in Taiwan and then shipped to the United States.

Shamballa, that *he was there!* Yes, Venusian-hearted
Lanto, one of the original Keepers of the Flame, played
a role in the earliest efforts of Sanat Kumara to fetch
humanity from their darkened descent.

The beloved Lanto *was there* at the LORD's side with
his ingenuity on the Second Ray to woo a piteous people
back to the adoration of the Trinity and the threefold
flame of Life in order that Christ-centered intelligent
life might begin again their Godward evolution on
earth.

The bands who volunteered to accompany Sanat
Kumara on his mission to the dark star sought nothing
less than the rekindling of the Divine Spark in mankind
who, through de-evolution, had lost the original fire and
animating intelligence (genus) of their Divinity. This
they purposed to do from the altar of Shamballa through
the Great One who had exiled himself on planet Earth
for the sole purpose of keeping the flame of Life.

"Ah Shamballa, city of my dreams and my Love—
alabaster… Buddha's glistening…white geometry—floral paths, rock formations, waterfalls leading to Guru's
tender heart. Gobi Sea, island home so long, too long
away: how the soul longs to return to thy light, but the
froward heart, my God! does not allow it.

"Alas, I, too, confess—in this vision of the Golden
City—I am too far from my home away from Home.
O LORD Sanat Kumara, I who would save must needs
be saved. Help me, Great Guru!"

Such is the cry of lightbearers who also came with

Lanto to be world teachers but lost touch by neglect, mists of forgetfulness, letting go of the outstretched hand of the Ancient of Days. Today these urgently seek their LORD, his name unknown, only the Great Light remembered and his figure, powerful beyond this world, at the altar of Shamballa.

And the Chohans, these Lords of the Seven Rays who take their leave from Holy Kumaras Seven, blaze a trail to his heart of fire.

Thus, before his ascension Lord Lanto determined that the light from his own heart flame should shine forth physically as living proof to his disciples that the threefold flame, as in past and coming golden ages, is the Word that is made flesh and that it can be thus expanded and intensified by the priority of the adept.

Affirming with (or aeons before) the proverbial Job, "Yet in my flesh shall I see God!" Lanto, by the dynamism of his decrees from the heart, his devoutness to the living Word as the Universal Christ ever with him, and his consecration of the chakras* to the sacred fire of the Mother did achieve what none other in earth's recorded history since the Fall had done:

Lanto so adored the Trinity in the tripartite light of his innermost being that the intense glow of that Divine Spark could actually be seen through his flesh form emanating a soft golden glow through his chest. This he maintained in honor of Sanat Kumara until his ascension around 500 B.C.—"a memorial to all genera-

---

*seven spiritual centers of light and consciousness in the body of man tions" who are the issue of the I AM THAT I AM—in order that the original lightbearers might recall the mission to illumine the dark star.

Throughout the nineteenth and twentieth centuries Lanto has stood faithfully behind the efforts of Saint Germain to liberate mankind through his release of the Ascended Masters' Teachings on the I AM Presence and the violet fire. On July 3, 1958, the Ascended Master Confucius succeeded Lord Lanto as hierarch of the Royal Teton Retreat. With attainment far beyond that required either of retreat hierarch or Chohan, Lanto accepted from Kuthumi the office of Lord of the Second Ray on that date (this blessed brother who had worshiped the God of Peace as Saint Francis having already in 1956 joined his Lord in the service of the World Teachers).

On October 30, 1966, in cooperation with the God

Confucius Temple, Taipei, Taiwan.

Built in 1854, destroyed by the Japanese in 1895, and rebuilt on the same site in 1925.

and Goddess Meru, Lanto was granted the dispensation by the Karmic Board for a "mighty transcendent golden flame of illumination" to pulsate 300 feet into the atmosphere over the colleges, universities, divinity and theological schools of America and the world whose students and faculty were and would be receptive to knowledge from higher spheres.

Any students of any school of higher learning may call this flame into action on behalf of the faculty and student body. The yellow section of dynamic decrees for the Second Ray disciple found in the Keepers of the Flame decree book is ample for the task, even as its use enhances the auric splendor of the gifts of wisdom and knowledge. So, too, the Second Ray should bring great joy and Chinese/American laughter to those who, bringing happiness to it, so find their mission in keeping the golden flame of illumination with Lanto for the re-education of a world of wonderful people.

And so, through Wisdom's Ray let happy hearts be harnessed to the mission of the Secret Love Star.

Inasmuch as the wisdom of Lord Lanto is excelled by few ascended beings serving this earth, as *he is* the embodiment of the Second Ray, his flame should be invoked daily on behalf of oneself, one's family, and the youth of the world.

As you give the following prayer dictated by the Master, angels of the Second Ray will cut right through to bring order out of chaos in any situation, personal or planetary.

You may wish to compose your own prayer asking
God for help for yourself and loved ones, naming such
conditions which are the result of the misuse of the
crown chakra and the third eye as the following: ignorance, mental disorders, density or retardation, diseases
of the brain and the central nervous system, possessing
demons of insanity and addiction affecting the mind,
body and emotions, and all learning or psychological
problems.

Then give "Lanto's Prayer" with tenacity and let it
gather a momentum all its own as you repeat it until all
illusion is devoured by the golden flame of illumination
from the heart of Almighty God—focused by his servant-
Son in heaven, your elder brother on the path of the
Second Ray who loves you!

Lanto's Prayer

In the name of Almighty God
I stand forth to challenge the Night,
To raise up the Light,
To focus the consciousness of Gautama Buddha!
And I AM the thousand-petaled lotus flame!
And I come to bear it in his name!
I stand in Life this hour
And I stand with the scepter of Christ Power
To challenge the Darkness,
To bring forth the Light,
To ensoul from starry heights
The consciousness of angels,

Masters, Elohim, sun-centers
And of all of Life
That is the I AM Presence of each one!
I claim the Victory in God's name.
I claim the Light of solar flame.
I claim the Light! I AM the Light!
I AM Victory! I AM Victory! I AM Victory!
For the Divine Mother and the Divine Manchild
And for the raising-up of the crown of Life
And the twelve starry focal points
That rejoice to see the salvation of our God
Right within my crown,
Right within the center of the Sun
Of Alpha—It is done!

After giving this prayer with all the love of your heart for the liberation of the youth of the world, you would do well to meditate on the great causal body of Lord Lanto for the purpose of drawing his Electronic Presence around yourself, or even your city, expanding his golden lotus flame through your own crown and heart chakras by using the music that is the keynote of the Royal Teton Retreat—"Song to the Evening Star" from the opera *Tannhauser* by Wagner.

In his great desire to answer those questions of modern-day seekers: Who am I? Why am I here and where am I going? Lord Lanto and the Masters of the Far East dictated instruction on the psychology of the soul, published as a series of *Pearls of Wisdom* entitled *Understanding Yourself.* He teaches that it is contact with the

Holy Christ Self, the Real Self of each one of us, that enables the soul to reestablish the chord of true identity and divine direction in life:

"The soul has been neglected, the soul must be awakened. And man, too, must awaken himself to the soul's consciousness. He must never permit the desecration of the beautiful soul which the LORD God made in his own image. The restoration of the son to the image of the Father is the precious way of salvation which is implemented by the power in hand of the living Christ-identity vouchsafed to every man.

"When every eye shall see him as he is, they shall place their fingers upon the body of his substance, they shall feel the symmetry of the Spirit that is within him, they shall feel the electronic throb of his heartbeat as the essence of his life pours through the garment he wears and floods their souls with identification with higher realms. Then shall man truly come to know who and what he is."

In his basic lectures, the Lord of the Second Ray invites to the Royal Teton Retreat "all who pursue Wisdom, though Her veils and garb be varied as She passes through all levels of learning—all who seek Her knowledge as that true knowledge which comes forth from the fertile Mind of the Creator."

"Come to Wisdom's fount," he says, recalling the cry of Isaiah—"Ho, every one that thirsteth, come ye to the waters…"—"and make ready while there is yet time for you to become all that Wisdom has held in store for you throughout the ages."

In the splendor of the Royal Teton are held conclaves attended by tens of thousands of lifestreams from every continent who journey there in their finer bodies. Smaller classes and tutorials are conducted by angels and adepts who prepare students for the initiation and counsel of the Masters. It is the initial retreat of the Great White Brotherhood to which the neophyte may ask to be taken.

For souls who are studying between embodiments to show themselves approved unto God—as workmen rightly dividing the word of Truth that needeth not to be ashamed before the Holy of Holies—Lanto explains, there are "cubicles within our retreat where students may study alone—and some do for decades as they rise from the screen of life [depart the world of form through the change called death] in meditation upon the Word in science and religion.

"Theologians who have not known or understood the fullness of the mission of the avatar Jesus Christ (and who have been ignorant of Christ's true Doctrine) will sometimes spend years and years (calculated in your time) putting on those simple concepts which come so easily to souls of light in your midst.

"These are sincere devotees of the way of Christ. And gradually, little by little, they excel. They come to understand that the wisdom and knowledge of Christ are found out through a self-awareness in Him—made possible by the great love Jesus imparts as he regularly instructs disciples here in the way of the Universal Christ, whose incarnation he was during the Galilean mission.

"Thus, in their study, wisdom also becomes the component of transmutation, as an adjunct to the violet flame. And through the violet flame and the atonement of the mind in wisdom's law, there comes about the shedding of the snakeskin that has been put upon these sincere ones by those fallen angels called serpents who have entered the pulpits of life to purvey a gospel that is, in effect, anti-Life and anti-Christ.

"But, blessed hearts, there are some children of God who have heard the false gospel for such a long time that they have absorbed the fear of these fallen angels (truly wolves in sheep's clothing) who tremble before the altar of the Almighty, who fear the final judgment, who fear then to stand before the brilliant light of the Avatar Christ Jesus. They know not the true presence of the living Master. They know not the light of His Holy Spirit or His Love!

"Yet, blessed hearts, you must understand that some men's religion is a discoloring of the aura of Christ, a disfiguring of the blessed visage of the Son of God. Thus some, by their skillful momentums weaving webs of false teaching, controlling crowds by tears, emotionalism, strong body movements and their lust after the power of Christ, do in their false doctrine dismember the Body of Christ dividing brother from brother on the interpretation of scripture—and yes, they would, if they could, split, divide and saw asunder Christ's own Universal Body on earth!

"Thus it is in this idolatrous sense of self as the deliverer (while mouthing 'in the name of Jesus') that they partake of Communion—desiring yet to live off his Blood, thinking to escape the inevitable consequences (karma) of the assimilation of His Body and His Blood as a means to the ungodly ends of the control of His little ones.

"Therefore understand how even those who are children of the light could be so encumbered and so burdened by a false clergy—which cloaks its passivity to the warfare of the Spirit it ought to be waging, by taking the sacred name of Jesus in vain—vainly repeating it to sanctify their ungodliness before a credulous public who are too ready to receive the kingdom in clouds of glory, praising Jesus and not at all eager to demonstrate their faith by works—the serious work of casting the money-changers and the drug dealers and the possessing demons out of the temples of their children.

"And rock music and country at the altar tells it all. It tells what spirits are upon the preachers, to whom they give allegiance and to what low levels of compromise they are willing to go to keep their followers. Let them renounce it all and follow the LORD in solitude as Moses, Elijah and Jesus have done. And let them know that the real empowerment requires the sacrifice of money, position, power, fame, and an idolatrous cult of 'yea, Lord' yes-men and -women also beset by the same low order of entities which followed Jesus everywhere he went, repeating in vain his blessed name over and over for fear that the LORD would exorcise them. And He did!

"To all of the pastors and sheep led astray, we say with Jesus, 'Father, forgive them, they know not what they are about.' But to the serpents who have contrived a false Christianity that strips the people of their true spiritual defenses in time of ultimate danger and death from nuclear war with the placebo, 'Jesus is coming,' the entire Spirit of the Great White Brotherhood says with the Ascended Master Jesus Christ:

"'WOE TO YOU FALSE PASTORS who Destroy and Scatter the sheep of my pasture... I will visit upon you the evil of your doings for thus saith the LORD the I AM THAT I AM the Almighty!'

"So declares Lanto at the Royal Teton Retreat with the World Teachers Jesus and Kuthumi flanking him, saying, 'Amen. I AM Alpha and Omega, the beginning and the ending.'

"After all, blessed hearts, Christianity today is as much a social institution as is Judaism. And people gather together in their churches as centers of fellowship while the delicate truths and the piercing light of the sacred mysteries—even the mystery of the piercing of the Body of Christ—escapes them and becomes merely the repetition of words they have heard and mere human sentiment that they entertain for a season.

"But it passes away, never having penetrated the heart, never having given unto them the reality that we the Ascended Masters are alive forevermore and that He is the same yesterday and today and forever!—yet expanding, ever expanding by the magnificence of the co-measurement of the Son of God with the living Word, with the Eternal One, with the light behind the light of Brahman!

"Yes, Jesus is coming 'with clouds,' and 'every eye shall see him.' But look for him to descend into your temple from the cloud of the Mighty I AM Presence above you. Look for him in the One Sent and the One promised, the LORD OUR RIGHTEOUSNESS (Jer. 23:6) who is the Universal Christ personified in you as your beloved Holy Christ Self.

"For, by this sign of the Person of the Trinity, we also conquered, we also were resurrected, we also made our ascension. And so shall you. For this same Christ of Jesus is also *your Real Self!* Therefore, look for his Second Coming as day by day he returns to his temple in the hearts and minds and spirits of the living saints.

"But remember it is written that 'all kindreds of the earth shall wail because of him' (Rev. 1:7) and their wailing is the wailing of the demons possessing the people both in and out of the churches. These are they who *will not* eat his flesh and drink his blood of the New Covenant—who will not take responsibility for the full cup of discipleship in his footsteps leading to joint-heirship—neither are they willing to self-sacrifice to attain the inheritance of that Christhood and Him dwelling bodily in them!

"No, when it comes down to it, they want to be saved by the *name* of Jesus without the person of Jesus. And their weeping and wailing in the churches and synagogues and at the wailing wall is no sign of the LORD's coming or of His Holy Ghost, but the crying of the same genre of demons who said, 'Let us alone; what have we to do with thee, thou Jesus of Nazareth? art thou come to destroy us? I know thee who thou art, the Holy One of God.'

"Therefore today from the Royal Teton Retreat, and from the pulpits of the nations, Jesus rebukes the proud spirits which possess the pastors and the people and which mourn and defy his coming in his true apostles, saying: 'Hold thy peace and come out of them!'

"Thus, blessed hearts, understand that there are many levels which we have provided for the sincere and the pure in heart as they take their leave of this octave and must prepare again (through study under the Chohans in their retreats) for a life (reembodiment on earth) which will be to them the opportunity to enter the path of true discipleship and true Christhood.

"Let us concern ourselves, then, with the needs of those who are trapped in the orthodoxy of the major world's religions. Let us understand that the false priesthood have succeeded in transmitting to the followers of God their own fear. That fear paralyzes, that fear makes for pride, even spiritual pride that closes all of the apertures of self to the fresh winds of the Holy Spirit....

"You see, blessed hearts, this confusion of the Lord's

Doctrine is not merely a burden of narrow-mindedness. It is not merely the burden of those who themselves are dense after the density of the planet. It is a situation where the children of the light who ignorantly follow the false pastors are carrying the weight of karma of these fallen angels who have placed themselves in positions of leadership in the world's religions.

"And therefore, when you see the followers of the blind leaders of the blind, it is the followers (and not their leaders) who represent the Lamb slain from the foundation of the world. *They* are the children of the Lamb; and as such, they are His little lambs and they know not why they bear such a burden of ignorance, of heaviness, even of densification and unknown diseases in their flesh.

"And thus it is that as long as the leaders in Church and State, in science, religion, education, industry and the labor movements are themselves the fallen ones, purveyors of gross darkness and darkening concepts, downward spirals that through art and music lead to the death vibration—so long will those who follow after them for social tradition and for human creature comforts be bearing the entire weight of the karma of the Watchers and their godless creation.[1]

"Can you not see how these serpents have contrived to be 'karma-dodgers' and to place upon the children of the light worldwide—who indeed are the faithful—their own guilt, their own self-condemnation, their own fear of death and hell, *and therefore* the rigidity of their orthodox interpretations of the original and vital principles of the living Word incarnate?

"Therefore we come. We come as Brothers of the Golden Robe. We come to deliver the renewed light, the original Mandate, the true essence of the Blood of the avatars, the Christed ones of the ages!

"We come to reinfuse the sweet children of the light with that which is due them, for it was theirs from the beginning—the Everlasting Gospel of God, the Lost Teachings and the Lost Word of the fairest Lord Jesus, and the revolutionary and prophetic message of Saint Germain."

Through our experiences with Jesus and Saint Germain at the Royal Teton Retreat in the heart of America's Rocky Mountains, we can see that the ties that bind the seed of light from the Far East to the Far West run deep.

And what with the Lady Kuan Yin, Goddess of Mercy, serving on the Karmic Board (which convenes here at the solstices) and the annual New Year's Eve and Wesak addresses of the Lord of the World, Gautama Buddha, broadcast from the great council hall (as from Shamballa and a valley in the Himalayas), complementing the service of Jesus and Saint Germain—what with the golden flame of illumination and the Chinese-green fire for the precipitation of the abundant Life focused here—the souls of all nations and planetary systems are at One and at Home.

Let us go there!

It is now New Year's Eve, when Masters from around the world come for a great convocation and solemn council. We arrive early—just as the sun is setting, tinting the snowy peaks of the Grand Teton a golden pink.

Lord Lanto greets us warmly as we bow to him and welcomes us to this ancient palace of spiritual splendor.

While we await the New Year's Eve address of beloved Gautama Buddha, we go to a massive etheric amphitheater where tens of thousands of unascended

Gautama Buddha,
2nd–3rd century

Lao Tzu,
Keichyu Yamada, c. 1906

The three great branches of Chinese religious and moral thought—Buddhism, Confucianism and Taoism—had their origin in the sixth century B.C. Gautama Buddha (c. 563 B.C.–483 B.C.) and Confucius (c. 551 B.C.–479 B.C.) were contemporaries.

Although it is not certain whether Lao Tzu, founder of Taoism, is a historical figure at all, tradition says he was born 604 B.C., and a first-century B.C. historian records a supposed dialogue between the aging Lao Tzu and the younger Confucius.

souls are gathered. Lanto leads us out of the great council hall, down the corridor to a door which opens into the starry night where tier upon tier of seats rise from a central stage. The amphitheater was recently constructed, he says, for the "lightbearers who, on earth and in America today, are a part of the body of believers who are seeking the LORD God in churches and not finding him in doctrine or dogma."

He takes the lectern at the center of the platform and begins to teach these Truth-starved souls:

"...Let us understand that illumination and its flame must not be snuffed out in this land—as youth are in delirium and their senses dulled by drugs and rock, and think of no other thing but lyrics that take them down and down again to a lower level and therefore deprive them of the blossoming of the yellow fire of the crown! Let us realize that there is a movement, a force— and I must say, it is the tremendous force of 'hell' itself moving across the land to take a stand against the light— against the wisdom of the heart!

"Who shall pursue the fount of wisdom? Who shall be able to rise and mount the ladder of the chakras when these drugs and the downward-spiraling beat does take the youth even beneath their feet to subterranean levels of hellish fires of fallen ones—who themselves long lost their wings, blackened now with other things, and therefore dwell in places of insects' origins and biting and stinging things that ought to be no more but are—fed as they are by mass ignorance?

"I come to pierce the veil of ignorance!... If I had my say, I would tell you that unless the flame of illumination be understood as the apex and culmination of all of life and the key to immortality, unless it be revered, all else must go down.

"Think upon it, blessed hearts. One may tell you the law; but without the understanding, did you always obey it? Nay. It requires a teaching, a reasoning of the heart, a motive that comes through understanding and understanding alone. You may know the truth, but the truth that sets you free is the truth that is understood by illumination's flame."

Speaking on behalf of himself and the Mentors of the Spirit serving with him on the Second Ray, Lord Lanto adds:

"We look to increase understanding. We look to the students to increase self-understanding. To understand the self is to know the self in relationship to God. That relationship must be discerned, of course, by an appreciation of who and what the Self of God is. For you cannot understand a relationship between yourself and any part of Life except you have understanding of the two parts....

"Thus, the understanding of the Self must be found by an approximation of the Holy Christ Self. Even though you know not that Self, you know that you can pray for oneness with that Self, to put on the vestments of that Self. You know that the Self is the mediator between light and darkness, between heaven and earth and between God and your outer self-awareness.

"Therefore, when the view of these two becomes dim, you must flee to the tower of the Christ consciousness and pray earnestly at the altar of the Lord for the putting on of the garment of that consciousness of your

Confucius presenting the young Gautama Buddha to Lao Tzu,
Quing dynasty

From the thought of these three masters came the cultural golden age of China, during which she was the preeminent world civilization. To the uncivilized West she brought such things as paper, printing and gunpowder, as well as bathing and noodles.

Holy Christ Self. And when you have that consciousness put on, you have the point of contact with the realistic assessment of your present state of evolution and how far you must go to get to that God whom only your Christ Self can reveal to you.

"For it is He who has said: 'I AM the open door which no man can shut.' It is the Universal, or Cosmic, Christ speaking through the Christ of Jesus and the Christ of you who says: I AM the Door: by me if any man enter in, he shall be saved, and shall go in and out, and find pasture. I AM the Way, the Truth, and the Life: No man cometh unto the Father, but by me....

"I am your teacher, friend, and mentor of old; and I have come to claim you once again. At any hour of the day or night when you would be free of the bondage of mortality, call to me and I will send forth that golden ray to quicken, to awaken, to hallow the sacred ground beneath your feet made holy by your endeavor to be the fullness of the God flame."

To grateful applause, Lord Lanto exits the platform and excited whispers fill the audience. It is now nearly midnight and Gautama Buddha is seated on a golden throne, the Lords of Karma standing beside him. The Lord of the World is ready to address the members of the Brotherhood gathered in the great council hall as well as invited guests who fill the amphitheater. These see clearly through the now-transparent mountain wall directly into the hall where we have been ushered to our seats for the event.

A hush descends over the starlit amphitheater as he begins to speak. Soon the Seven Chohans rise, step forward, and bow, acknowledging their obeisance to the God flame. They present a scroll to Lord Gautama and the Lords of Karma.

These presiding Masters open the scroll and read it; in a moment the Buddha looks up and explains that this is a request made by the Chohans to open universities of the Spirit in their respective retreats where thousands and tens of thousands of students may be summoned to attend courses in Ascended Master law.

He outlines the plan for those "who will diligently pursue the path of self-mastery on the seven rays systematically, mastering most especially the First and the Seventh Rays whereby they might establish the Alpha and the Omega of their identity—the will of God, the divine blueprint, the inner plan for twin flames—and immediately begin an action of personal and world transmutation" through the violet flame.

Studies are to begin with El Morya at Darjeeling for a fourteen-day cycle, then a fortnight with Saint Germain at the Royal Teton Retreat. The student will alternate these periods between the two centers until he successfully passes certain levels and receives an opportunity to study with the other Chohans.

The Lord of the World announces that he and the Lords of Karma have approved this petition and that "in this hour it is formally granted."

The crowds in the amphitheater leap to their feet,

cheering the dispensation as the mountains resound with the shouts of the people's acclamation. So great is the desire of their souls to attend the Mystery Schools of the Brotherhood!

This is a most opportune dispensation for the unification and enlightenment of the lightbearers of the world. The Royal Teton Retreat thus becomes a launching pad for thousands of souls to reach the star of their own God Presence through the Teachings of the Ascended Masters. Here the I AM Race of all nations and kindreds and tongues are welcomed and they do gather nightly, for the Grand Teton is the sign of the rising SUN—the Spiritual Unity of Nations—to all lightbearers whom Saint Germain has called, making himself heard like the town crier in every city, town, hamlet and home:

"Lightbearers of the world, unite!"

May they respond with the scientific statement of their universal religion taught by the Lords of the Seven Rays—and may it be Wisdom's smile that turns on the universal age.

———————

Before leaving the comfortable and comforting sphere of light that is the auric field of Lord Lanto, we must not forget nor neglect to apprise our readers of the most wonderful counsel offered by the Lord of the Second Ray to disciples seeking Love/Wisdom's initiations leading to the restoration of twin flames to the path of Oneness.

Concerning twin flames and their uniting at inner levels for the fulfillment of their divine plan (whether or not they are joined together on the outer, i.e., in physical embodiment), Lanto does instruct at this university of the Spirit the "male" and "female" whose spirits were made in the beginning by Elohim out of the white fire ovoid—twin flames having, by definition, the identical electronic blueprint.

Having laid the foundation for their understanding of the path of Love's reunion in the white fire body (i.e., the causal body) of the I AM THAT I AM, Lord Lanto reminds that it is through their diligent transmutation of the records of the karma of past lives that twin flames achieve the best results.

The hierarch requires that twin flames exercise and acquire the mastery of the Science of the Spoken Word in the giving of violet flame decrees for the clearing of all blocks to their united service in furtherance of the world plan of the Lords of the Seven Rays for universal peace, enlightenment and freedom.

When twin flames have advanced together in Lanto's classes on "marriage counseling" for those pursuing the marriage made in heaven, he brings many "couples" together for initiation—i.e., a transfer of light from the Great Central Sun to enhance their efforts and accelerate their minds and chakras to become greater instruments of light of the Universal Christ.

Having taught them the mantra of twin flames who are the Christed ones: "I AM Alpha and Omega in the white-fire core of Being," they are set to receive his blessing. And we are privileged to observe this ceremony in part and to hear his invocation and lecture for our edification:

"Elohim of God, come now! I, Lanto, summon thee in this hour to the Royal Teton Retreat and to our mountain. Thus, come to the Grand Teton, O Elohim. Intensify these foci of seven rays upon the brows of twin flames.

"Beloved ones, as I speak, my Electronic Presence here, I am in the Great Hall of the Grand Teton, one with Elohim—the Alpha of myself in the retreat, the Omega sealing the Messenger speaking my word here in the Chapel of the Holy Grail.

"Therefore, the arc is that thou might come—thou and thy twin flame—that thou mightest enter this hall this night while the body sleeps and truly stand at inner levels with thy twin flame for this dispensation of the alignment of the inner being and the fiery ovoid and the chakras by the hand of Elohim, who shall place their hands on the brow of the male and female form. For out of Elohim in the white-fire core of being thou didst come forth in this form as the polarity of being.

"We speak, then, of the universities of the Chohans opened. We speak of our course intensive under the Second Ray at the Royal Teton Retreat. Beloved ones, Cosmic Christ illumination is intensifying now within the crown chakra. For those who gather must know that the cosmic cross of white fire is drawn—the vertical bar now being the channel of the chakras and the raising of the sacred fire; the horizontal bar, beloved ones, the extending of this light by the Sacred Heart of which John the Beloved spake last night.

"See, then, how the summoning of the sacred fire of the Divine Mother in the Hail Mary, in the *Sri Mata*, O beloved, does raise that fire to the point of the heart, even as you draw it from the Central Sun of your I AM Presence.

A frontier pass on the Silk Road near Lanchow, China

Lord Lanto, together with his more renowned contemporaries Confucius and Gautama Buddha, held the God-consciousness for the nation of China for centuries. The yellow flame of illumination reflected in the Chinese people burns in the retreat of Archangel Jophiel and Christine, located south of the Great Wall near Lanchow, China. This flame is the primordial light of the yellow race which when harnessed through the illumined ones gave cultural impetus to China at a time when the rest of the world, having either rejected or missed altogether the Christ-flame in the ones sent, was karmically locked in an age of barbarism. The greatness of China is reflective of the consciousness of Lanto, the Master who endowed her, and of the Masters who endowed him—the Ancient of Days, Lord Himalaya, Gautama Buddha and Lord Maitreya.

"Therefore, beloved, the descending sacred fire and the ascending must be extended by these arms, strong and instruments of the Holy Spirit in action. Thus, you see what capacity you have in these hands—you, twin flames, two pairs of hands to anchor the Alpha, the Omega. See, then, that the work of the hands provides the vessel for the fire that must be released.

"Let the matrix be perfected. The word *matrix* comes from the word *womb.* It is the Cosmic Egg of the Cosmic Virgin where thou shalt perfect the alchemy of those heavenly patterns that must be brought forth in order that the flame might be passed heart to heart.

"It is not difficult to understand. When thy brother hath need of Christ in the gift of the cup of cold water, the cup is essential to contain the liquid. You do not offer the cup of water in your hand or by drops: a vessel is required. Thus, this liquid light is passed and, when given in the name of Christ, it is always charged with the light of his heart and the light of the heart of your own Holy Christ Self.

"Beloved ones, the gift of spiritual fire must have the vessel, whether as service, as action, as handiwork, as profession. Consider then, beloved, what is thy daily occupation, and see to it that on the path of karma yoga, balancing that karma, you are giving and giving again and giving.

"And do you know, beloved, the joy of joys? When you realize that your whole life is the building of the vessel and then you come to the beloved or to the sick, the sinful, the dying, and the needy, and you realize that—building upon the mantra of the Word, building upon the living fire invoked by the dynamic decree, building again by the actions of devotion and service—'I have become my own handiwork. I am the vessel of Elohim. We are that vessel—the "I" and the "thou" of twin flames sharing in the God-fire in the mighty caduceus.'

"Thus you come, beloved. And it is no longer the cup or the handiwork that you offer but yourself alone. And so you say to those in need, 'I AM the vessel.* Here is the Light of my heart. I give it freely. I AM in Christ the One.' And you say, 'Lo, this is my body which is broken for you.'

"Thus, the breaking of the seal and the letting flow of the light of the chakras—each chakra a wafer of the Alpha/Omega. Thus, seven wafers of Cosmic Christ consciousness. And the wine is the essence of thy life. No less might thou give.

"Any lesser gift is not the perfect offering unto your Lord. For ere he send you to the multitudes, he himself will come disguised in any and many forms to test the readiness of the givingness of thyself, to test the strength of the vessel, the equanimity and joy, the sense of mercy, but also the sense of the protection of this the great light that is the gift of Elohim.

"Thus, beloved, carefully give the light to one who may contain it, who has a vessel—however meager. For

---

*The I AM THAT I AM in me is the vessel, and I myself am the Master's vessel, because He has called me and because I have answered.

those who come to the well of Life must bring their pots, their cups. They cannot receive if they are empty-handed. Thus, learn the Law, beloved. Thou canst not give this cup of water to those who are empty, devoid, having only a negative vortex through which the light does pass, as through a sieve, and then pass into the astral plane.

"Thus, give as God gives. Let the fire now be unto the sons and daughters of God. Let it be unto you as Christ did bless at the Last Supper, transferring himself—he, the vessel.

"Now into new vessels must this Messenger and your twin flames pour yourself. Thus, watch and pray, for the pouring is out of the eternal fount, and the light does descend. And by the knowledge and the understanding of the Real and the unreal, this light will be vouchsafed unto those who are Real, those who have lamps trimmed, already containing the fire of the wise virgins. Thus, unto them who have shall more be added, and sons and daughters of God shall become this Son.

"At the Royal Teton Retreat this night you shall receive the first impetus of Elohim for the alignment of twin flames. Each successive night for fourteen days this alignment shall increase until you may go forth better able to carry the spiritual fire. This can be accomplished by Elohim only as commensurate with the works that are brought by yourselves—the work of the hands, that which is in the causal body, that which is attainment.

"And those who have not the attainment will not be

rejected but taken into the hall of our university to study in the way in which we teach, from many aspects of the infinite Mind, how to build from the very foundation to the top of the pyramid, how to begin to build so that one may have at least one cup that may receive some light.

"It is the age of the World Teachers. It is the age of the Chohans and the Maha Chohan. It is the age of your victory if you will make it so. The temple doors have been opened with the ascension of Lanello, and the universities of the Spirit are opened now, where thousands may come to the retreats of the Seven Chohans—this in the hour of the victory of your beloved Saint Germain.

"Thus, I, Lanto, speak to you of the mysteries of God that you may rejoice in prayer and meditation and call to the angels of the blessed Mother Mary to take you to this great retreat of light where tutors are waiting to tutor and test your souls by a most magnificent Love.

"May you pray for the lightbearers in all the earth to be cut free by the mighty Archangels to join you in the universities of the Spirit, that there might indeed be a great swelling of a cosmic revolution on earth and that the cosmic spin of the planet might also be restored because you have dared to accelerate your chakras. For the chakras of thyself and thy twin flame will hold the electromagnetic balance for the increase now of the spin of this planet until the etheric plane is once more tangible, even as it is becoming tangible to yourselves.

"Thus, having given you an opening of the door of

the University of Wisdom's Flame, I, Lanto, seal you and look to welcome you shortly for the continuation of my dissertation.

"I am rejoicing in the flame of Jesus upon the hour of your resurrection to new Life. For I AM the Resurrection and the Life of the Great White Brotherhood in the earth as in the heaven, in Spirit and Matter, through this bowl and your own.

"In Christ's own Victory, by the rose of your heart, O beloved ones pursuing the Sacred Heart, I am one grateful Chohan of the Second Ray in this hour of the seventh dispensation. May you rejoice as one grateful chela to know Wisdom face to face."

Portrait of a Man (self-portrait),
Paolo Veronese c. 1570, J. Paul Getty Museum, California

3

PAUL THE VENETIAN
the Artist

Gift of the Discerning of Spirits

The Ascended Master Paul the Venetian, Lord of the Third Ray and initiator of our hearts, relates a very touching personal experience from his life as an artist in which his sensitive soul, at one with God, bore the unknown grief of another and then the comfort of the Resurrection Spirit that had the power to heal even an angel veiled in flesh:

"I remember so dearly the day when I first developed enough of the divine sense to feel that God and I were one. It had been a cloudy morning, and I had worked long and hard to try to portray the face of an angel, but somehow it was as though the celestial beauty escaped me and there was a jangle in my nerves and senses and feelings.

"This was strange, because I had for some time developed a feeling of serenity, of calmness, of knowing, and now here I was desiring out of that calmness and serenity and knowing to portray a celestial being, and I needed to drink deeply of the fountain of peace.

"For some reason, which did not seem to break through to my outer senses, I could not still my mind, and so with some measure of disturbance, shall I say, I closed up shop. I put away my brushes and frankly there was sadness in my every movement. It was not a state of utter discouragement, it was just an unusual state of unrest in my feeling world, almost a dire foreboding that something undesirable would happen.

"I left the studio and I walked out into the street, and it seemed to me as though every thought of my heart was known by all whom I met, and certainly my glances must have appeared furtive, as though I were a criminal seeking to hide from the eyes of prying mankind.

"This now drove me almost to a state of desperation and I wandered away from the busy thoroughfare of the streets of the city seeking the reasonable quietude of the country. As I reached the edge of a field near an old churchyard, it seemed as though the feeling of oppression began to lessen and the clouds were now thinning a bit and a gentle breeze was blowing.

"And in the stillness of the approaching country I began to feel the awakening of the sense of peace, so familiar and so dearly loved. And as I wandered farther and farther into the fields and forest regions, I began to ponder as to whether or not the oppressions of the city could be responsible for my condition, and then I reasoned quite suddenly that I ought to be strong enough to hold a sense of beauty in the midst of the ugliness and garrets of the city.

"And I decided that this was not it either, yet I enjoyed my newfound serenity, and I felt that if perhaps I could quiet the possibility of its return I would be able to go back once more to the room and create the angelic face.

"But this was not to happen, for I heard a terrible sound of sobbing, and for a moment my heart trembled for mankind. This sobbing came from a graveside where a young lady, prone now upon the ground, cried as though her heart would break. I debated with myself as to whether or not it would be propriety for me to speak, being a stranger unto her, and to say unto her, 'Dry your

Feast in the House of Levi, detail,
Paolo Veronese 1573, Galleria della Academia, Venice

tears, daughter, be of peace.' And somehow I could not for a moment seize the courage—and this, too, was unusual.

"And then I decided that I would enter into simple prayer for her. And as I prayed, the sun came out with greater glory and it was as though the hands of the angels were drawing back the curtain of dark clouds. And with this change in the environment of the little cemetery, the young lady suddenly ceased to sob and gazed up with wonder. Her sorrow and her grief were plainly stamped upon one of the most beautiful faces that I have ever seen, and there was my angel—the face that I sought.

"Buoyantly now, I re-create that moment. But I knew that I must paint out that grief, and therefore I must seek somehow to bring a ray of hope, some measure of consolation to her heart. And hesitantly at first, I broke a smile upon my face and she returned it. And I said to her, as I tenderly took ahold of an apple blossom from a nearby tree, 'Daughter, there is a resurrection in Nature, and all things do pass and go through their cycles, only to return once again to the fullness and the dawn of bloom, and in the resurrection your father dear shall return to you.'

"And she sobbingly said, 'I know it, kind sir. I know it, but I am so lonely now.'

"And I took her by the hand, and as I prayed, I felt a surge of the Christ radiance go through me, and I watched as every line of her face reflected consolation, mercy, acceptance of the Resurrection Spirit. And then

I noted that through my arm and hands was a great puls-
ing energy, and I felt my heart beat with greater expectation. Truly the 'whole eye' spirit was activated.

"And the young woman suddenly burst into a smile
of greater happiness, and she said, 'Oh, I do not feel
lonely any more. I will go home now to my mother, who
has been distraught with my grief, and I will no longer
mourn; for I feel something within myself, something
that encourages me to believe you. I do not know why.
Your words have meaning to me, and I am no longer sad.'

"And now as the sun came out in greater measure,
blooming full orbed, I witnessed the transformation that
was a miracle never to be forgotten throughout all the
days of my life until I won my ascension. The face of
an angel shone now in all of the glory and magnitude
of God. And I said, 'Truly God is veiled in flesh,' and
I returned and painted my angel."

"Paolo Veronese," as he was known in his last life as
the Italian Renaissance painter (1528–1588), exercised
the gift of the discernment of spirits in art. He broke away
from the tradition in religious art of making the figures
of Christ and his apostles stiff and unreachable. He was
a spiritual revolutionary who waged his battle against
the forces of anti-Life in the arts and who saw Beauty as
the most powerful catalyst for enlightenment.

Through his discernment and execution of delicate
nuance in his paintings of Jesus, the twelve, various biblical figures and the saints, he effected a subtle change
in attitudes toward the sacred. Never did he become

irreverent, never did his figures lose their aura of holiness; however, by endowing them with lifelike expressions and associating them with easily identifiable places and things, he put them within the reach of the common people. Their lives lived as real people became a goal towards which more might aspire. By a fresh perspective, he approached serious and sacred subjects with a simple familiarity that eroded the idolatry inherent in previous medieval and Renaissance art.

This was not to be accomplished, however, without inciting the wrath of the powers that be, those who were carrying on a tradition in art and religion of warped concepts from which Paolo would break free.

On one occasion he was summoned before the tribunal of the Inquisition under suspicion of heresy for the "irreverences" in his painting of the Last Supper, which included in it a dwarf with a parrot, guards in German armour, dogs and a jester. He stood firm before his accusers in defending the creative freedom of the artist, saying, "We painters take the same liberties as poets and madmen take." The question was not resolved until Veronese changed the title of his work to *Feast in the House of Levi*.

The Master transcended the traditionally flat, lifeless and grim aspects of medieval art by creating new colors as well as by contrasting colors in a way that had never been done before. No more somber, depressing shades, but translucent hues conveying light and vibrancy—almost an intoxication with rich color.

He experimented until he perfected a technique of pigment preparation for preserving paint that is unsurpassed; and the magnificent colors radiate from his work to this day. Veronese became renowned for his biblical scenes, historical subjects, festivals and pageants refreshingly executed with joy and a sweeping grandeur, so much so that he took his place as the third of the Renaissance giants in Venice, along with Titian and Tintoretto.

Near the close of his life, his Guru, the Maha Chohan, advised Paul that through the Christic disciplines of Love on the path of the Third Ray, self-imposed for many lifetimes, he had earned his release from Earth's schoolroom and was ready to enter into the realms of immortality. After his passing at the age of sixty, he retired to the Château de Liberté, where his soul entered the ritual of the ascension April 1588, rising, whence it had descended, to the Sun of Aries, truly having earned the God-control of the divine art of Being.

In previous embodiments Paul served in the government of Atlantis as the head of cultural affairs. Before the continent sank, he established a focus of the liberty flame in Peru which gave impetus to the culture, beauty and wealth of the Incan civilization. He embodied in the Incan empire as an artist who, true to his colors, used paints that did not fade. Later he embodied as an Egyptian master of esoteric architecture and worked with El Morya, then a master mason, at the time of the building of the pyramids.

His love has been fulfilled in his works. As he said,

"The fullness of love cannot be love unless it is action. Contemplated love or the mere repetition of words may occupy one's fancy, but love in action is the measure of a heart united with mind and soul."

Paul the Venetian and the Brotherhood of the Third Ray of Divine Love with whom he works from ascended octaves are no idle dreamers but pragmatists in the way of the Holy Spirit. It is the Third Ray through which the qualities of tact, diplomacy, arbitration, patience, forbearance, unity, brotherhood, culture, beauty and the perfecting of the heart manifest. And it is the pink/rose flame of this ray with white-fire center that pulsates to externalize the divine plan in the chalice of man's being through the Body (white) and Blood (ruby) of the Universal Christ.

Since his ascension, Paul has tutored students of art, music, architecture, engineering, and the culture of the Divine Mother which antedates Lemuria and goes back to the earliest golden ages of earth. All that he teaches as technique for the creation of beauty, symmetry, and design in form is both to the ritual and the goal of the balance of the threefold flame—heart, head, and hand—and the extolling of the qualities of the tripartite flame of Liberty, the fleur-de-lis that is the signet of every son and daughter of Sanat Kumara.

Until recently, these activities took place at the Château de Liberté, Paul's vast retreat on the etheric plane in southern France that lends itself to the function of gallery, museum and archives of art and artifacts from many cultures and civilizations. A Versailles of its own splendor, it contains endless classrooms where great works of art of all ages are displayed. Paintings by Paul, his students, and other masters abound. Here workshops for musicians, writers, sculptors, students of voice as well as crafts of all kinds have been held and Ascended Masters of all the rays have introduced new techniques in every field of art.

A magnificent painting of the Holy Trinity by Paul graces the main hall of the retreat. Begun before and completed after his ascension, it portrays the majestic figure of the heavenly Father, the Son in the likeness of Jesus, and an impressive white dove with a nine-foot wing span as a focus of the Holy Spirit. Beneath the painting, inscribed in gold letters, are the words "Perfect love casteth out fear."

Currently certain classes formerly held at the Château de Liberté under the direction of the Lord of the Third Ray are taking place in the Temple of the Sun over Manhattan in connection with the dispensation of the universities of the Spirit announced by Gautama Buddha New Year's Eve, December 31, 1985.

This is the etheric retreat of Paul's spiritual Mother, who is the Goddess of Liberty—the Cosmic Being behind the statue, so named for her complete identification with the God consciousness of liberty. It was she who first enshrined the liberty flame on earth and, just prior to the sinking of Atlantis, transported it from her then-physical Temple of the Sun to the Château de Liberté.

It was the Goddess of Liberty who inspired the idea of the Statue of Liberty as a gift of the people of France to the people of the United States, which was dedicated on Bedloe's Island October 28, 1886. A symbol of their friendship and more, it was the spanning of the arc of liberty from the Château de Liberté back to the Temple of the Sun with the intent that the descendants of Atlantis reembodied at both her East and West gates (at France and the United States) would hold high her torch

The Square of St. Mark's, Venice, Antonio Canale Canaletto, 1740

From the time Paolo Caliari arrived in Venice until his death at sixty, a period of thirty-three years, he was the chosen painter of the Most Serene Republic. Dubbed Veronese after his native city Verona, he adopted Venice and encapsulated in his works of art the brilliance of her cultural zenith. The rich variety of color in her markets and harbor became his palette. He rejoiced in her as she in him.

until Liberty's culture should once again appear in a golden age founded upon the balanced and expanded threefold flame in the hearts of the freedom-loving people of these sister nations.

Seventy-six years later, in a dictation given in Washington, D.C., September 30, 1962, an Ascended Master of the Fifth Ray announced the bestowal of another gift from France to America, this time from Paul the Venetian:

"There has been held a beautiful and wonderful session at Chananda's retreat in India and a decision was made on the part of beloved Paul the Venetian whereby there was transferred from his retreat in France this day, at the hour of eleven o'clock your time, the full pulsation of the great liberty flame.

"This flame was permanently placed within the forcefield of the Washington Monument; and the pulsations of the liberty flame are intended to grace the heart of America as a gift from the Brotherhood and from the heart of beloved Paul the Venetian....

"It is given as a treasure from the heart of France, from the spiritual government of France to the spiritual government of Amer-

The Washington Monument

ica.... The liberty flame is a gift of greater magnitude than the former gift of France, the Statue of Liberty, as a tribute to that great being, the Goddess of Liberty. It is incomparable, for the flame itself shall penetrate the structure of the monument, rising high into the atmosphere above it; and all who visit there shall become, even without knowing it, infused by the pulsations of the liberty flame within the heart of America."

In addition to making a pilgrimage to this shrine, you may call to the angels of the Third Ray to take you to the university of the Spirit at the Temple of the Sun for the development of the heart chakra and the gift of the *discernment of spirits* on the Third Ray. Truly, this training awaits you, as do your Teachers—when you are ready.

It is Paul the Venetian with the Maha Chohan himself who will tutor your soul in discerning the foul spirits of demons below and the fiery spirits of angels above, both of which may work through people according to their up-and-down moods and vibrations.

The Master is devoted to the perfecting of the soul and the development of the intuitive and creative faculties of the heart. His path brings together the teachings of the Lords of the First and Second Rays by making practical the will and the wisdom of God through the science of Love as it applies to every challenge we face today—from drugs to terrorism to pornography to nuclear war or economic debacle, even cataclysm and the putting down of the Divine Woman (and the Feminine Ray) in both sexes and little children.

Beloved Paul will also teach you to "try the spirits, whether they are of God," as John admonished us to do, "because", as the apostle said, "many false prophets are gone out into the world." And by the Holy Spirit he will show you how to exorcise those spirits if they are not of God and how to harness their forces if they are. This training, which prepares you for self-mastery through God's love, involves the initiations of the Ruby Ray under the Maha Chohan and Lord Maitreya and a working knowledge of the ritual of exorcism taught by the Ancient of Days.

In order to bind evil spirits in the name I AM THAT I AM, in the name Jesus Christ, you must establish a strong heart-tie to the Sacred Heart of beloved Jesus and to the Immaculate Heart of his Mother, Mary. It is essential that you develop a close working relationship with Archangel Michael and his legions of blue-flame angels as well as with the cosmic Mother-figure called Astrea, even as you learn to wield the *sword* of the sacred *word* in giving dynamic decrees.

This you can do. And this we do, for Jesus has taken us to Paul the Venetian's retreat in southern France— once a physical focus on the Rhône River, later frequented more on the etheric plane where over the years it did become a vast enclave of light and the proving ground of the greats of the Renaissance in art and music who occupied the "practice makes perfect" cubicles, as Paul called the chambers he set aside for those who brought

The Marriage of
Saint Catherine,
Paolo Veronese,
1574–1576

forth the heavenly patterns in the classics of every field, including literature, drama, and architecture.

Here we studied the spiritual skills involved in taking control of the circumstances of our lives by the all-power of Love's creative forces and the Holy Spirit's alchemy of the Seventh Ray.

You can see that Paul's current university of the Spirit curriculum—and the path of the Third Ray itself—is by no means for artists alone: it is for the soul as the artist of life, her own life, who must move from the canvas of karmic impressionism through that of the stark realism of abstract astral recordings to ethereal pastels and inner actualities appearing until the inner blueprint of Life is rendered on the clean white page of her victorious overcoming in Christ.

Indeed, the path of the artist is the path of Life. So is the Third Ray discipline the inescapable synthesis of the divinity of Christ within the humanity of the son of man. This, the paradox of earthly existence, must be confronted before the disciple of the mysteries may pass on to the retreat and Fourth Ray disciplines of Serapis Bey. Dichotomies in the psyche must be faced and defaced if necessary. For here, resolution of the soul's essential unity is the law of hourly becoming.

Thus the path of the Third Ray, under the direction of the Great Lord, the Maha Chohan, who is the supreme artist of our lives, encompasses the divine art of the creation of man—by God and man as co-creators —and the decision to "uncreate" by the sacred fires of transmutation all that is unholy and ungodly.

And therefore, the Cosmic Clock and the all-consuming violet flame are foundational to every course at Paul's retreat which, *enfin*, is a course in self-expression that leads to God Self-expression. The purpose of this ritual, then, is the making, or remaking, of genius in every field. And the discipline of psychology as the study of the soul's progressions, octave by octave, is the circle of life that is drawn around the whole of this course we run with the Third-Ray Adepts and the Holy Ghost.

Now examine the Master's approach and you will soon see that you are in the presence of a Master Psychologist for whom the Divine Art in all its ramifications has become the modus operandi to the attainment, by himself *and* his students, of Cosmic Consciousness:

"People feel a sense of worthlessness and that only the few have the ability to invent and to create," he says. "But I am here to tell you that locked in the heart of every one of you is a unique idea of Love that you can bring forth for the benefit of your fellowman and the progress of the culture of the Divine Mother. It may be an invention, it may be a poem, it may be a geometric design, but it is a gift which only you can bring forth.

"Unfortunately, many of you have held that gift in your heart for a succession of embodiments simply because no one has told you that you could release it, that you could bring it forth, that you are beings of ultimate creativity....

"Do not doubt that you, even in your present state, can rise quickly—no matter what your level of attainment—to greater self-mastery and greater control of the fires of creation. For when you come right down to it, the fires of creativity held within the forcefield of a man determine what he can accomplish in his earthly span.

"Some dissipate their creativity in lust for money and things and worldly desire and pursuits, and in acquisitiveness that is the disease of the human race. We then must exercise the mind in nonattachment, and our devotees give mantras to affirm that 'the earth is the LORD's and the fullness thereof, the world and they that dwell therein.'

"They must come to understand not merely intellectually but also in their feelings that because all things are God's, all things are theirs to command and to use to amplify his will and his wisdom. To acclaim the universe within and without as God's and then to use it to implement his glory—this is the great satisfaction of the devotees of Beauty.

"By the power of the seven rays from the heart of the Maha Chohan, by the illumination of the Buddha through the World Teachers, we stand in life this hour to anoint each child of God to receive the tabernacle of the two witnesses within his being.

"Our call goes forth to the children of God across the margent of the world and to all those who will hear and respond to the calls of the students of light to come Home. And all who answer the call shall receive the blessing of the Seven Chohans and the opportunity to attend classes in our retreats."

Here Paul addresses one of his classes on sharpening the tools of the spiritual senses:

"What tremendous import there is in the development of the spiritual senses. The old senses must pass away to give place to the new. Transmutation, transcendence, and transfer all speak of translucence, even of transparency; for the idea of seeing through a glass darkly but then face to face is always the miracle of a moment when opacity yields to translucency and translucency to transparency. The thinning of the veil and the clarification of nebulous concepts together with their reduction to orderly simile will provide the son of light with a golden rule by which he may measure his doings—his goings and his comings—and his progress in a universal sense....

"Therefore, as I come, I bring to you an understanding of your own soul's psychology in relationship to El Morya and beloved Lord Lanto. For you see, your hearts wax fervent in love for the will of God, in joy in the presence of El Morya, and in the study of the wisdom teachings. But there is a general confusion, if I might say, among the students (which is akin to the confusion on this planetary home) that the contemplated action, the happiness, the enjoyment of another's attainment is the equivalent of the attainment of the Third Ray—Love itself.

"Some actually suppose that the words 'I love you' carry the full force of its commitment and fulfillment. Not so. It is a mantra that must be fulfilled by a keen perception of the needs and demands of every part of Life and what ought to be the next givingness of self....

"Let us, then, carefully define what are those spirals yet to be completed—the contemplated life's journey. Each one has a sense of self-knowledge of that which is to be accomplished. Do not think that thinking about it will make it so! Thinking about it and yet not achieving it will result (in the hour of transition) in the necessity of going back into embodiment to begin again the process of coming to understand that the mighty work of the ages must be here on earth a shrine to the living, to the free, to the little ones, and to the LORD himself who dwells with his people.

"Now, therefore, I would converse with you concerning the *step not taken*—the step contemplated and often resisted until resistance itself becomes habit and a momentum and a coil wound tight around the spine of being. And this pole of being, once set with that habit, becomes an act no longer reviewed or questioned. It simply becomes a self-acceptance, 'Well, this is the way I am. People will have to accept me the way I am. This is my level of service. This is all I intend to give. Others will have to do the rest.'

"Well, the fallacy in this is not self-knowledge and defining one's potential, for it is good to understand one's capacity and not to commit more than one can. But the fallacy is, beloved heart, the sense that one can rest on any plateau or arrive at a set of definitions for one's life or personality, seal them with a sealing wax, make the imprint of the seal of oneself and say, 'As it is, so it is. So be it. I have spoken.'

"Now, this is the human ego that would hold captive and prisoner the soul to a certain level of the knowns, a certain level of stability. But unknowingly it would keep the soul there, and it would convince the soul that no other progress can or should be made and that its current level of attainment is sufficient unto all things.

"How can this state of mind, I ask you, be reconciled with the upward-spiraling, self-transcending movement of the galaxies, of God himself, of the Ascended Masters and their circles of chelas, all of whom and all of which are moving through Cosmos at colossal speeds toward the Central Sun?

"Let us take care, then, that self-assessment does not result in the inertia of rest and that such inertia is not

The Annunciation, Paolo Veronese, c. 1580

Veronese's biblical scenes were nearly always set in Venice and peopled with sumptuously attired Venetians. The artist, who has been characterized as both absurd and adorable, was less concerned with historical accuracy than with infusing his subject matter with the same new life that Renaissance Italy was imparting to Europe. Despite his great fame, he was noted for his simple, affectionate, and pious nature, which was perhaps responsible for the love that grew between Venice and Veronese.

confused with the lawful state of samadhi or of nirvana. Contrary to any human opinion whatsoever, these higher states of consciousness are those of movement even within the point and the heart of absolute rest....

"My service to life and to you, then, is to show you the way of Love, especially to coalesce the teachings of the Lords of the First and the Second Ray. For here at the point of Love is the leap, then, into the fiery core of Serapis Bey, and then the going forth therefrom to bring into precipitation, by the light of the Fifth, the Sixth and the Seventh Rays, all that has been builded from within.

"Why, this is the moment to step forth and to realize that no longer are thoughts or dreams or wishes to be left in jars upon a shelf and admired as a collection of some long-lost culture of ancient Egypt or Greece or China. Now these vessels come alive....

"Let each one then consider starting at the bottom of the stairway of Love and enjoying each upward step. Let there be a savoring and a resting at each step, as with each Montessori exercise so joyfully entered into. Let us not skip the steps and leap and bound with pride that we may move as a mountain goat or a she-lion. But let us know that every step contains the lawful angles and the mathematics of life; and fifty steps higher, one will need the fortitude gained on the second step of life. Therefore, let us not overlook these lessons.

"Alas, beloved ones, it is almost without exception that here and there in past embodiments you have skipped a step or two. And this is why you find yourself sometimes doing something for which you have such a stinging remorse within your heart, as the hot tears run down your cheeks and you realize the word that has escaped your mouth or the sharp feeling that has crushed another. You long to draw it back, and you say to yourself, 'How could I have let go of something that so easily has hurt another?'

"Well, my beloved, have compassion for your own soul, and self-correct. It is because of a lost step. Go back, then, and learn the art of patience and of the lever of control of the movement of forces in your being. Do not allow yourself to be triggered by sudden information that someone brings to you about another which may or may not be correct, which may be exaggerated or distorted. But rather hold the reins of an emotional fury. Hold back then, and in wisdom consider all things. And let only the word of the innermost Presence of Love be the healing in every situation."

Healing on the Third Ray, Paul tells us, is achieved through the multi-disciplines of the seven rays. One of these, which he himself teaches, is the alchemy of the creation of Beauty, the precipitation from the Universal into form, by the work of the hands in balance with head and heart, of some very tangible gift one purposes to lay upon the heart's altar of the Friend. This gift becomes a veritable materialization (even as it is the spiritualization) of the gift of the discernment of spirits.

For true art, fine art, as Paul discovered early in his career, is just that: the discernment not only of the spirits, or Muses, of art as these cosmic teachers have been identified, but also of the spirit of the work of art itself by which God and man can endow their handiwork as a crystal chalice for the flame of the Holy Spirit—tended by angels or elementals.

This ritual of Love and its interchange through art (as Above, so below) as demonstrated by the Master is a study which we can never get enough of. Truly, in the life of Paul the gifts of the Spirit, all nine of them, become gifts of form, light and symmetry capturing exquisitely not only the Beauty of God, but also the sound of harmonious spheres fashioned into one vessel.

To hear Paul lecture on this theme of being a co-creator with Love is to know that the creation of Beauty in some form is essential to the nurturing and development of the Child in us all and to the maturation of the soul on the path of the ascension.

Practicing the precepts that he preaches, Paul tells us of his own handiwork—a work of Love's art, to be laid upon the altar of his Guru:

"The Spirit of God takes delight in the work of his own hands. He is joyous because of the perfection and the quality of perfection which manifests in that which he has created. This beautiful manifestation of God's perfection is a chalice of light forever!

"Speaking of chalices, I want to tell you that for a period of seventeen years I have been at work at inner levels in constructing a beautiful chalice to present to the Maha Chohan. And this very day it has been taken to him in his home in Ceylon. There it stands in his retreat.

"The base of this magnificent chalice—which, incidentally, is snow-white in color—is set with three rings of precious stones, all resembling diamonds. One band, beloved ones, is pink; another is pale yellow; and the other is a radiant blue. These three concentric rings around the base of the chalice are charged with the wisdom of God, the will of God, and the love of God.

"The symbol therein is this: the will of God can be a great comfort to those who understand it, for when the will of God is understood, men will say, 'God is good.' When the wisdom of God is understood, the 'why' God has permitted this and the 'why' God has permitted that will be answered in a manifestation of the great divine Law, flooding forth into the consciousness of men; and that, too, will be a chalice of comfort to them. For they will drink the comfort of divine Wisdom. Could divine Wisdom be comfortable? I challenge you, beloved ones, could it be?

"Then last but not least, the radiance of divine Love itself will be partaken of as a feeling—a feeling of infinite care, a care for each of the creatures of God, regardless of the size or dimension of that creature. The Father, in giving Life, has given himself to all; and because he has given himself, he gives the infinite possibility of expansion to all. And the leaven of the Christ light poured out into the heart's chalice of each individual is the greatest comfort they shall ever have.

"Although they may seek on land and sea; in husband, in wife or in home; in brother or in sister; in name and fame or fortune or place; wherever they will go they will never find any place so wonderful, so magnificent, and so comforting as their own heart. There the Life that God has created and sustained is flooding over the brim, hoping to express the perfection of which it is capable.

"It gives unto the stewardship of individual man the power to choose for himself to walk through the narrow gate that leads to the fullness of his own God-identity and the outpicturing upon the screen of Life of the verdured perfection of God. Such a one manifests then for all time as a man of God, a *man*ifestation of Liberty's flame—the fleur-de-lis of Love, Wisdom, and Power—a *man*ifestation of eternal comfort.

"You will then be a being of beauty and a joy forever, for you will have become an Ascended Being, a Christ—a Cosmic Christ—infinite in conscious action. You will rise in the arms of infinite Love until you, as the Maha Chohan does, will be able to render a service to a portion of Life everywhere.

"In the great perfection of Life that swells through this galaxy, flooding out through the grateful Cosmos, you will be a part of the flame of omnipresent Life. That flame, like music and perfume and light, weaves upon the screen of Cosmic Law *all* of the unfolding mysteries of God made known to you from within and from without forever by the charge of divine Love.

"Now, my beloved ones, this beautiful cup, which I have worked on for so many years, has been given into the keeping of the Maha Chohan. I shall not further describe it to you today for a very special reason. The reason is that I ask those of you who are spiritually perceptive and love the Father to call unto God with fervor and determination until, while you sleep at night, God himself shall direct your journey unto the Great Lord's Temple of Comfort in Ceylon; and your own eye shall behold the work of my hand.

"And then I think that you will be grateful that I did not try to describe it for you in words, for you will see an Ascended Master jewel of perfection resting there. The Great Divine Director and the members of the Karmic Board who have all witnessed it have said that it is indeed a splendid thing.

"I hope now that you, too, shall realize this day that you are a splendid thing, a manifestation of God—not a puny personality, not a human creation full of faults and flaws, but a child of light, splendid in all your dimensions—the work of God's hands, the work of your own Divine Presence manifesting now and always joy forever, forever, and forever!"

The beloved Master Paul has promised an important initiation to those who come knocking at the door of his retreat in southern France ready for a greater increment of the love flame:

"I will take you by the hand and show you my castle. I will show you the works of art that have been brought forth by chelas unascended and ascended. And we will go through many rooms, and lastly I will take you to the room where there is that frame that hangs. In some cases it will be an empty frame, in some cases it will have a canvas in it. It will be your frame, the frame of your identity waiting for you to bring forth the genius of your soul. And when you see that frame, if it is empty, you will want to fill it.

"And so I will take you to that place, 'The Atelier,' where you can work with other artisans who are learning the art of living Love by the discipline of the hand and the discipline of expression so that you can draw the image of your own Christ-perfection. And when it is the best that you have to offer, it will be placed in your frame."

This is the essence of the path of the Lords of the Seven Rays—teaching us how to unfold the image of the Christ in all that we do. And you can make the call each night to go to their retreats in your finer bodies while you sleep to learn how to do just that. El Morya explains that you can adapt the following prayer as you call to be taken to one of the retreats of the Seven Chohans each night:

> In the name of the Christ, my own Real Self,
> I call to the heart of the I AM Presence and to the
> angel of the Presence, to Archangel Michael and
> Beloved Kuan Yin, to take me in my soul and in
> my soul consciousness to the retreat of Paul the

Venetian in southern France (or to the university classes currently being held at the Goddess of Liberty's Temple of the Sun) according to the direction of my Holy Christ Self and the Maha Chohan.

I ask to receive the instruction of the Law of Love and to be given the formula for the victory of the Love flame within my heart—especially as it pertains to the gift of the discerning of spirits. And I ask that all information necessary to the fulfillment of my divine plan and that of my beloved twin flame be released to my outer waking consciousness as it is required. I thank thee and I accept this done in the full power of the risen Christ. Amen.

4

SERAPIS BEY
the Architect

Gift of the Working of Miracles

Serapis Bey, Chohan of the Fourth Ray, was a high priest in the ascension temple on Atlantis. While other Masters with their circles of devotees transported the various flames they guarded on the continent to focuses across the earth, establishing both etheric retreats and mystery schools adjacent to temples built to the Divine Mother (at a time when the flames were still enshrined in the physical octave), Serapis and his band, leaving Atlantis well before the final cataclysm, bore the ascension flame to Luxor, Egypt.

The hierophant tells us why, out of the seven, he originally chose to serve on the white ray of the Divine Mother: "When I was a chela determining on what ray I would serve, what ray I would preserve in the office of preserver of Life, I contemplated all, but I came to the light of purity, and I said—master of geometry that I was—'The shortest distance between two points, point A and B, is purity. Purity I shall be.'"

To the students who make it to Luxor, Serapis introduces himself with characteristic directness: "I am the hierophant of Luxor, Retreat of the Ascension Flame. I am known among the Brotherhood as the disciplinarian, and among my disciples as the fiery Master, and among those who have rejected the disciplines of our retreat by various and sundry names."

El Morya describes Serapis as "a Spartan if I ever saw one—whose fiery determination has saved many a soul from the mush of self-indulgence. His chelas reflect the fierceness of their Master as they are immovable in

Statue of Leonidas at the site of the Battle of Thermopylae, Greece

their dedication to purity focused as the Mother light."

And indeed Serapis was a Spartan—most famous of them all, Leonidas. This king of Sparta (whose name means "Son of the Lion") was sent by his countrymen to maintain the pass of Thermopylae against the vast invading army of the Persian king Xerxes in 480 B.C. Three hundred Spartan warriors marched with him, expecting the rest of their allies to follow at the conclusion of the Olympic games, which were taking place simultaneously. Meanwhile, he was joined by six thousand troops—his forces now seven thousand strong as they reached the pass.

By holding this narrow passage between the mountains and the sea, Leonidas was acting to protect the nearby Greek fleet from being outflanked in combat. He and his men faced the Persian hordes, which numbered anywhere from the 250,000 modern scholars have calculated to the 1.7 million the Greek historian Herodotus claimed.

For two days Xerxes suffered heavy losses without breaking Leonidas' resistance. Then a local man, Ephialtes, led Xerxes to a path through the mountains, and a hand-picked force of "Persian Immortals" attacked the Greeks from the rear. Leonidas at once informed the fleet, dismissed all but 1,400 men—700 Thespians, 400 Thebans and his own 300 Spartans—and prepared to die, declaring that he and his Spartans would not abandon their post. Then, with the handful of troops under his command, he charged the myriads of Persian soldiers.

Leonidas fell in the thickest of the fight. "And now there arose," Herodotus records, "a fierce struggle between the Persians and the Lacedaemonians [Spartans] over the body of Leonidas, in which the Greeks four times drove back the enemy, and at last by their great bravery succeeded in bearing off the body."

At the end, the Greeks were left with only a tiny hillock on which to fight. Here "they defended themselves to the last," Herodotus said, "such as still had swords using them, and the others resisting with their hands and teeth; till the barbarians… overwhelmed and buried the remnant left beneath showers of missile weapons."[1]

The Persians killed every Spartan and Thespian, but the Thebans laid down their arms and surrendered. Afterwards, Xerxes ordered that Leonidas be beheaded and his body crucified. But no such ignominy could mar his image. His heroism and selfless devotion to the flame that was Greece—the greater cause and glory more precious than life itself—had secured him a singular place in history, and in the imagination of his own and succeeding generations. By his superlative discipline and sense of timing, the Greek fleet was able to retreat and later defeat the Persians in a sea battle.

A monument in the shape of a lion was erected on the spot where the 300 had taken their last stand. A stanza immortalizing them reads, "Go tell the Spartans, thou that passeth by, / That here, obedient to their laws, we lie."

And so we are told that after bearing the flame to Egypt from Atlantis (prior to his life as Leonidas), Serapis continued to reincarnate in the land of the Nile for the perfecting of the Work, forgoing his own ascension until about 400 B.C. As the Egyptian pharaoh Amenhotep III (reigned c. 1390–1353 B.C.), he constructed the physical temple that is at Luxor on the Nile.

The temple is actually built to correspond to the outline of the human skeletal framework, traced according to anthropometrical methods and precisely proportioned. Its courtyards and rooms closely correspond to the body. As R. A. Schwaller de Lubicz, who spent over fifteen years studying its architecture, has said, "The Temple of Luxor is indisputably devoted to the Human Microcosm. This consecration is not merely a simple attribution: the entire temple becomes a book explaining the secret functions of the organs and nerve centers."[2]

In truth this temple displays the idea of the rebirth

Amenhotep III, reigned c. 1390–1353 B.C.

Known as "the magnificent" and as the "Louis XIV of ancient Egypt," Amenhotep III ruled Egypt at the height of her power. His reign was so peaceful that he went to war only once. His massive construction projects included the main portions of the temple of Luxor.

Temple of Luxor, colonnade of King Amenhotep III, view from the great forecourt, eastern Thebes

of the divine man based on his transformation through the universal Mother Principle. And to those who have eyes to see and ears to hear, the mysteries are unveiled. The Principle and Presence of the Mother in the matter body is taught by the Lord of the Fourth Ray as in metaphor he raises our consciousness to the plane of causation:

"Out of the Word is Mother and the Word is Mother and in this Word was the soundless sound that passing through her lips became the AUM of the creation. Thus the science of sound and the science of the Word are known in the white-fire core of the Fourth Ray. And Alpha stepped forth and Omega was the One and through her the beginning became the ending."

"For the sake of her children's restoration to the House of Spirit," he explains, "Omega entered the Matter universes. And our Dear Mother became one with the Matter cycles below even as She is in—for her Blessed Being constitutes—the Matter cycles Above. And now in the last days the Mother, even the Great Kali, strips from her own all violations of Her Matter Body by the dark ones.

"Therefore I give you this prayer to sustain you through the rigorous initiations of the Fourth Ray: 'Even so, come quickly, Dearest Mother, to liberate our souls forever from the bondage of the senses, the illusion of time and space and the violators of thy Word incarnate in our souls! Come, Blessed Mother, Come.'"

Thus we learn at our nightly class at Luxor that the Fourth Ray of Alpha and Omega embodies the quintessence of every other ray. It is the white on white which outlines Mother's many faces in all her sons and daughters.

In this bas-relief of white fire, Purity—and this is one of the many-virtued names of our Divine Mother—reveals a higher beauty and a truer harmony of Love in music and art, and a technology beyond any achieved through the applied sciences of today. This purity, Serapis says, is the fierce innocence of the Mother that reaches the "stars" (i.e., the fallen angels) and with the laser beam of the Ruby Ray annihilates their star wars and their game plans.

Immersed in the beauty and power of the Divine Mother, we are left in silent meditation to contemplate his closing words:

"And She is the All, and the sacred fire of the creation is both her servant and her Lord."

In addition to purity and the rituals of soul-purification, the qualities of the Fourth Ray of God's heart are the desire for the perfection of the inner patterns to be outpictured in the matter matrix and the desire for self-discipline under one's spiritual hierarch in order that one might attain the pristine goal.

Devotees of the Fourth Ray take delight in the archi-

Panel of the Ara Pacis (Altar of Peace), bas-relief, 9 B.C., Rome

Mother Earth as the embodiment of fertility with rich gifts of children, animals, and the fruit of the land. She is flanked by two figures personifying winds.

tecture of the Matter cosmos, the music of the spheres, the science of sound and the precipitation of the Word, which also come under the guardianship of the mentors of the Fifth and Seventh Rays. These studious ones meditate upon the blueprint of the soul and its tracings upon the molecules of the four lower bodies. Out of mathematics, geometry, astronomy, astro- and nuclear physics, biochemistry and the wonders of Divine Science mirrored in the physical sciences, they derive an inner satisfaction equal to none of communing with the Law of the One and the alchemy of the Word "made flesh."

Beloved Serapis, great initiate of the Mother flame, administers the gift of the *working of miracles*—Mother's miracles—to the lightbearers of earth. This gift, in order to be received, requires utmost Love; for only Love begets self-discipline in the sacred fire that is neither brittle nor fanatical nor self-demeaning. The abundance of every good and perfect, miraculous gift of God is derived from the white light of the Mother, whose sacred fire breath is at the heart of every atom and sun center.

Intense devotion to the Presence of God will result in the natural bestowal of the gift of miracles. As Serapis has said, "In the past, many of the saints who levitated into the atmosphere did so by reason of the intensity of their magnetization of the energy of the God flame above. The floating into the air of these saints was an attest to their devout and intimate relationship with the God Presence."

Serapis cautions against becoming enamoured of the gifts that result from attainment on the Path. The ascension and the abilities attendant on the raising of the Kundalini fire must be desired ordinately, he says. Some desire them inordinately and resort to a haphazard use of various forms of yoga, when they could

Head of Serapis, detail, Hellenistic style of Egyptian art

The Graeco-Egyptian god Serapis gained prominence around the third century B.C. His cult spread throughout Egypt and later into Asia Minor and even Italy. During the Graeco-Roman period in Egypt, approximately forty-two temples were erected to him. King Ptolemy I selected him as the official god for Egypt and constructed a temple to him at Alexandria.

Yet Serapis is one of the most mysterious of the Egyptian gods. Scholars have suggested numerous translations for his name. His country of origin is unknown. The secrets of his cult, kept by his temple priests, lie buried with the other great mysteries.

achieve the *siddhis,* i.e., powers, naturally by fulfilling the Seventh Ray requirements for the ascension.

For the daily application of the violet flame in dynamic decrees is the joyful noise made unto the LORD that purifies the aura and chakras, transmutes the records of karma—when combined with Community service—and facilitates the balancing of the threefold flame as the requirements of the path of personal Christhood are adhered to.

The raising up of the sacred fire—the Mother light sealed in the base-of-the-spine chakra—is accomplished through various techniques of meditation with bija mantras. This raising of the Kundalini under the Ascended Masters' tutelage is not a sudden burst of fire, but a gentle rising of strength and consciousness. And you feel the consciousness of God a part of yourself along this spinal altar. And it gives you the strength of mind and will and body to achieve your ends.

You have meted out to you a quotient of sacred fire daily. As you spend it, so will be your increase or decrease.

Serapis Soleil,
artist unknown

It is yours by free will. And therefore, squandering light in any of the seven chakras simply sets you back from the gain you advanced by all of your other disciplines.

Serapis teaches that dynamic decrees as well as meditation combined with the visualization and acceleration of the white light and the violet flame in all of the chakras are very important keys to the integration of the soul faculties as well as the nine gifts of the Spirit within one's being.

Truly, the violet ray—as the highest light of the physical spectrum, bursting forth as the transmutative fires of the Holy Spirit—clears the way for the restoration of the white light of the Fourth Ray and its sacred fire in the soul and all her members.

Thus, ask to be taken to the violet flame room at Luxor as you set for yourself goals of acceleration on your Homeward path. Can't make a decision? Don't know which way to go? Or what to do with your life? Take up your copy of *The Science of the Spoken Word* and give daily "Ten for Transmutation." The ten decrees to the violet flame in that chapter may be said by you in multiples of nine times each as mantras of the Holy Spirit.

Establishing your violet flame session nightly before retiring and concluding with a call to Archangel Michael, Kuan Yin and the mighty Seraphim to take you to the heart of Luxor and the violet flame room will do much to focus your heart and mind one-pointedly to achieve the goals of your life which were set before you by Jesus or one of the servant-Sons in heaven prior to your soul's descent into embodiment.

The reason that such Seventh Ray rituals work is that the violet flame transmutes the records of karma and misqualified energies—the very substance of which blocks your vision and your decision-making. According to the law of cycles, only so much substance can be taken from you each day. And each day your decree momentum builds, and as it builds, your capacity to sustain the action of the violet fire in your four lower bodies increases by geometric proportion.

"The real miracle and first lesson of alchemy at Luxor is the separating out of the Real from the unreal in the psyche (soul) of the individual," explains Serapis. "What is real in you, what is unreal? I charge you this day, students of the Most High God, to give answer; for you are not students of Serapis Bey or Morya or Saint Germain, but you are students of the Almighty, of the Christ, and we stand as mentors and fellow servants of the Most High God.

"I charge you, then, this day to take a page in your book of Christhood, to make two columns. The first column—Myself, What Is Real; the second column—Myself, What Is Unreal. You will head the first column with the word *God, the I AM THAT I AM; Christ, the only begotten Son.* This is that which is real within you. You will head the second column with: *the human ego, the human will, the human intellect, the human pride.*

"And then you will list the virtues of the light, the virtues of the Christ and of God in the first column, which you know to be real and to be outpictured within you. And in the second, you will list those faults, those sins which are not real. Then you will return to the first column and list those attributes that you desire to have as real, that you know exist, that you honor and adore, but which you have not yet mastered. These you must also claim as yourself, as reality; for unless and until you claim them, you cannot be them. And thus, you will clearly mark the truth and the falsehood of identity.

"This is the starting place of the ascension. That which is in the first column must rise, that which is in the second must be transmuted before the energy thereof can rise.

"Then step by step each day, with rejoicing in your heart, you take the power, the dominion of the God qualities you have listed in the first column and all energies that you have listed there and you use them as your authority, your substance, your collateral to invoke the grace of God, his will, and his healing to remove the stain of sin and all unreality which you have listed as the misqualified energies and momentums in the second column. This, then, becomes an objective and practical exercise in the demonstration of the science of the laws of God."

From his Ascension Temple, the beloved hierarch of Luxor initiates candidates for the ascension, assigning tutors to walk with their charges every missed step on the paths of the seven rays. This he does, stickler that he is, in cooperation with the other Chohans. And the line is drawn: the chela may not pass until he fulfills that neglected, long-forgotten or suppressed missed step. This process can be tedious and trying—more for the chela than the Master, I am certain!

Now, to Serapis' classes come the artists, musicians, sculptors, architects, planners—those who serve on the Fourth Ray as well as the most staunch disciples of every ray—to express purity, harmony, rhythm, balance and perfection in any undertaking. Military and intelligence strategists and all who serve in the armed forces, security and police departments of the cities—all receive special training here in the defense of the flame of Life.

To these and to all who seek entrance Serapis clarifies the rigors of the highest path to attainment, the path of the white light, of a purity that is won through service, self-sacrifice, and surrender to the all of God.

Serapis Bey's methods of discipline are tailor-made for each candidate for the ascension. After an initial interview by himself or one of Twelve Adepts presiding in his mystery school, devotees who come to his retreat are assigned in groups of five or more to carry out projects with other initiates whose karmic patterns (graphically illustrated in their astrology) forecast the maximum friction between their lifestreams. This test must be given in order that they may choose to be or not to be centered in God. Soon it is clear that *all* idols of the tyrant self or karmic past must be surrendered if one is to merge with the confluent stream of the Law of the One.

Each group must serve together until they become harmonious—individually and as a cohesive unit of hierarchy—learning all the while that those character traits that are most offensive in others are the polar opposite of their own worst faults and that what one criticizes in another is apt to be the root of his own misery.

Aside from this type of group dynamics, individuals are placed in situations (both in the retreat and in their day-to-day activities) that provide them with the greatest challenges, according to their changing karmic patterns. In this course of Serapis one cannot simply up and leave a crisis, a circumstance, or an individual that is not to his liking. He must stand, face and conquer his own carnal mind and misqualified energy by disciplining his consciousness in the art of nonreaction to the human creation of others, even as he learns how not to be dominated or influenced by his own human creation.

When souls who have been placed in close proximity precisely because they have rubbed each other the wrong way for lifetimes have succeeded in smoothening their rough places, finally preferring God Harmony to all lesser gods of gosh awful tears and tirades, they proceed to chambers of advanced learning. Here in the presence of Serapis the alchemical secrets of the Tree of Life may at last be made known to those who, weary of the world of desire, have subdued the passions and polarizations, conceding only to "be still and know that I AM God."

These, then, are ready to undergo the rigors of initiation that will eventuate first in the soul's alchemical marriage to the Holy Christ Self and then in the reunion with her God Presence and causal body through the ritual of the ascension.

Serapis has explained to us how important it is, especially in this Dark Cycle of the descent of earth's karma, that we the lightbearers come to his etheric retreat at Luxor and strive to win our ascension both from inner levels and on the outer, conscientiously applying what we have learned "out of the body" in the performance of the daily tasks at hand: "For we count not one, but a number of ascensions each year as absolutely indispensable to the holding of the balance of Life upon earth."

Before God, you may declare the ascension to be your goal at the conclusion of this life, and call to your Mighty I AM Presence that your divine plan might unfold and that you might indeed be found worthy to be a candidate for initiations of the sacred fire and the Mother flame under Serapis Bey. Most assuredly, this call will compel an answer.

Serapis points out the need for divine humility in all aspirants on the path to the ascension and cites the Master Jesus as the perfect example: "I recall full well when the Master Jesus came to Luxor as a very young man that he knelt in holy innocence before the Hierophant, refusing all honors that were offered him and asking to be initiated into the first grade of spiritual law and spiritual mystery. No sense of pride marred his visage—no sense of preeminence or false expectation, albeit he could have well expected the highest honors. He chose to take the low road of humility, knowing that it was reserved unto the joy of God to raise him up.

"To raise an individual is a glorious thing when that individual lies prone in hope, in faith, and in charity, awaiting an act of God to reconsecrate the self to the simple quality of humility. For there is an act of false pride which manifests as false humility and causes individuals to appear humble whereas in reality they reek with pride. This false humility is often manifest in subtle ways and it is a mockery of the real....

"I urge upon all, then, that they seek the banner of divine humility. If the Masters and the Divine Presence of men through the mediatorship of the Christ have ever recognized any of the errors of men that have hindered them from becoming that which they long to become, they have recognized their pride. Pride takes many forms and true humility but one. True humility must be worn eternally. It is not a garment you place upon you for a moment, for a day, or a year, or when passing a test. It is an undergarment with which God himself is clothed, and unless it surround thee thy hopes of attainment are slim indeed."

There are thirty-three initiations which every ascending soul must pass, including the major ones of the transfiguration, the crucifixion, the resurrection and eventually that of the ascension itself. The negative spiral of limitation that opposes the ascension process, which man himself has created, can be overcome by the correct qualification of God's energies as he calls upon the law of forgiveness and invokes the sacred fire to transmute the errors of the past. Thus the impure elements of what is called the electronic belt (the conglomerate 'core' of a man's karma and his carnal-mindedness) are consumed daily by the alchemy of dynamic decrees, and the purified energy ascends to the causal body.

Serapis Bey tells us, "You ascend daily." Our thoughts, our feelings, our daily deeds are all weighed in the balance. We do not ascend all at once but by increments as we pass our tests and win our individual victories. The entire record of all our past lives and momentums of both good and evil must be counted; and then, when we have brought at least 51 percent of all the energy that has ever been allotted to us into balance with the purity and harmony of the Great God Self, we may be offered the gift of the ascension, which is indeed by the grace of God. The remaining 49 percent must be transmuted, or purified, from the ascended octaves through service to earth and her evolutions performed by the soul after the ascension.

"You need not expect, precious ones," Serapis says, "that as the swoop of a great bird of paradise, heaven will come down to you and raise you instantly up into the light. Each day you weave a strand of light substance back to the heart of your Presence by the shuttle of your attention; each strand strengthens the anchor beyond the veil and thus draws you into a state of consciousness wherein God can use you more as an effective instrument for good."

There are several other requirements for the ascension besides the balancing of 51 percent of one's karma: the balancing of the threefold flame; the alignment of the four lower bodies so that they can be pure chalices for the flame of the Holy Spirit in the world of form; the achievement of self-mastery on the seven rays of the Christ; the attainment of mastery over sin, sickness, and death, and over every outer condition; the fulfillment of one's divine plan; the transmutation of one's electronic belt; and the magnification of the Mother energy of the Kundalini.

Serapis Bey reminds us of one more requirement. He says: "The ascension must be desired and it must be desired ordinately. It must be desired not as a mechanism of escape from responsibility or from worldly duties. It must be desired as the culmination of a lifetime of service in the will of God, and men must be willing during their final embodiments upon the planet—the time of their escape from the round of the centuries—to give the very best of service to the light and to help usher in the kingdom."

Saint Germain has promised us that everyone who sincerely tries can make his ascension in this lifetime or at least in the next if there are extenuating circumstances that require another incarnation. At the time of her passing from the screen of life, the soul will be taken to temples of the Brotherhood and tutored on the inner planes so that the succeeding embodiment can be the victorious one. The only exception to the Master's promise would be if the individual, in order to fulfill his divine plan, is required to take embodiment at some future time so that he can complete a specific mission of service agreed upon before his Holy Christ Self and the Lords of Karma.

At the close of their final embodiment of service to earth's evolutions, candidates who have been accepted for the ascension rite come to the Ascension Temple at Luxor to receive the initiation that will reunite them with their God Presence. Accompanied by ascended and unascended masters, the initiate is bidden to the flame room by the Lord of the Fourth Ray where he must stand on a dais in the center of a large circle with Masters, adepts, seraphim and brethren in attendance on the periphery.

At a certain moment when all is in readiness the individual's cosmic tone is sounded, and the current from Alpha is released from the circle on the ceiling and the current from Omega rises from the base. The moment the individual's tone is sounded, and simultaneous with the bursting forth of the flame formed by the caduceus action of both currents, the seraphim in the outer court trumpet the victory of the ascending soul with a magnificent rendition of the "Triumphal March" from *Aïda*. The discipline that is the keynote of this retreat is felt in their precise, golden-tone rendition of the piece.

The ascension flame is an intense fiery white with

a crystal glow. The Easter lily is the symbol of the flame and its focus in the Nature kingdom, and the diamond is its focus in the mineral kingdom. While the melody of the flame is the "Triumphal March," the keynote of the retreat is "Liebestraum" by Franz Liszt and the radiance of the Electronic Presence of Serapis Bey and his twin flame pour through the aria "Celeste Aïda."

We are grateful to have a description of the changes which take place during the ascension recounted to us by the hierarch of the Ascension Temple. Serapis says, "Although the form of an individual may show signs of age prior to his ascension, all of this will change and the physical appearance of the individual will be transformed into the glorified body. The individual ascends, then, not in an earthly body but in a glorified spiritual body into which the physical form is changed on the instant by total immersion in the great God flame.

"Thus man's consciousness of the physical body ceases and he achieves a state of weightlessness. This resurrection takes place as the great God flame envelops the shell of human creation that remains and transmutes, in a pattern of cosmic grids, all of the cell patterns of the individual—the bony structure, the blood vessels, and all bodily processes which go through a great metamorphosis.

"The blood in the veins changes to liquid golden light; the throat chakra glows with an intense blue-white light; the spiritual eye in the center of the forehead becomes an elongated God flame rising upward; the garments of the individual are completely consumed, and he takes on the appearance of being clothed in a white robe—the seamless garment of the Christ. Sometimes the long hair of the Higher Mental Body appears as pure gold on the ascending one; then again, eyes of any color may become a beautiful electric blue or a pale violet....

"Lighter and lighter grows the physical form, and with the weightlessness of helium the body begins to rise into the atmosphere, the gravitational pull being loosened and the form enveloped by the light of the externalized glory which man knew with the Father 'in the beginning' before the world was.

"This is the glory of the ascension currents. It is the glory of attainment which Jesus demonstrated....

"These changes are permanent, and the ascended one is able to take his light body with him wherever he wishes or he may travel without the glorified spiritual body. Ascended beings can and occasionally do appear upon earth as ordinary mortals, putting on physical garments resembling the people of earth and moving among them for cosmic purposes. This Saint Germain did after his ascension when he was known as the Wonderman of Europe. Such an activity is a matter of dispensation received from the Karmic Board." Generally, however, ascended beings do not return to the physical plane unless there is some specific service requiring this change in vibratory rate.

Some who have earned their ascension volunteer

to surrender this blessing temporarily and continue to reembody in order to assist those who are still in the process of overcoming. This is called the bodhisattva ideal. There are many in both the unascended and ascended octaves who have volunteered to remain with the evolutions of earth until every last man, woman, and child is free in the ascension.

However, "one of the demands of the Lords of Karma is that a stated number of individuals must graduate each year in order to renew the grant of light that is necessary to maintain the stability of the planet," Serapis tells us. "Therefore, do not feel that you are being selfish if you decide to ascend rather than to remain behind with the evolutions of earth. As each soul ascends, an increment of that light is anchored on Terra. Your ascension can bless and benefit each one on earth and the planetary body also. The victory of each individual contributes to the victory of the whole."

Serapis says, "The ascension is the fulfillment of the will of God for every man."

Knowing full well just how rigorous is the path of the soul's ascent, Serapis Bey released his *Dossier on the Ascension* in a series of dictated letters he sent to his chelas worldwide. In this divine document—a treasure of the ages—the hierarch of Luxor explains the requirements for the ascension and offers to the faithful "the benefit of our thoughts, our feelings, and our release of the ascension flame into tangible manifestation." In this work the beloved Master releases a safe portion of the

Fourth Ray teachings which he gives in his beginning classes at Luxor to those who are applying to become candidates for the ascension.

He wrote: "The future is what you make it, even as the present is what you made it. If you do not like it, God has provided a way for you to change it; and the way is through the acceptance of the currents of the ascension flame."

The ascension is the goal of every soul of light evolving on planet Earth and throughout the galaxies of time and space. Truly it is the goal of Life itself—Life begetting life in order that it may ascend.

Jesus' prophecy to Nicodemus of the ascension of the 'descendants' of God is also the plain truth: "And no man hath ascended up to heaven, but he that came down from heaven, even the Son of man which is in heaven. And as Moses lifted up the serpent in the wilderness [the sacred fire of the Kundalini sealed in the base-of-the-spine chakra—and raised it to the third eye as the winged serpent, i.e., caduceus], even so must the Son of man be lifted up: *That whosoever believeth in him should not perish, but have eternal life.*" (John 3:13–15)

And so, beloved, when the Son of man, who is your Holy Christ Self, is lifted up in you (as the Sun, or light, or Christ consciousness) even as the 'serpent', or life-force, was raised upon the spinal altar of Moses, then you will be called by the Father to ascend to him, even as you came down (descended) from heaven.

Believing in the Christ of Jesus allows the Saviour

to assist you in the process of raising up the same light of this blazing Sun of Righteousness (Jesus' own causal body) whereby you too have eternal Life through the ascension flame! This is the victorious ascent to God from whom the children of the Sun descended.

And it takes place through the vision of the Ascended Master Jesus Christ—every eye that shall see him and that shall believe in him receives thereby the arc of transfiguring light from his ascended Presence whereby each one who *sees and believes* is caught up in the rapture of the currents of the ascension flame! And so it was that the people who beheld the brazen serpent, symbol of the raised sacred fire, were healed of their snakebites.

In reality the son of man is a flaming spirit who descended into physical form to master the conditions and trials of everyday life—his karma and his lower self. When he shall have successfully overcome the human will, the human ego, the human intellect, having replaced them by their divine counterparts, the Divine Ego, the Divine Will, and the Divine Mind, by the grace of God and his leave he shall then ascend back to the heart of the Father—victor over time and space.

The ascension is the highest gift of God, the sum of the nine gifts and the summum bonum of each and every gift, for it is the power of the nine squared. It is given to us more by his grace than by our works, although both are necessary, for works as well as words form a chalice that is upheld to receive God's grace. And by faith man becomes that living chalice by his words *and* his works.

Jesus walked the path of the ascension so that all could follow his example. The Bible records but a few of the many who have ascended into the light. Enoch, the seventh from Adam, "walked with God: and he was not; for God took him." Elijah the prophet "went up by a whirlwind into heaven," having been parted from Elisha by a chariot of fire and horses of fire. Melchizedek, King of Salem and Priest of the Most High God, Mary the Mother of Jesus, John the Beloved Disciple, Gautama Buddha, Zarathustra, Confucius, St. Thérèse of Lisieux, and Pope John XXIII are only a few of the ascended saints in heaven who upon their ascension joined the ranks of the immortals to become one with the entire Spirit of the Great White Brotherhood.

Serapis' lectures are the plain truth and the simple logic that proceed from the ascension flame itself: "Men cannot build immortal bodies out of mortal substance. They cannot build out of mortal thoughts immortal ideas. They cannot build out of mortal feelings divine feelings that enfold the world and create the great Pyramid of Life."

Man asked for and was granted the gift of free will. As in the parable of the prodigal son, we have taken the Father's pure energy and misqualified it. Now we must purify and redeem all our errors of the past back to our first embodiment in Matter.

"Immortality is of a high price," advises Serapis,

"and it demands the allness of men from the smallness of men.

"In order to ascend, you must abandon your past to God, knowing that he possesses the power, by his flame and identity, to change all that you have wrought of malintent and confusion into the beauty of the original design which, by the power of his love, did produce the fruit of eternal goodness. Cast aside illusion, then, veil after veil of the 'personal person,' and possess the willingness, in the name of Almighty God, to change your world!"

With his usual candor, Serapis continues: "Men require 'spunk' and a straight spine. There is no question they have pampered themselves, and that with illusion. Straight talk and straight thought will do much to clear the way, and it will not place any individual outside the citadel of hope but wholly within it.

"Men stay on the merry-go-round of human thought and feeling because they fear lest they fall off. But it will keep on going. So jump off the round of delusion and the mad whirl of human confusion. Come to Luxor, to the place where I AM."

And when we do come, he instructs us in this wise, "You should love purity with an utter devotion because purity is your freedom. In fact when you step into the flame, you find etched in fire and in crystal the permanent identity of the permanent atom of the permanent molecule of being. And you find that all else is consumed.

"And you stand to face the Presence, and behold,

in the mirror of eternal Life you see God face to face and you say, 'Lo, I AM made in his image. I AM the image and the likeness of the Holy One.' For in that fire you see yourself as God is—not as you were yesterday in the human consciousness or today or tomorrow—but you see yourself in the foreverness of the invincibility of that cosmic honor flame."

"Actually, the process of the ascension is one of utter forgiveness," explains Saint Germain. "It is one of transmutation and transformation. It is the drawing-in of holy energies and the purification of all abused energies of the past. It is a regenerative process that begins not only in the physical form but also in the very heart and soul of man. It is the Christ-command to the great Cosmic Law itself to draw within the form the magnetic properties that will attract more and more of God to the individual monad."

Summarizing the *Dossier on the Ascension* that has already become the handbook of those rare initiates carefully culled from planet Earth by the hand of God's destiny through the final steps of the ascension, Serapis Bey says in his unpretentious manner:

"We have thought to convey in this Dossier the understanding that spiritual exercise alone without obedience to karmic precepts and the divine plan for man may be of limited value to the aspirant. We have also pointed out that both approaches to salvation come to the shining apex of manifestation in man's glorious ascension in the light when all of the spiritual signets are set in place as God wills it. This includes the use of the cosmic honor flame from the heart of God whereby men in honor prefer one another and recognize the meaning of true brotherhood and service....

"The divine geometry, through the symbol of the pyramid, draws the aspiring consciousness of man into the idea of an ascendant life. To ascend is to blend in cosmic unity with the heart of the Eternal. It is the destiny of every man. Those who understand this will rejoice in the consolation of their own ultimate freedom from every earthly travail as cosmic purpose is enthroned in consciousness both now and forever. My hands will be extended in loving welcome to thee at the hour of thy victory."

5

HILARION
(the Apostle Paul) *the Healer*

Gifts of Healing

We see the figure of the Master Jesus appearing to Saint Paul on the Damascus way—"a light from heaven, above the brightness of the sun, shining round about me," as he described his experience to Agrippa. And he heard the voice of the Master saying, "Saul, Saul, why persecutest thou me? It is hard for thee to kick against the pricks."

It was a blinding light and a purging light that descended on Paul. It was for the rebuke of his human consciousness that had persecuted the true servants of God. It was for the purification of his sight that he might behold the Son of God. It was the light of conversion that turned him around and set him on the path of his own personal walk with the Master Jesus Christ. By the power of the Logos Jesus bore, the Master was calling and recalling Saul to his point of origin in the I AM Presence.

Whatever else Paul was outwardly, inwardly his soul was ready!

As he had been prepared of the Spirit, so he had readied himself through diligent application to his studies in this and previous lives. You will remember that Paul was a citizen of Cilicia, a learned Jew brought up at Jerusalem at the feet of Gamaliel, who was a Pharisee of the council and doctor of the law.

Familiar with the path of learning and the learned, the soul within, quite apart from the outer mentality, was no stranger to its spiritualization by the Word. Though the mind of Saul was prejudiced against Christ (by hereditary and environmental factors that cannot permanently alter the soul's direction except she give consent), the image of the apostle Paul, his fiery destiny, was already etched within his spirit.

In his own words Hilarion speaks of the great turning point in his life as Saul of Tarsus through the intercession of the Saviour:

"That Great Doctor of the Law, the Lord himself, who appeared to me on the road to Damascus, allowed even me to experience that blindness which accrues from the dead ritual of the untempered zealot.

"He took away my blindness to the things of the Spirit. Ah, indeed I was blind to the light indwelling in his chosen disciples. So great had been the darkness in me that I must persecute that light which was about to swallow up the whole damned philosophy of Serpent and his seed. How my soul longed to be rescued, though I knew it not!

"Of the same measure that I fought with fury the Light that would deliver me was my longing to be free. It was a question of polarization. And when men are polarized to the anti-Christ position, if they be truly of God and of Christ who is All and in all—though they deny him, yet by his Holy Spirit he will repolarize them

The Conversion of Saul, Vincenzo Camuccini, Basilica of St. Paul Outside the Walls, Rome

out of the deadness of their words and more words unto the Alpha and Omega of the living Word.

"Oh, how I love that Christ who is All and in all! O thou Great Deliverer of my soul, I walk the earth in the power of thy love seeking my instruments through whom I might convey that conversion of the Holy Ghost that came upon me in the encounter with my Lord.

"He chose me as an ensample. Yea, the tears yet stream upon my face when I think of my former estate, the proud Saul of Tarsus."

The mission of Paul, persecutor of Christians, he having consented to the heartless stoning of Saint Stephen, was confirmed through one Ananias to whom the Lord appeared saying, "Go thy way: for he is a chosen vessel unto me, to bear my name before the Gentiles and kings and the children of Israel. For I will shew him how great things he must suffer for my name's sake."

And so Saul, who had been struck to the ground and blinded in his encounter with the Master on his way to Damascus as he was yet "breathing out threatenings and slaughter against the disciples," was now prayerfully waiting for instructions in the house of Judas—and for the one who would restore his sight.

Ananias, following the Lord's directions to the street called Straight, entered the house "and putting his hands on him said, Brother Saul, the Lord, even Jesus, that appeared unto thee in the way as thou camest, hath sent me that thou mightest receive thy sight and be filled with the Holy Ghost."

By the act of this messenger, Paul had the immediate proof that the voice he had heard midst the blinding light was none other than that of Jesus himself: "Saul, Saul, why persecutest thou me?"

Thus, it is recorded that through the Lord's instrument, Ananias, "immediately there fell from his eyes as it had been scales, and he received sight forthwith and arose and was baptized." And the disciples fed him and he was strengthened and he stayed with them "certain days."

But the more abundant proof of the Master's voice that yet echoed in the chambers of his heart—"I AM Jesus whom thou persecutest: it is hard for thee to kick against the pricks.... Arise, and go into the city and it shall be told thee what thou must do"—is that straightway after his conversion and baptism of the Holy Ghost "he preached Christ in the synagogues, that he is the Son of God."

After many days of this, even to the confounding of the Jews in Damascus, proving to them that this Master Jesus is the "very Christ," the Jews took counsel to kill him: "But their laying await was known of Saul. And they watched the gates day and night to kill him. Then the disciples took him by night, and let him down by the wall in a basket."

It is axiomatic: the presence of the Holy Spirit in the power of conversion side by side with persecutions is the greatest proof of our oneness with Christ— "The servant is not greater than his lord: If they have persecuted me, they will also persecute you."

To what end was the conversion of this Saul of Tarsus? Clearly, it had to have been for a very special purpose that the Master Jesus personally undertook the tutoring of Paul, whose experiences and writings in Christ dominate the New Testament.

In Truth, his mission was to build Christ's Church upon the Rock of his personal encounter with the Lord—to convert the 'Gentiles', their leaders, and the children of light and to elucidate Christ's Person and

St. Paul Preaching to the Thessalonians, Gustave Doré

Presence as the living Saviour in sermons and letters delivered throughout Asia Minor and the Mediterranean over a period of thirty years.

But this Paul had still another mission—one to be gleaned from his example and that of the resurrected Christ working with him throughout his life as the Lord's ministering servant. It is their integral relationship that affords insight into the bond of Ascended Master and unascended disciple and through it the fusion of heaven and earth—as when a nova appears in the firmament to beckon us to the higher calling through the I AM THAT I AM.

Paul's direct and touching relationship with his Lord shows the intended friendship and personal initiatic path Jesus holds for every one of us—once we allow ourselves to be fully converted (the word means "turned around, transformed as a new creature in Christ") and subject unto the Universal Christ in life and death and eternity.

The Eastern term for the office Jesus held and still holds is *Guru*, meaning God-man, the dispeller of darkness—the incarnation of the Word (Avatar) who is Teacher, Initiator par excellence.* There is no higher office held on the initiatic scale by one in physical embodiment (though the degrees of attainment by the officeholder may vary according to the quality of his

---

*When lowercased, the term *guru* is applied to a leader or teacher in any field, just as we think of the Messiah as the title and office of Christ although it is used lowercased to describe a deliverer of the people.

heart and his endurance on the initiatic path). The Eastern term for the office held by Paul is *chela*—servant of
the God-man, devotee of the light of Christ in the One
Sent, the Living Master who wears the mantle of Guru.

Paul's experiences as a direct chela of the Ascended
Master Jesus Christ show the ardor necessary to with-
stand the rigors of giving birth in the midst of Jewish
law and Roman paganism to the 2,000-year Piscean
dispensation of *Christ-I-AM-ity*—and the challenge of
every chela following in the apostle's fiery wake to
deliver the Everlasting Gospel to those bound by still
other cults of orthodoxy and idolatry, East and West.

Now, this term *Christ-I-AM-ity* is used by Jesus to
describe his doctrine and the way of deliverance he proclaimed to us as the religion of the Cosmic Christ who
overshadowed him. The Piscean Master's religion is the
path of the Universal Christ weaving through the hearts
of millions of souls tethered to the One through the
affirmation of their Being in Christ. *Christ-I-AM-ity*: the
way of the Sons of God using the power of the sacred
name I AM to affirm their God Identity on earth as it is
in heaven.

Thus it is written in akasha. Thus it behooved
Christ, then and now, to teach his own the mysteries
concerning their incarnation of the Word.

The Ascended Master Hilarion, whether in the historical limelight as Jesus' apostle Paul or in his not so
well-known final incarnation as Saint Hilarion, did not
think it robbery to take upon himself the mantle of his

Lord. Overshadowed by Christ, he could do naught but perform healings in the manner of his Teacher.

By being the vessel of Christ, offering the totality of his being unto his Lord (Guru), he became that Christ, that Lord, and that Guru. Even so, we say, "I and my Guru are One," and the answer returns over the figure-eight flow of our Oneness: "I and my Chela are One."

"Even so, Lord Jesus, 'Drink me while I AM drinking Thee,'" says the aspiring soul seeking the Divine Union, the alchemical marriage with her Lord.

Therefore, having so become, having so entered and merged with the heart fire of Jesus, Hilarion holds the office of Lord of the Fifth Ray. This means that Hilarion embodies the Christ-flame, the Christ-standard, and the Christ-consciousness of the fifth aspect of the light-emanation of God and that he is qualified to transfer this attainment to his students, line upon line, cycle by cycle.

You who would be the unascended disciple of the Ascended Master Hilarion—studying for a season under his tutelage at his university of the Spirit as he imparts to you the mysteries and the initiations of his Lord and Master and Guru—you may also aspire to embody by increments the Christhood of the Fifth Ray, taking to yourself the mantle of God as you are able, as you are willing, as it is practical for you to incorporate* into your life, or lifestyle, the calling of the Lord of the Fifth Ray which you would make your own.

---

*unite with and take into your body

This path is one where you and you alone decide just how much of the Law of Christhood embodied by, and governing the path of, the Guru will be engrafted to your soul through the Guru. At such time as you have by your own self-discipline (applying the precepts of the Lord of the Fifth Ray) so appropriated the essential light of the Lord and the Ray, chakra by chakra, the Ascended Master by Cosmic Law is compelled to take you as his chela.

Until the would-be chela has diligently prepared himself for the calling of this discipleship, he must remember the words of Jesus: "You have not chosen me, but I have chosen you," signifying that until the chela is ready it is the Guru who decides, and not the chela, if the commitment to the relationship is to be entered into. But when the chela is ready, even though she know it not in her outer mind, the Guru will surely appear. As we have seen, this was the case with Saul of Tarsus.

Now you may learn of this chela become Guru and see if you would qualify yourself to be his right-hand man or woman in a glorious mission marked by gifts of healing transmitted in this true lineage—this "apostolic succession" whereby the mantle of the healing Masters of the Fifth Ray may one day be claimed by you!

"And God wrought special miracles by the hands of Paul: So that from his body were brought unto the sick handkerchiefs or aprons, and the diseases departed from them, and the evil spirits went out of them." (Acts 19:11, 12)

Paul was indeed the Lord's chief exorcist, so much

Statue of St. Paul, Basilica of St. Paul Outside the Walls, Rome

so that in certain quarters his name was invoked along with the name of Jesus. At Ephesus, for example, some itinerant Jewish exorcists would say, "I command you by the Jesus whose spokesman is Paul."

On one occasion when the seven sons of Sceva, a Jewish chief priest, attempted to exorcise in this manner, the evil spirit replied, "Jesus I recognize, and I know who Paul is, but who are you?" To their astonishment "the man with the evil spirit hurled himself at them and overpowered first one and then another, and handled them so violently that they fled from that house naked and badly mauled." (Acts 19:13–16, Jerusalem Bible)

Though Jews and Greeks alike were greatly impressed by this episode and the name of the Lord Jesus came to be held in great honor, for those who were going about exorcising in the name of Jesus and Paul without first having established the foundation of a Master-disciple relationship through conversion, baptism and oneness with Jesus' Sacred Heart, this calamity was and is a warning that all who would appropriate the power of the Lord and his apostle without accepting the responsibilities of the path of discipleship may meet with similar consequences—or worse.

It also illustrates the lesson that possessing demons will submit to the Lord and his apostle only through those who have their mantle of authority, in other words, through an established hierarchy where the chain of command leading back to the Cosmic Christ is clear and unbroken. Possessing demons are likewise familiar with the false hierarchy of Antichrist and his fallen angels to which they give allegiance except when challenged by the superior Christ Presence.

Therefore, all ye who would deliver the sweet children of Jesus from the toils of the possessing demons of drugs, suicide, and dread diseases, seek ye first the kingdom of God and His righteousness—and His righteous Son—lawfully, wisely, lovingly, selflessly, having no desire for personal glory, and all these powers (gifts, graces, siddhis) shall be added unto you, even as you surrender to Christ's perfect love in the will of God.

Now, there was one called Elymas the sorcerer, who withstood the messenger of God when he journeyed to Salamis with Barnabas, sent by the Holy Ghost. And he surely lived to rue the day, for he himself was judged along with his demons, with whom he identified fully and from whose arrogance he refused to separate himself out, nor did he seek deliverance from this hellish state through the one sent.

The following account demonstrates the responsibility of the individual to denounce the forces of Antichrist which would use him and to separate himself bodily from them, lest he meet with the same judgment as is due them in the Day of Vengeance of our God— which cometh as a thief in the night.

It is clear that if the individual will not bend the knee before the living Christ or the Spirit of Christ in his true representative, then the apostle will not exorcise him against his will (without his consent). Nevertheless, the demons themselves will be judged, with or without his accord; furthermore, when the hour of the Lord's judgment is come, he himself will indeed be judged—whether he fall to the right or to the left of the plumb line of Truth— and by his words and his works shall he stand or fall.

Students of the Word, if they would progress Christward, must reconcile themselves with this Truth. Therefore, consider the events of Paul and Barnabas' trip to Salamis, where through their instrumentation the judgment of the willing 'host' (the carrier of the demons) and the binding of his discarnates took place simultaneously:

"They traveled the whole length of the island, and at Paphos they came in contact with a Jewish magician called Bar-jesus. This false prophet was one of the attendants of the proconsul Sergius Paulus who was an extremely intelligent man. The proconsul summoned Barnabas and Saul and asked to hear the word of God. But Elymas Magos—as he was called in Greek—tried to stop them so as to prevent the proconsul's conversion to the faith.

"Then Saul, whose other name is Paul, looked him full in the face and said, 'You utter fraud, you impostor, you son of the devil, you enemy of all true religion, why don't you stop twisting the straightforward ways of the Lord? Now watch how the hand of the Lord will strike you: you will be blind, and for a time you will not see the sun.'

"That instant, everything went misty and dark for him, and he groped about to find someone to lead him by the hand. The proconsul, who had watched everything, became a believer, being astonished by what he had learned about the Lord." (Acts 13:6–12, Jerusalem Bible)

On another occasion Paul's exorcism of a damsel resulted in his being thrown in prison. This slave girl, "possessed with a spirit of divination," followed Paul and those traveling with him for many days, crying, "These men are the servants of the most high God, which shew unto us the way of salvation!" One day Paul lost his temper* and turned around and said to the spirit, "I command thee in the name of Jesus Christ to come out of her!" And the spirit came out of her right then and there.

---

*See Jerusalen Bible for this translation.

When the girl's masters saw that there was no hope of making any more money out of her fortune-telling, they dragged Paul and Silas before the magistrates, claiming that "these men, being Jews, do exceedingly trouble our city, and teach customs which are not lawful for us to receive, neither to observe, being Romans."

Paul and Silas were beaten and cast into the inner prison, their feet fastened in the stocks. At midnight, as they sang and prayed, "suddenly there was a great earthquake so that the foundations of the prison were shaken and immediately all the doors were opened, and every one's bands were loosed."

The keeper of the prison escorted them out, fell down before them trembling, and asked, "What must I do to be saved?"

"Believe on the Lord Jesus Christ," they replied, "and thou shalt be saved, and thy house." Then they preached the word of the Lord to him and all his family and that very night they were baptized. (Acts 16:16–34)

Not only did the Lord put upon his messenger the gift of conversion for the select ones He would heal and enlighten, but through Paul He also withheld that power of the Holy Ghost from those who would not receive the Christ through this one sent. Nevertheless, in the presence of all adversity, even unto the mouthing of demons, Paul was emboldened to "speak and hold not thy peace" by the Master Jesus. (Acts 18:5–11)

The restoration of the life-force and the light of the chakras in the impotent man at Lystra healed by the

Holy Ghost at the hand of Jesus through Paul shows the power of the spoken Word delivered in "a loud voice" as a command from on high to restore wholeness through the light of Alpha and Omega:

"And there sat a certain man at Lystra, impotent in his feet, being a cripple from his mother's womb, who never had walked.

"The same heard Paul speak: who stedfastly beholding him, and perceiving that he had faith to be healed, said with a loud voice, Stand upright on thy feet! And he leaped and walked." (Acts 14:8–10)

To perform works such as these, the disciple of Christ who studies under the Ascended Master Hilarion must begin by gathering momentum in the reciting of Jesus' mantra given to John the Revelator: "I AM Alpha and Omega, the beginning and the ending, saith the LORD I AM THAT I AM: which is, and which was, and which is to come, the Almighty." (Rev. 1:8) Then he must study to show himself "approved unto God," as Paul admonished his student Timothy, "a workman that needeth not to be ashamed, rightly dividing the word of Truth."

Indeed, the preparation of the ministering servant must be complete if he is to face Christ's adversary in the world. For this force of Antichrist, when challenged, will unleash all of its Death and Hell against the one who comes in Christ's name to liberate his children of the light from their control.

The Keepers of the Flame lessons and the whole body of the Ascended Masters' teachings is the preparation provided. And Summit University is the mystery school where the soul may learn how to perfect herself in the precepts of Jesus' Lost Teachings. This is the door that is opened to you who knock. It leads to the fount of Truth and the New Day, when you can claim the mantle of your Lord and Saviour and work his works on earth, as he has called you to do with the helpful and comforting support of his brothers and yours—the Lords of the Seven Rays.

Think of it! Paul not only took to himself the mantle of the Holy Spirit but he received the divine approbation of the Lord to wear it in Jesus' name—and for this grace you ought to pray. Paul had to have had the sense of his self-worth in Christ, which could have been imparted to him only by Jesus, in order to take on so mighty a mission—and succeed. And for this, too, you ought to pray—diligently.

Because of Paul's all-consuming passion for the Lord's mission, Christianity has survived in a form that has prepared Christ's followers to receive the Lost Years, the Lost Teachings and the Lost Word as they are being restored today. Paul, by his example in putting on Christ Jesus, almost more than by his words, prefaces and anticipates John's vision of the Everlasting Gospel and the new heaven and the new earth.

We read in Paul's letter to the Galatians—and he stressed this—how he did not receive his knowledge of Christ's message from the other Christians of the day:

The fact is, brothers, and I want you to realize this, the Good News I preached is not a human message that I was given by men, it is something I learned only through a revelation of Jesus Christ. You must have heard of my career as a practicing Jew, how merciless I was in persecuting the Church of God, how much damage I did to it, how I stood out among other Jews of my generation, and how enthusiastic I was for the traditions of my ancestors.

Then God, who had specially chosen me while I was still in my mother's womb, called me through his grace and chose to reveal his Son in me, so that I might preach the Good News about him to the pagans. I did not stop to discuss this with any human being, nor did I go up to Jerusalem to see those who were already apostles before me, but I went off to Arabia at once and later went straight back from there to Damascus.

Even when after three years I went up to Jerusalem to visit Cephas and stayed with him for fifteen days, I did not see any of the other apostles; I only saw James, the brother of the Lord, and I swear before God that what I have just written is the literal truth.

After that I went to Syria and Cilicia, and was still not known by sight to the churches of Christ in Judaea, who had heard nothing except that their onetime persecutor was now preaching the faith he had previously tried to destroy; and they gave glory to God for me. (Galatians 1:11–24, Jerusalem Bible)

If Paul did not gather his knowledge of Christ's message from the chroniclers and Christians of his day, should not we also be willing to seek and find the Master himself—in the secret chamber of our hearts where his voice can still be heard and known? And in the dictations of the Lords of the Seven Rays, who only confirm the law and the Divine Self-knowledge that God said he would write in our inward parts?

Can we not also learn to read the code of our spiritual identity, as scientists learn to read the genetic code of a law that governs even the numbering of the hairs on our heads?

Whence cometh the Lord to Paul with his message? We know that Paul was called by Jesus and taken up in the spirit to the Master's etheric retreat over the Holy Land (at Arabia). Here, night after night and throughout the days of his sojourn his soul was tutored for his assignment to lay the foundation of the Church for the two-thousand-year Piscean dispensation.

Thus, by stages Paul put on the mantle of his Lord and accomplished His works as His instrument in healings, miracles, prophecies, preachments and fiery conversions. This was the true path Christ meant his apostles to walk—as the Ascended Master Hilarion once told us:

"If the light that is in thee be filled with the momentum of God and if the gears of the chakras be oiled with the holy oil of Gilead, then by the very vibration of your life you can intensify the currents of God, you can be one with God, *you can be God incarnate as Jesus Christ was.*

"This is what I learned from him as he became my inner and outer Guru. This is what I understood: that I, too, could become the Christ as the instrument of the Saviour—that where I walked he would walk, that where I stood he would heal, that where I spoke he would speak. This I learned, and yet I understood the unworthiness of the lesser self in the state of sin that is made worthy by grace, by transmutation, by fiery baptism and by the balancing of karma in service to Life."

Now, as for Hilarion (d. c. 371), his was the soul of Paul come again for his final incarnation to fulfill the law of balancing his karma incurred in the persecuting of Christians and the consenting to their death. In obedience to his Lord and out of love for His own, he once again accepted the gift of His mantle to teach and preach and heal. Thus, by grace, through the Lord's intercession, he settled his accounts with life and went above and beyond the call of karmic duty to bless untold thousands, the Lord working in him and through him.

Hilarion spent twenty years in the desert in preparation for his mission and only then wrought his first miracle—God working through him, he cured a woman of barrenness enabling her to bring forth a son. From that day forward, he carried out a healing ministry.

He healed children of a fever by invoking the name of Jesus, cured paralysis and cast out many devils. Crowds would gather to be healed of diseases and unclean spirits. They followed him even into the most desolate and remote places. He tried many times to hide, but they always found him, compelling him to follow his true calling, for the love of Jesus.

Once, he sailed away and hid in Sicily, but a devil cried out through a man in St. Peter's Church in Rome, "Hilarion the servant of Christ is hiding in Sicily. I will go and betray him." Still possessed of the demon, he set sail for Sicily and went directly to Hilarion; throwing

St. Hilarion, Abbot, I. Romney, c. 1814

himself down in front of his hut, he was cured. The saint couldn't hide from the people and he couldn't hide from the devils!

As Jerome said of him, "A city set on an hill cannot be hid." Hilarion had become that city by his devotion to Christ and by that devotion he magnified the Lord.

Jerome, whose biography of the saint provides most of the information we know about him, records: "The frequency of his signs in Sicily drew to him sick people and religious men in multitudes; and one of the chief men was cured of dropsy the same day that he came, and offered Hilarion boundless gifts; but he obeyed the Saviour's saying, 'Freely ye have received; freely give.'"

And then the Lord did something truly extraordinary through him. It was on the occasion of a great earthquake, and the sea was threatening to destroy the town. According to Jerome, "The sea broke its bounds; and, as if God was threatening another flood, or all was returning to primeval chaos, ships were carried up steep rocks and hung there."

The townsfolk, seeing these mountains of water coming towards the shore, ran and got Hilarion, and, "as if they were leading him out to battle, stationed him on the shore. And when he had marked three signs of the Cross upon the sand, and stretched out his hands against the waves, it is past belief to what a height the sea swelled, and stood up before him, and then, raging long, as if indignant at the barrier, fell back, little by little, into itself."

You can imagine how the crowds flocked to him all the more after that alchemical feat—Christ's alchemy through him, you see. No doubt they said of him what they had said of his Master before him, "What manner of man is this, that even the wind and the sea obey him?"

Toward the end of his life the people's saint, for they had claimed him as their own, retreated to a spot in Cyprus so remote that he was convinced no one would find him there. It was even haunted—the people would be afraid to approach, he thought. But one paralyzed managed to drag himself there, found Hilarion, was cured, and spread the word.

And so it was that the saint ended his days in that valley, with many people coming to see him. After his

St. Hilarion Castle, Cyprus

Hilarion spent his final days in a cave on this mountain.

passing, his followers buried him there, as was his desire, but within several months his closest disciple, Hesychius, secretly dug up his grave and carried his body off to Palestine!

Alas, they deified the miracle worker instead of internalizing his example and teaching on the crystallization (Christ-realization) of the God flame. And he became the crystal and the crystal returned to the mist —and they missed it. They missed the whole point of his mission, his sacrifice, and his victory!

As with Jesus, they wanted the loaves and fishes. They wanted to be fed and delivered of their transgressions (karma) come upon them through their diseases— without paying the price. Yes, whatever was free they would take, but they didn't want the personal responsibility of internalizing the Word, of *being* and *becoming* the Christ—perhaps with "groanings" and "travail," as Paul says, as we also wait the Lord's adoption of our souls unto Himself. (Romans 8:22, 23)

"I *must* work the works of Him that sent me"—thus Jesus taught and fulfilled the requirements of being a disciple of the Cosmic Christ and he expected those who would call themselves his disciples to do likewise.

Yes, the greatest scientists who have ever lived, Jesus and the saints of East and West, including the Seven Chohans, stand before the people, and the people just take the miracles and the healings but never ask how or why or, "Can I do it, too, Lord?"

Instead they want to know who amongst them will

be greatest in the kingdom, while Christ is looking to bestow his mantle for world regeneration upon anyone who will apprentice himself to him and Saint Germain and the Maha Chohan and the other Chohans to learn the science of healing and longevity with good health and the art of the miraculous abounding like roses falling from Nada's chair!

The fiery spirit of Hilarion performed, the Lord working through him, those works which equaled those of Jesus Christ. This testimony of his Sonship, had he proclaimed it in words rather than deeds, would have been considered blasphemous in his day even as it would in ours.

As a false theology denies the present potential of Sonship to every child of God, so too the works of a "Christed one"—i.e., one anointed by the LORD, the Mighty I AM Presence through Jesus Christ—are frowned upon lest, by the very empirical proof offered by the lives of the saints, that false doctrine of only one son of God—stemming from Antichrist's deliberate misinterpretation of the "Only Begotten of the Father, full of Grace and Truth"—should be rendered of no use.

The soul of Paul, already as the apostle, was the recipient fully of the gifts of the Holy Spirit. In him were fulfilled the promises of our Lord: "He that believeth on me, the works that I do shall he do also; and greater works than these shall he do; because I go unto my Father…"

Because none dare say it and none dare tell it, we

say it and we tell it: You too can do the works of Jesus Christ, you too can become the fullness of that Christ which he became—if you will to submit yourselves unto his Law and his Love.

This is the message today not only of Jesus but of Hilarion and the other Lords of the Rays. The whole point of their path is to reveal this Christhood on each of the seven rays and to show you how to unlock your present potential to attain it.

To this end Hilarion invites to his retreat all who espouse the cause of Truth, all who are the voice of Truth (and often the lone voice), all who are messengers of Truth in the media or any field where unless defended, Truth is set aside by the lies and distortions of the serpent class. The Healing Master bids them to come in their finer bodies to attend classes in his Temple of Truth at the isle of Crete. This retreat of the Great White Brotherhood is located on the etheric plane at the site of the original Temple of Truth where vestal virgins once kept the flame of Truth as oracles of the Divine Mother, beloved Vesta.

The flame of Truth enshrined at Hilarion's retreat is an intense bright, fiery green—the color that compels precipitation, actualization, practicality, healing, and rejuvenation. The flaming blue of the power of God combines with the golden ray of the intelligence of God to focus the green flame of healing and scientific wholeness. The musical keynote of the retreat is "Onward, Christian Soldiers."

The Lord of the Fifth Ray together with the Brotherhood of Crete sponsors teachers of Truth, servants of God, religious leaders and missionaries, as well as those practicing the healing arts, scientists and engineers in all fields, mathematicians, musicians, and those specializing in computer and space technology.

He, with the Fifth-Ray Masters, works steadfastly to draw their consciousness into a greater and greater appreciation of the full spectrum of Truth, which most have experienced but in part. To take them from a partial knowledge of Truth to self-awareness in the Divine Wholeness of Truth is the goal of these brothers whose motto, we must remember, is "And ye shall know the Truth and the Truth shall make you Free, i.e., Whole."

Hilarion is especially concerned with helping atheists, agnostics, skeptics and others empirically centered who, often through no fault of their own but thanks to the blind leaders of the blind in Church and State, have become disillusioned with religion and life in general.

"The agnostics cry out today against the trivia of this age and quite frequently they take a stand for principles of the light," he says. "The atheists deny while the agnostics struggle to see. In our temple at Crete, we have determined to bring new meaning to life through the avenues of science and to stop the perpetual harassment of those forward-moving individuals who seek to assuage some measure of human grief"—even though they may not conform to some people's version of Truth or science or religion.

"My responsibility," Hilarion once told us, "is to release through the fiery core of my heart, energies for healing, for science, for truth, for the enlightenment of souls by the law of mathematics of the energy flow, the energy systems that can and will contribute to wholeness and the integration of souls with the Life that is God here on the planet Earth."

Speaking on behalf of the healing Masters who had been deliberating with the Karmic Board and other Cosmic Beings concerned for the fate of mankind, Hilarion said, "There has never been a time in human history when mankind have been so plagued by disease of every form. Often these are diseases which are not perceptible to the people themselves, for they are the diseases of the mind, the diseases of character, diseases within the subconscious.

"This energy of malfunction, of disturbance, of an unnatural activity within the cells of the body of God on earth is reaching alarming proportions—in fact it is an alarm that has sounded across the Cosmos itself. For if mankind be not whole, then how can they be over-comers in this age? How can they solve the larger problems on the world scene when their four lower bodies are so far from the center of reality?

"We have seen, then, that Saint Germain and Morya, Masters of the age, require the support of the healing Masters and of Cosmic Beings from many sectors of Cosmos. We have seen that the dream of Morya to free the earth, that the fires of transmutation and freedom for the Aquarian age in the hand of Saint Germain cannot be realized unless mankind be made whole, unless there is a quickening.

"And therefore we have appealed to the Holy Spirit, to the Maha Chohan. This noble one was summoned to our meeting by the Goddess of Liberty, the spokesman for the Karmic Board. And we placed the dilemma before the Maha Chohan. And he gave his reply, stating that he was aware of the proportions, and his concern was also a mounting one....

"His statement was that at the very foundation of the problem of disease, of sickness of every type was the estrangement of the soul from the flame of the Mother, the estrangement of the soul from the Spirit Most Holy. In the light of this assessment he pointed out how troubling world conditions, manufactured to a large extent by the fallen ones, were specifically calculated to separate the soul from the security of the Divine Mother and from the energy flow of the Holy Spirit."

Then Hilarion gave us an important key: "Will you remember, then, when all else fails, especially when you find that somehow there is a distortion in your mind, in your vision, in your ability to cope with life that you instantaneously invoke in the name of Jesus the Christ the sealing of the mind with the dispensation of the emerald-teal ray?"

Hilarion explained that this dispensation, when

invoked, is performed by a special legion of angels assigned to the task who seal the mind and mental body in a forcefield of brilliant emerald-teal light, glowing now as green, now as an aspect of the hue of blue.

"Inasmuch as I am the Chohan of the Fifth Ray, inasmuch as the Chohans of the Rays are the guardians of the Christ consciousness of their ray, it was given to me to organize legions of light for the protection of the Christ Mind in the children of the light by the flame of Truth. Therefore, you may call upon this contingent of healing forces to reinforce the Christ consciousness and to saturate the minds of mankind with the healing flame.

"Know, then, that in answer to your call I come forth with millions of angels and ascended hosts of light, some even newly ascended..., who have determined to join in this specific endeavor of locking the light of healing around the consciousness of mankind for the protection of that light, that Logos, that logic of the Divine Mind that it might mesh with the lower mental body, the brain, chakras and central nervous system, and be accessible to the race."

Hilarion speaks often of the guarding of the mind as well as the spirit:

"In the matter of bodily health, the state of the mind and spirit must be considered. How foolish it is for men to ignore the content of the mind and to fail to examine that which they allow to fall into it; for the mind can be a pit and a snare because it is of the earth, earthy. Men should carefully watch the intake of their minds, for out of all that is absorbed therein are often compounded those animallike qualities which later appear 'out of nowhere' to crush the evolving Christ consciousness, both in its infancy and as it approaches a mature perfection in the soul.

"A man must consider how he becomes his own worst enemy. Unless this be done, his progress may be slow; for within the circle of his being, he will find lurking the most crafty of enemies.

"There are many victims of maladies of the mind and spirit who attribute to outside forces the distortions which they themselves have taken into their worlds. Let us seek to cast out of each blessed monad the negativities that have entered there in order that the eyes may see with singleness of vision the beauty of the emerging Christ."

In his love of healing and the healing arts, the flow of his thought is a never-ending stream of the panacea of Peace men have sought but seldom found. Hilarion is living proof that the all-cure of God can be known, the elixir of youth imbibed, and the sunbeam of Truth followed to its Source:

"O beloved ones, the healing ray is everywhere present. You cannot wander far upon this earth and not be in the presence of Life. And Life is healing. Life in its essence, when understood, always brings healing.

"There is no need for incompleteness; there is no need for a lack, for an incomplete manifestation in the four lower bodies when Life is understood. Life with all the fullness of God himself comes to all each day in every breath, and the secrets of healing are themselves lodged within this divine pneuma.

"Sometimes I wonder at mankind's lack of ingenuity in the discovery of the healing ray, for it is the most obvious of all of the seven rays, I think. I think, too, that in one another, in holding the balance of life for one's fellow man, the discovery of true healing may be known. For to see perfection in each one is to see the power of healing flood forth in all of its glory.

"Sometimes failure, on the part of those who would heal, comes because they have not held to the perfect image with enough tenacity, enough determination to hold a concept until the manifestation does appear. Mankind have trained themselves to wait for the springtime, to wait for the harvest, and they know it will come—to wait for the birth of a child. And the period of gestation of all forms of life is known unto them. And by scientific conclusion they know that at a certain hour, a certain time all will be fulfilled, all will appear in divine order.

"But when it comes to the unknown, there is hesitancy, there is doubt. And people wonder, How long must I wait to outpicture the perfect image? And because there is no precedent or set time for the full-blown image to appear, they become disturbed in their feelings and they dash in pieces the matrix which Divine Love will surely fulfill in each one (in the cycles of time and space) as he holds to the immaculate design.

"For, there is no limit to that which you can outpicture by the power of Love if you will hold intact within you the perfect design."

Justice Lifts the Nation, mural, old Supreme Court Building,
Lausanne, Switzerland

As a lawyer on Atlantis, Nada defended the downtrodden and
oppressed. This mural of the archetypal female figure of Justice
carries the fervor of her fiery determination to defend the freedom,
liberties and divine rights of all people then and now.

6

LADY MASTER NADA
the Judge

Gifts of Diverse Kinds of Tongues and the Interpretation of Tongues

Assisting Saint Germain in his "great gathering of the elect" who will serve with him in the cause of world freedom is beloved Nada, Chohan of the Sixth Ray. This Ascended Lady Master also serves on the Karmic Board as the representative of the Third Ray. Through both offices she teaches Jesus' path of personal Christhood through ministration and service to life.

On Atlantis Nada served as a priestess in the Temple of Love. The etheric counterpart of this temple, which is designed after the pattern of a rose, is centered above New Bedford, Massachusetts. Each petal is a room, and in the center there burns the flame of Divine Love—tended by brothers and sisters of the Third Ray for the healing of earth's evolutions by Love, which Jesus says is the fulfilling of the law of karma.

In other embodiments, Nada took up the avocation of law and became an expert in the defense of souls oppressed by the spoilers in the earth. During her meditations upon the Law of God and in the course of her ministrations in the temple, she perceived the Law "as the certain defense which the Mother must use to protect her children from the wiles of this world, from the fallen ones who seek also to use the Law to their unjust purposes."

In her final incarnation 2,700 years ago, Nada was the youngest of a large family of exceptionally gifted children. The beloved angel Charity appeared to her at a very early age and taught her how to draw God's love from the flame in her heart and to radiate it into the Nature kingdom for the blessing of life. The Archeia of the Third Ray also taught Nada to expand her threefold flame for the quickening of the chakras of her brothers and sisters, that by a heightened inner awareness they might bless the people and uplift the culture of the Divine Mother on earth through the arts.

In a dictation given August 28, 1982, Nada told her story:

"As I was embodied in a large family of many brothers and sisters of great talent, I saw how each one in pursuing his career needed love and ministration and the keeping of the flame of the sacred fire in order to be successful.

"And thus, although the choice was given to me to pursue my own career, unbeknownst to my brothers and sisters I quietly kept the flame in deep meditation and prayer as well as outer helpfulness, in [by way of] contacting the great spheres [causal body] of their divine plan, and in accelerating through the mighty Archangels Chamuel and Charity in the understanding that the adversaries of Love are many, and that Love is the full power of creativity, and that the success of the career son or daughter of God depends upon the

Charity, mosaic

Gentle tutor of Nada's final incarnation, the Archeia Charity taught her to draw forth the love from her I AM Presence and the threefold flame of her heart and to radiate it into Nature to the elemental builders of form. Beloved Archangel Chamuel and Charity, twin flames of the Third Ray, also administered initiations of the Ruby Ray to Nada when she practiced the healing arts on Atlantis. Her healing retreat is over the area of New Bedford, Massachusetts.

defeat of Love's adversary, point counterpoint.

"And therefore, in the course of defending the Christhood of my brothers and sisters, I had to advance in my own self-mastery to confront the fallen ones who attempted to thwart them in their most magnificent lifestreams and their offering to the world. Thus I understood Love as the consuming fire of the Holy Spirit that does indeed challenge and bind the wicked in the way!…

"I can assure you that at the conclusion of my incarnation when I saw the victory of each one of my brothers and sisters, the fullness of my joy was in a heart of Love expanded, keeping the flame—keeping the flame and knowing that I was needed, that I was essential to their victory.…

"It seemed to the world, and perhaps even to my own, that I had not accomplished much. But I took my leave into the higher octaves thoroughly understanding the meaning of the self-mastery of the pink flame. Thus it was from the point of the Third Ray that I entered into the heart of Christ and saw the application [on the Sixth Ray] as ministration and service."

As Lord of the Sixth Ray of Ministration and Service, the Ascended Lady Master Nada assists ministers, missionaries, healers, teachers, psychologists, counselors at law, professional people, public servants in government as well as those devoted to serving the needs of God's children in every branch of human and health services. You will also find her at the side of businessmen and -women, blue-collar, skilled and unskilled workers, farmers, ranchers, defenders of Freedom and revolutionaries of Love in every field.

Of course, Nada loves them all because she teaches the principle and practice of the sacred labor as the effective means to achieve the goal of the ascension. Fittingly, the mottos of her disciples are "I serve," "The servant is not greater than his Lord," and "I am my brother's keeper."

Nada tells us of the initiations and joy of selfless service:

"Understand this formula of selflessness: To know when you have become selfless is to not be aware of the choice of selflessness. By this I mean that the natural course of your life is always the preferring of the love of God, the service of that God incarnate. To be aware of self, its pleasures, its privileges, its preferences, and then to make a choice to forgo that self is a step on the path of selflessness which must indeed be taken....

"But once you have reached that center, you are no longer aware of choosing between the Self—the Real Self—and the not-self. For you have become that living Self and you identify with all preferences to be that Self, to be immersed in that Self, to be the hands, the heart, the head of the Lord wherever you are needed, wherever it is required, filling in for God, supplying every need and therefore supplying each aspect of the Christ which someone may lack fulfillment in for the mastery of the threefold flame.

"Your preference is then in supplying the tenderness and compassion, perceiving the need because your sensitivity to God has been refined not only by the All-Seeing Eye, but by the exercise of the secret rays, letting those rays flow through you and fearing not the pain of the crucifixion, but altogether transforming that pain into the bliss of communion."

The gifts of the Holy Spirit which Nada administers are those of *diverse kinds of tongues* and the *interpretation of tongues.* These gifts involve the mastery of nuances of vibration in the five secret rays and their almost infinite combinations with the elements of the seven rays as the qualities of the Word are released through the petals of the chakras.

As pertains to human, divine, and angelic tongues, these gifts involve the mastery of speech, communication and the delivery of the Word. They range from the mastery of earth's languages for the transmission of the Word universally to all to proficiency in the tongues of angels as spoken by angelic messengers through the empowerment of the Holy Spirit.

Such releases given from an enraptured, exalted, or altered state are dictations (sometimes ex cathedra) for the initiation of souls and the transfer of the sacred fires from the altars of heaven. These fires, grounded through the anointed, are surely for the blessing of the saints who labor in Love under the weight of planetary karma they bear, or for the binding, surely, of the embodied seed of the fallen angels whose hour for the final judgment has come.

The gifts of tongues also facilitate understanding between peoples and figure in the art of diplomacy and just plain getting along with your neighbor—the soft answer that turneth away wrath, the bridling of the tongue that James admonished—comforting a child or the wounded soul or dealing in the power of the LORD's Spirit with the Devil's railings and possessing demons.

Thus the Science of the Spoken Word in all of its very human and divine ramifications is Nada's forte, which she conveys with the gifts of tongues and the interpretation thereof. So, too, it must be borne in mind that once the Word is spoken, instantaneously it becomes the manifest Work of the LORD through His mediators on earth.

Following in Jesus' footsteps, beloved Nada had assumed the full Chohanship of the Sixth Ray by December 31, 1959. Nada serves in Jesus' retreat in the etheric octave over Saudi Arabia, where many disciples of the Lord have received their training directly from his Sacred Heart, face to face, during the Saviour's two-thousand-year occupancy of that office.

Here in the home of the Prince of Peace Nada instructs and gives exercises in the God-mastery of the emotions and the quieting of the inordinate passions of the desire body. Using Jesus' mantra "Peace be still!" she demonstrates the use of the solar plexus for the release of the power of peace through the seven sacred centers. Here, too, she unveils the mystery of Jesus' saying "He that believeth on me, out of his belly shall flow rivers of living water."

As Nada directs disciples in the application of the radiant purple-and-gold flame of the Sixth Ray—a key step in the nine steps of precipitation taught by the Master Alchemist Saint Germain and the priesthood of the Order of Melchizedek (as well as by the Seven Mighty Elohim and the elemental builders of form)— she stresses the path of devotion (*bhakti* yoga) through the reestablishment of a personal heart-tie to Jesus. This Love-tie, she says, is *the* key to "believing on him." And in this case, believing *is* seeing—seeing just how to put on his consciousness, to assimilate his Body and his Blood, and to internalize his Word.

Oneness with the Christ of Jesus, chakra by chakra, reinforced through the individual Christ Self, is the open door to the disciple's instrumentation of that flow of light from the Great Central Sun by which sons and daughters of God hold the balance for earth and her evolutions. The flow of light out of "the belly," which means through the solar plexus, or place of the Sun, is of spiritual significance:

Here the belly refers to the womb as the matrix, or place prepared, for the soul's alchemy of bringing forth the Divine Manchild—the Christ consciousness of the universal age. This realization of the self as the instrument of the Greater Self with its attendant putting on of the light of the Great Central Sun (the Son of God) leads to the God Self-realization of the Mother seen as the soul who is Woman, "clothed with the 'Sun.'"

By this Sixth Ray alchemy of Christ's Love combined with the Ruby Ray action of the Third Ray—present in the Manchild who has the gifts of the Holy Ghost while he is yet in his mother's womb—Nada, assisted by her angels and devotees, contributes to the mitigation of world tension and the astral weight of the mass consciousness. Thus, this path of practicing the presence of the Lord—pursued by his own who abide in his heart as he abides in theirs—is the Sixth Ray aspect and action of the transmutation of personal and planetary karma.

Nada tells us of a beautiful ritual whereby through a simple call we can help alleviate the stress and strain weighing not only upon our brothers and sisters but upon our own body temple:

"God in man is yours to commend into the arms of the Holy Spirit. Thus I commend you each one. Will you commend one another into the arms of the Holy Spirit and understand that that Holy Spirit is the immaculate image of Father-Mother God?

"And when you commend yourself ere you fall asleep at night, ere you walk the pathway and the ways of the world, when you commend one another into the arms of the Holy Spirit, you are sealing each one in that certain matrix of perfection that is a shield and a guard through all testing, through all trial, through all tribulation.

"Thus did the Lord Christ proclaim upon the cross, 'Into thy hands I commend my Spirit, O God.' Thus, you see, he sealed his soul in the perfection and the protection of the Holy Spirit. This you must do each day for the selfhood of each one entrusted to your care, for all mankind, for the planetary body, for elementals and each blossom rare that my angels now place within the crystal chalice of your hearts."

In an age of Aquarian freedom the demands upon those who would tame its soul fires are great. True Love for the brethren in Christ engenders a desire for self-mastery and self-control in the timing and teamwork of the Lord's Word and Work—in order that the achievements of Community might reflect the Christhood of initiates who have translated the nine gifts of the Holy Spirit into the nine steps of alchemy for the building of the temple of God and man.

Nada offers this sound advice for our soul's mastery of alchemy in this age:

"The vortex of every endeavor must contain an intense will. When balanced with Alpha and Omega in the individual or twin flames or friends, the increase of the periphery is as great as the fire of the center. Let the central flame therefore reveal all ingredients of the goal, for the very alchemy itself depends upon the formula. If the formula does not contain the capacity to bless life, to heal life, to increase wisdom, it will be a self-limiting one.

"Therefore, in business, in service, in any activity, consider: How far will the light travel? How far will the effort expended reach? Will all the earth be blessed because I have lived this hour and striven for the highest? Or will only those in my immediate circle find temporal comfort?

"It is so true, beloved hearts, that mastery, as a quality, of itself has many dimensions. And the wisdom and intelligence of the mind that guides and directs an effort, that sets forth the goal and the means to achieve it, are principally to be considered as the most important ingredients. Combined with the love, then the power, the intelligence and the planning (the understanding of all phases of a project or design) will mean that you have discovered a limitless formula that will multiply and multiply itself long after you have walked the earth or that will rise and fall again.

"Thus, neither the soul nor the goal itself can rise any higher than its own matrix. Rather than pursuing many little endeavors, concentrate, then, on that which will reach the star of your I AM Presence. Let your Christ Self calculate the mathematical formula: How much effort and planning, how much involvement will it take for the rocket of the soul to mount and accelerate to the vibration of the I AM Presence?"

This self-assessment of resources, will, and goals is nowhere more vital than in family planning.

The Goddess of Liberty has stated the position of the Karmic Board that parents ought not to bring forth more children than "you are able to care for and for whom you may adequately express your love." Nevertheless, abortion as a means to birth control is deemed a violation of the sacred flame of Life, which every Keeper of the Flame has vowed to keep. Therefore, other means to predetermining the family circle must be intelligently studied and applied, for when life, sacred life, is at stake, one does not act haphazardly as though the bearing and rearing of children were a matter to be left to the fates or the gods.

The worth of the individual as the potential to be God in manifestation is incalculable. Its violation at any level is fraught with far-reaching karmic consequences, as Jesus warned, to any who offend even one of these little ones. Thus, tenderly Nada sponsors the world's children, individual by individual, often in answer to their prayers, or cries of anguish in abandonment. And she has legions of angels who personally attend the little ones and the youth.

It must be remembered, however, that unless the child is taught to pray and does pray daily, or someone does pray for him daily in his stead, the angels are not permitted to overstep their bounds to intrude or inter-cede in his life. By the justice of this Cosmic Law, which often seems unjust, accidents and calamities do happen. As you say, "There are no free lunches," so the Ascended Masters say, "There are no favorite sons." God is no respecter of persons but does respect his covenanted free will vouchsafed to all equally who abide in the Matter spheres.

The decision to have or not to have the intercession of angelic hosts and Ascended Masters in the life of the family and the children and between husband and wife is a daily one which can only be made by you. It involves communion with the I AM Presence and a conscious desire expressed in prayer for the will of God to take command in every situation.

When wrestling with possessing demons of addiction and terminal diseases on behalf of loved ones, there is simply no replacement for a strong and dynamic decree momentum which can be acquired quite rapidly by fervent hearts who will study and apply the teachings recorded in our book on *The Science of the Spoken Word.* Those facing family difficulties of any kind should include in their list of options for the resolution of crisis the daily, concerted application of this unfailing Law and light. Decrees work if you work.

Nada tells us of her answer to one child's prayer. Know, O blessed reader, that she will answer your heart's call just as simply and beautifully as she did this little girl's. If you are burdened, do not give up, but take this moment to implore her immediate help in Jesus' name.

"I remember many years ago when a little girl who did not even know of the existence of the Masters of Wisdom prayed to God and said, 'O Father, if thou hast any servant upon this earth or anywhere in the universe that will love me and help me, thou dost not need to come thyself, but send them and I will receive them as thyself.'

"And when she prayed thusly, I was sent. And I appeared to her at first only as in a dream. She saw me surrounded with roses, and having a parochial background she fancied that I was Mother Mary. And so, in one of her dreams Mother Mary came also with me, and then she was confused and said, 'Oh, you have a sister.'

"Do you understand the sweetness and simplicity of the child mind?

"And so eventually she found two spiritual friends who guided her destiny and assisted her through the entire school system. Upon her graduation, she became an artist of most ethereal pictures and followed the course of art all the days of her life.

"I want you to understand that within that artist there were many beautiful pictures unborn, paintings that never graced the canvases of the world. And if these could have been seen by humanity, they would, I tell you, have paid all that they had just to prize one of them."

Nada is especially concerned that incoming souls receive the necessary spiritual, practical and academic education and that parents understand the need to give their children loving but firm and creative discipline as a prelude to their discipleship under the Cosmic Christ.

Consequently, Nada is very much involved in the initiation and sponsorship of twin flames and the Aquarian-age family. And she draws her circle of love around homes of light where father and mother set the example of the Path and children are tutored in the Law from birth by right standard and right action.

Regarding the problems of crime and the burdens of drugs upon our children, Nada has said: "The love that must be instilled, beginning with yourself, is a love so tangible for God in the person of one another, for God in the person of his saints, his angels, the Masters, Nature, and the simplicity of life itself, that in the presence of such love the abrogation of the laws of God is altogether unthinkable."

Her sponsorship of the brothers and sisters of the Order of Saint Francis and Saint Clare is uniquely toward self-mastery of the sacred fire on the path of the Divine Mother that their service might suffice unto the calling of "kings and priests unto God." Such attainment may also be the lot of householders during and after the childbearing years, if they so choose to consecrate their marriage. For great is our God and great are his dispensations to those who espouse the highest path of the initiates: Christhood through the Son of God.

In a recent dictation with Mighty Victory, Nada spoke of her sponsorship of twin flames:

"I come in the person of the Mother flame, as Chohan and member of the Karmic Board, to teach you and to walk with you. I come as the initiator of twin flames and soul mates and community members of the sangha of the Buddha and the community of Christ. For, beloved, the initiations of the Ruby Ray are tough. Therefore, we have recommended partnership, two by two, as Jesus sent his disciples, who also received some of these tests.

"Whenever there is the action of going forth two by two, one is the bearer of the Alpha flame and the other of the Omega, forming a circle of light that cannot be penetrated, like an impregnable fortress....

"Realize, then, that the conferring by the Lords of Karma of opportunity and initiation for twin flames is to that end that the twin flames together [might] enter the path of initiation of the Ruby Ray. Thus, with or without companion (known or unknown to you), it is well to call upon the Lords of Flame, Holy Kumaras, for those initiations [to be given] to yourself and your beloved."

Since the sinking of Lemuria and subsequently Atlantis, circles of Masters and disciples sponsored by the Great White Brotherhood have held the balance of light for earth's evolutions. Nada was one of those who kept the flame for the earth during the period of great darkness that covered the land. For, as we have pointed out, the priests and priestesses who tended the flames in the temples of Atlantis and on Lemuria (principally those who came to earth with Sanat Kumara) did carry those flames to other locations.

These keepers of the flame have continued to reembody as initiates of the sacred fire serving on the ray and in the temple of their calling. Whether in physical embodiment or from the ascended state, they maintain the balance of Alpha and Omega in the Spirit-Matter cosmos through the Guru-chela relationship.

Let us now enter their course and run with the torchbearers of the seventh age and its hierarch, the Ascended Master Saint Germain.

Atlantis, Auriel Bessemer

SAINT GERMAIN
the Alchemist

Gifts of Prophecy
and the Working of Miracles

Enter Saint Germain May 1, 1684,
God of Freedom to the earth.
Draped with a cloak of stars,
He stands with his twin flame,
The Goddess of Justice,
Against the backdrop of Cosmos.
He is come to ignite the fires of world transmutation
In hearts attuned to the cosmic cyphers
And to avert personal and planetary cataclysm.
He pleads the cause of God-Freedom
Before the councils of men
And presents his case before
The world body of lightbearers.
He offers a ransom for the oppressed—
Gift of his heart—and of his mind,

Rarest jewel of all our earthly souvenirs—
And of his causal body:
Sphere upon sphere of the richness of himself
Harvested from the divine, and the human, experience.
All this he offers.
Like a beggar with his bowl piled high,
He plies the streets of the world
Eyeing passersby
Hopeful that even one in every million
Might take the proffered gift
And hold it to his heart in recognition
Of the Source, of the Sun,
And of the alchemy of the age so close.
Yes, as close as free will and the Divine Spark
Is our extrication from the dilemma
Of doubt and deleterious concepts and death.
And as far, as far as the toiler's envy
Of our Love tryst is from grace,
So, without him, is the morning of our deliverance
From tangled entanglements of karmic crisscrosses
Of our doodling and dabbling for centuries' boredom
With personalities far less, oh yes, than his.

Enter Saint Germain
Into our hearts forever, if we will only let him.

———————

He lived to make men free.

That, in a phrase, sums up Saint Germain's many embodiments. Although he has played many parts, in each life he has brought the Christ/light in prophecy and the alchemy of freedom to liberate the people of earth.

Enter Saint Germain January 1, 1987.

He comes to the fore as the Lord of the Seventh Ray and Age. He comes to initiate us in the gift of *prophecy* and the gift of the *working of miracles*—that we might foresee by the Spirit of the prophets what is coming upon us and turn the tide by the miracle violet flame.

More than fifty thousand years ago, a golden-age civilization thrived in a fertile country with a semi-tropical climate where the Sahara Desert now is. It was filled with great peace, happiness and prosperity and ruled with supreme justice and wisdom by this very Saint Germain.

The majority of his subjects retained full, conscious use of the wisdom and power of God. They possessed abilities that today would seem superhuman or miraculous. They knew they were extensions of the Central Sun—Life-streams issuing from the Great Hub of the Spirit-Matter cosmos.

For their wise ruler had charted for them on a great mural in the center of the capital city, "the City of the Sun," their cosmic history—that they should not forget the Source whence they had come nor their reason for being: To become sun-centers in this distant galaxy they now called home, extensions of the Law of the One. For they were part of an expanding universe. And their sense of co-measurement with the One sustained an ever-present cognition of the I AM THAT I AM.

Saint Germain was a master of the ancient wisdom and of the knowledge of the Matter spheres. He ruled by light every area of life; his empire reached a height of beauty, symmetry and perfection unexceeded in the physical octave. Truly the heavenly patterns were out-pictured in the crystal chalice of the earth. And elemental life served to maintain the purity of the Matter quadrants.

The people regarded their hierarch as the highest expression of God whom they desired to emulate, and great was their love for his presence. He was the embodiment of the archetype of universal Christhood for that dispensation—to whom they could look as the standard for their own emerging Godhood.

Guy W. Ballard, under the pen name of Godfré Ray King, recounted in *Unveiled Mysteries* a soul journey in which Saint Germain conducted him through the akashic record of this civilization and its decline.[1]

Saint Germain explained to him that "as in all ages past, there was a portion of the people who became more interested in the temporary pleasures of the senses than in the larger creative plan of the Great God Self. This caused them to lose consciousness of the God-Power throughout the land until it remained active in little more than the [capital] city itself. Those governing realized they must withdraw and let the people learn through hard experience that all their happiness and good came from the adoration to the God within, and they must come back into the light if they were to be happy."

Thus, the ruler (the embodied representative of the spiritual hierarchy of the earth under Sanat Kumara) was instructed by a cosmic council that he must withdraw from his empire and his beloved people; henceforth their karma would be their Guru and Lawgiver, and free will would determine what, if any, of his legacy of light they would retain.

According to plan, the king held a great banquet in the Jeweled Room of his palace, with his councillors and public servants in attendance. Following the dinner, which had been entirely precipitated, a crystal goblet filled with "pure electronic essence" appeared to the right of each of the 576 guests. It was the communion cup of Saint Germain, who, with the mantle and scepter of the ancient priest/kings, gave of his own light-essence to those who had faithfully served the realm to the glory of God.

As they drank to the "Flame of the most High Living One," they knew they could never completely forget the divine spark of the inner God Self. This soul-protection, afforded them through the ever-grateful heart of Saint Germain, would be sustained throughout the centuries until once again they should find themselves in a civilization where the cosmic cycles had turned and they would be given the full knowledge to pursue the Divine Union—this time nevermore to go out from the Golden City of the Sun.

Now a Cosmic Master from out the Great Silence spoke. His message was broadcast from the banquet hall throughout the realm. The resplendent being, who identified himself solely by the word *Victory* written upon his brow, brought warning of crisis to come, rebuked the people for their ingratitude to and neglect of their Great God Source, and reminded them of the ancient command to obey the Law of the One—Love. Then he gave them the following prophecy of their karma:

"A visiting prince approaches your borders. He will enter this city seeking the daughter of your king. You will come under the rule of this prince but the recognition of your mistake will be futile. Nothing can avail, for the royal family will be drawn into the protection and care of those whose power and authority are of God, and against whom no human desire can ever prevail. These are the great Ascended Masters of light from the golden etheric city over this land. Here your ruler and his beloved children will abide for a cycle of time."

The king and his children withdrew seven days later. The prince arrived the next day and took over without opposition.

As we study the history of Saint Germain's lifestream we shall see that time and time again the Master and his way of God-mastery have been rejected by the very ones he sought to help; notwithstanding the fact that his gifts of light, life and love—fruits of his adeptship freely given—his alchemical feats, elixir of youth, inventions and prognostications have been readily received.

The goal of his embodiments extending from the golden-age civilization of the Sahara to the final hour of his life as Francis Bacon was always to liberate the children of the light, especially those who in their carelessness in handling fiery principles of the Law had been left to their own karmic devices—in whose vices they were often bound. His aim was to see the fulfillment of his prayer offered at the final banquet of his reign:

> If they must have the experience that consumes and burns away the dross and clouds of the outer self, then do Thou sustain and at last bring them forth in Thy Eternal Perfection. I call unto Thee, Thou Creator of the Universe—Thou Supreme Omnipotent God.

As the High Priest of the Violet Flame Temple on the mainland of Atlantis thirteen thousand years ago, Saint Germain sustained by his invocations and his causal body a pillar of fire, a fountain of violet singing flame, which magnetized people from near and far to be set free from every binding condition of body, mind and soul. This they achieved by self-effort through the offering of invocations and the practice of Seventh Ray rituals to the sacred fire.

An intricately carved marble circular railing enclosed the shrine where supplicants knelt in adoration of the God flame—visible to some as a physical violet flame, to others as an 'ultraviolet' light and to others not at all, though the powerful healing vibrations were undeniable.

The temple was built of magnificent marble ranging in hue from brilliant white, shot through with violet and purple veins, to deeper shades of the Seventh Ray spectrum. The central core of the temple was a large circular hall lined in ice-violet marble set upon a rich purpled marble floor. Three stories in height, it was situated midst a complex of adjacent areas for worship and the various functions of priests and priestesses who ministered unto the Flame and mediated its voice of light and prophecy unto the people. Those who officiated at this altar were schooled in the universal priesthood of the Order of Melchizedek at Lord Zadkiel's retreat, the Temple of Purification, in the locale of the West Indies.

Through the heights and depths of the ages that have ensued, Saint Germain has ingeniously used the Seventh Ray momentum of his causal body to secure freedom for keepers of the flame who have kept alive 'coals' from the violet flame altar of his Atlantean temple. He has extolled and exemplified freedom of the mind and spirit. Endowing the four sacred freedoms with an identity of their own, he has championed our freedom from state interference, kangaroo courts, or popular ridicule in matters ranging from scientific investigation to the healing arts to the spiritual quest.

Standing on a platform of basic human rights for a

responsible, reasoning public educated in the principles of liberty and equal opportunity for all, he has ever taught us to espouse our inalienable divine right to live life according to our highest conception of God. For the Master has said that no right, however simple or basic, can long be secure without the underpinning of the spiritual graces and the Divine Law that instills a compassionate righteousness in the exercise thereof.

Returning to the scene of the karma of his people as Samuel, prophet of the LORD and judge of the twelve

Samuel Anointing David, Jan Victors

When the disobedient King Saul rejected the word of the LORD and the LORD rejected him from being king, "for rebellion is as the sin of witchcraft, and stubbornness is as iniquity and idolatry," the LORD sent Samuel to the house of Jesse in Bethlehem to anoint the shepherd boy David, youngest of Jesse's sons, to be king of Israel.

tribes of Israel (c. 1050 B.C.), Saint Germain was the messenger of God's liberation of the seed of Abraham from bondage to the corrupt priests, the sons of Eli, and from the Philistines by whom they had been defeated. Bearing in his heart the special sign of the blue rose of Sirius, Samuel delivered to the recalcitrant Israelites a prophecy parallel to his twentieth-century discourses— both inextricably linked with God's covenants concerning karma, free will and grace:

"If ye do return unto the LORD with all your hearts, then put away the strange gods and Ashtaroth from among you, and prepare your hearts unto the LORD and serve him only: and he will deliver you out of the hand of the Philistines." Later, when King Saul disobeyed God, Samuel freed the people from his tyranny by anointing David king.

True to the thread of prophecy that runs throughout his lifetimes, Saint Germain was Saint Joseph of the lineage of King David, son of Jesse, chosen vessel of the Holy Ghost, father of Jesus in fulfillment of the word of the LORD to Isaiah—"There shall come forth a rod out of the stem of Jesse, and a Branch shall grow out of his roots...."

We see, then, in each of Saint Germain's embodiments that there is present the quality of alchemy— a conveyance of Godly power.

So ordained the instrument of the LORD, Samuel transferred His sacred fire in the anointing of David and just as scientifically withdrew it from King Saul when

The Vision of St. Joseph,
Philippe de Champaigne

"Behold, the angel of the Lord appeareth to Joseph in a dream, saying, Arise, and take the young child and his mother, and flee into Egypt, and be thou there until I bring thee word: for Herod will seek the young child to destroy him. When he arose, he took the young child and his mother by night, and departed into Egypt." Matthew 2:13, 14

the LORD rejected him from being king over Israel. This unmistakable sign of the Seventh Ray adept, often in humble garb, was also present as the Holy Spirit's power of the conversion of souls and the control of natural forces in his life as the third-century Saint Alban, first martyr of the British Isles.

A Roman soldier, Alban hid a fugitive priest, was converted by him, then sentenced to death for disguising himself as the priest and allowing him to escape. A great multitude gathered to witness his execution—too many to pass over the narrow bridge that must be crossed. Alban prayed and the river parted—whereupon his executioner, being converted, begged to die in Alban's place. His request was denied and he was

Saint Alban and the Executioner, artist unknown

Alban was a prosperous Roman native of Verulam, which was
for many years one of the most populous cities in Britain. As the
Reverend Alban Butler tells us in his *Lives of the Fathers, Martyrs
and Other Principal Saints,* he traveled to Rome in his youth
"to improve himself in learning and in all the polite arts.…
Being returned home he settled at Verulam, and lived there
with some dignity." But Alban gave all this up when he became
a Christian and was sentenced to die.

The power of conversion delayed Alban's execution. After a river
had parted in response to his prayer, "the executioner was converted at the sight of this miracle… and throwing away his naked
sword, he fell at the feet of the saint, begging to die with him, or
rather in his place. The sudden conversion of the headsman occasioned a delay in the execution. In the mean time the holy confessor, with the crowd, went up the hill." There Alban fell on his
knees. "At his prayer a fountain sprang up, with the water whereof
he refreshed his thirst. A new executioner being found, he struck
off the head of the martyr."

beheaded that day alongside the saint.

But Saint Germain was not always to be counted in the ranks of the Church. He fought tyranny wherever he found it, including in false Christian doctrine. As the Master Teacher behind the Neoplatonists, Saint Germain was the inner inspiration of the Greek philosopher Proclus (c. A.D. 410–485). He revealed his pupil's previous life as a Pythagorean philosopher, also showing Proclus the sham of Constantine's Christianity and the worth of the path of individualism (leading to the individualization of the God flame) which Christians called "paganism."

As the highly honored head of Plato's Academy at Athens, Proclus based his philosophy upon the principle that there is only one true reality—the "One," which is God, or the Godhead, the final goal of all life's efforts. The philosopher said, "Beyond all bodies is the essence of soul, and beyond all souls the intellectual nature, and beyond all intellectual existences the One."[2] Throughout his incarnations Saint Germain demonstrated tremendous breadth of knowledge in the Mind of God; not surprising was the range of his pupil's awareness. His writings extended to almost every department of learning.

Proclus acknowledged that his enlightenment and philosophy came from above—indeed he believed himself to be one through whom divine revelation reached mankind. "He did not appear to be without divine inspiration," his disciple Marinus wrote, "for he produced from his wise mouth words similar to the most thick-falling snow; so that his eyes emitted a bright radiance, and the rest of his countenance participated of divine illumination."[3]

Thus Saint Germain, white-robed, jeweled slippers and belt emitting star-fire from far-off worlds, was the mystery Master smiling just beyond the veil—mirroring the imagings of his mind in the soul of the last of the great Neoplatonic philosophers.

Saint Germain was Merlin. The unforgettable, somehow irretrievable figure who haunts the mists of England, about to step forth at any moment to offer us a goblet of sparkling elixir. He the 'old man' who knows the secrets of youth and alchemy, who charted the stars at Stonehenge, and moved a stone or two, so they say, by his magical powers—who would astonish no one if he suddenly appeared on a Broadway stage or in the forests of the Yellowstone or at one's side on any highway anywhere.

For Saint Germain *is* Merlin.

Enter Merlin January 1, 1987, with his final prophecy to heroes, knights, ladies, crazies, and villains of the Aquarian Camelot.

Merlin, dear Merlin, has never left us—his spirit charms the ages, makes us feel as rare and unique as his diamond and amethyst adornments. Merlin is the irreplaceable Presence, a humming vortex about whose science and legends and fatal romance Western civilization has entwined itself.

It was the fifth century. Midst the chaos left by the slow death of the Roman Empire, a king arose to unite a land splintered by warring chieftains and riven by Saxon invaders. At his side was the old man himself— half Druid priest, half Christian saint—seer, magician, counselor, friend, who led the king through twelve battles to unite a kingdom and establish a window of peace.

The Bard, Thomas Jones, 1774

Dweller in the wild places, Merlin by legend asked his sister to build him a remote building "to which you will give me seventy doors and as many windows, through which I may see fire-breathing Phoebus with Venus, and watch by night the stars wheeling in the firmament; and they will teach me about the future of the nation." Sound like a description of Stonehenge? For centuries people believed that the ancient astrological observatory was built by Merlin himself. Scientists say it antedates the wizard by millennia. But who knows how old Merlin is anyway!

At some point, the spirit of Merlin went through a catharsis. The scene was one of fierce battle, the legend says. As he witnessed the carnage, a madness came upon him—of seeing all at once past/present and future—so peculiar to the lineage of the prophets. He fled to the forest to live as a wild man, and one day as he sat under a tree, he began to utter prophecies concerning the future of Wales.

"I was taken out of my true self," he said. "I was as a spirit and knew the history of people long past and could foretell the future.

I knew then the secrets of nature, bird flight, star wanderings and the way fish glide."[4] Both his prophetic utterances and his "magical" powers served one end: the making of a united kingdom of the tribes of the old Britons. His pervasiveness is recalled in an early Celtic name for Britain, "Clas Myrddin," which means "Merlin's Enclosure."[5]

By advising and assisting Arthur in establishing his kingship, Merlin sought to make of Britain a fortress against ignorance and superstition where Christ achievement could flower and devotion to the One could prosper in the quest for the Holy Grail. His efforts on this soil were to bear fruit in the nineteenth century as the British Isles became the place where individual initiative and industry could thrive as never before in twelve thousand years.

But even as Camelot, the rose of England, budded and bloomed, nightshade was twining about its roots.

Witchcraft, intrigue and treachery destroyed Camelot, not the love of Launcelot and Guinevere as Tom Malory's misogynistic depiction suggests. Alas, the myth he sowed has obscured the real culprits these long centuries.

'Twas the king's bastard son Modred by his half sister Margawse[6] who, with Morgana le Fay and a circle of like sorceresses and black knights, set out to steal the crown, imprison the queen, and destroy for a time the bonds of a Love that such as these (of the left-handed path) had never known nor could—a Reality all of their willing, warring and enchantments could not touch.

Thus it was with a heavy heart and the spirit of a prophet who has seen visions of tragedy and desolation, fleeting joys and the piercing anguish of karmic retribution endlessly outplayed, that Merlin entered the scene of his own denouement, to be tied up in spells of his own telling by silly, cunning Vivien—and sleep. Aye, to err is human but to pine for the twin flame that is not there is the lot of many an errant knight or king or lonely prophet who perhaps should have disappeared into the mists rather than suffer sad ignominy for his people.

Some say he still sleeps, but they grossly underestimate the resilient spirit of the wise man rebounded, this time in thirteenth-century England disguised as Roger Bacon (c. 1214–1294). Reenter Merlin—scientist, philosopher, monk, alchemist and prophet—to forward his mission of laying the scientific moorings for the age of Aquarius his soul should one day sponsor.

The atonement of this lifetime was to be the voice crying in the intellectual and scientific wilderness that was medieval Britain. In an era in which either theology or logic or both dictated the parameters of science, he promoted the experimental method, declared his belief that the world was round, and castigated the scholars and scientists of his day for their narrow-mindedness. Thus he is viewed as the forerunner of modern science.

But he was also a prophet of modern technology. Although it is unlikely he did experiments to determine the feasibility of the following inventions, he predicted the hot-air balloon, a flying machine, spectacles, the telescope, microscope, elevator, and mechanically propelled ships and carriages, and wrote of them as if he had actually seen them! Bacon was also the first Westerner to write down the exact directions for making gunpowder, but kept the formula a secret lest it be used to harm anyone. No wonder people thought he was a magician!

However, just as Saint Germain tells us today in his *Studies in Alchemy* that "miracles" are wrought by the precise application of universal laws, so Roger Bacon meant his prophecies to demonstrate that flying machines and magical apparatus were products of the employment of natural law which men would figure out in time.

From whence did Bacon believe he derived his amazing awareness? "True knowledge stems not from the authority of others, nor from a blind allegiance to antiquated dogmas," he said. Two of his biographers write that he believed knowledge "is a highly personal experience—a light that is communicated only to the innermost privacy of the individual through the impartial channels of all knowledge and of all thought."[7]

And so Bacon, who had been a lecturer at Oxford and the University of Paris, determined to separate himself and his thoughts from the posing and postulating residents of academe. He would seek and find his science in his religion. Entering the Franciscan Order of Friars Minor, he said, "I will conduct my experiments on the magnetic forces of the lodestone at the selfsame shrine where my fellow-scientist, St. Francis, performed his experiments on the magnetic forces of love."[8]

But the friar's scientific and philosophical world view, his bold attacks on the theologians of his day, and

Roger Bacon,
Gordon Ross, 1941

his study of alchemy, astrology and magic led to charges of "heresies and novelties," for which he was imprisoned in 1278 by his fellow Franciscans! They kept him in solitary confinement for fourteen years,[9] releasing him only shortly before his death. Although the clock of this life was run out, his body broken, he knew that his efforts would not be without impact on the future.

The following prophecy which he gave his students shows the grand and revolutionary ideals of the indomitable spirit of this living flame of freedom—the immortal spokesman for our scientific, religious and political liberties:

> I believe that humanity shall accept as an axiom for its conduct the principle for which I have laid down my life—the right to investigate. It is the credo of free men—this opportunity to try, this privilege to err, this courage to experiment anew. We scientists of the human spirit shall experiment, experiment, ever experiment. Through centuries of trial and error, through agonies of research... let us experiment with laws and customs, with money systems and governments, until we chart the one true course—until we find the majesty of our proper orbit as the planets above have found theirs.... And then at last we shall move all together in the harmony of our spheres under the great impulse of a single creation—one unity, one system, one design.[10]

To establish this freedom upon earth, Saint Germain's lifestream took another turn—as Christopher Columbus (1451–1506). But over two centuries before Columbus sailed, Roger Bacon had set the stage for the

Christopher Columbus

Columbus' "outer person and bodily disposition" were thus described by Bishop Bartolomé de las Casas, 1474–1566: "He was tall more than average; his face long and of a noble bearing; his nose aquiline; his eyes blue; his complexion white, and somewhat fiery red; his beard and hair fair in his youth, though they soon turned white through hardships borne; he was quick-witted and gay in his speech and, as the aforesaid Portuguese history says, eloquent and high-sounding in his business; he was moderately grave; affable towards strangers; sweet and good-humoured with those of his house... of a discreet conversation and thus able to draw love from all who saw him. Finally, his person and venerable mien revealed a person of great state and authority and worthy of all reverence."

voyage of the three ships and the discovery of the New World when he stated in his *Opus Majus* that "the sea between the end of Spain on the west and the beginning of India on the east is navigable in a very few days if the wind is favorable."[11]

Although the statement was incorrect in that the land to the west of Spain was not India, it was instrumental in Columbus' discovery. Cardinal Pierre d'Ailly copied it in his *Imago Mundi* without noting Bacon's authorship. Columbus read his work and quoted the passage in a 1498 letter to King Ferdinand and Queen Isabella, saying that his 1492 voyage had been inspired in part by this visionary statement.

Columbus believed that God had made him to be "the messenger of the new heaven and the new earth of which He spake in the Apocalypse of St. John, after having spoken of it by the mouth of Isaiah."[12]

His vision went back as far as ancient Israel, perhaps even further. For in discovering the New World, Columbus believed that he was the instrument whereby God would, as Isaiah recorded around 732 B.C., "recover the remnant of his people… and shall assemble the outcasts of Israel, and gather together the dispersed of Judah from the four corners of the earth."

Twenty-two centuries passed before anything visible happened that seemed to be the fulfillment of this prophecy. But late in the fifteenth century, Christopher Columbus was quietly preparing to set the stage for the fulfillment of this prophecy, certain that he had been divinely selected for his mission. He studied the biblical prophets, writing passages relating to his mission in a book of his own making entitled *Las Proficias* or *The Prophecies*—in its complete form, *The Book of Prophecies concerning the Discovery of the Indies and the Recovery of Jerusalem.* Although the point is seldom stressed, it is a fact so rooted in history that even *Encyclopaedia Britannica* says unequivocally that "Columbus discovered America by prophecy rather than by astronomy."[13]

"In the carrying out of this enterprise of the Indies," he wrote to King Ferdinand and Queen Isabella in 1502, "neither reason nor mathematics nor maps were any use to me: fully accomplished were the words of Isaiah." He was referring to Isaiah 11:10–12.

Thus we see that lifetime by lifetime, Saint Germain, whether his outer mind was continuously cognizant of it we know not, was re-creating that golden pathway to the Sun—a destiny come full circle to worship the God Presence and reestablish a lost golden age.

As Francis Bacon (1561–1626), the greatest mind the West has ever produced, his manifold achievements in every field catapulted the world into a stage set for the children of Aquarius. In this life he was free to carry to its conclusion the work he had begun as Roger Bacon.

Scholars have noted the similarities between the thoughts of the two philosophers and even between Roger's *Opus Majus* and Francis' *De Augmentis* and *Novum Organum.* This is made even more astounding by the fact that Roger's *Opus* was never published in his lifetime, fell into oblivion, and not until 113 years after Francis' *Novum Organum* and 110 years after his *De Augmentis* did it appear in print!

The unsurpassed wit of this immortal soul, this philosopher/king, this priest/scientist, might easily have kept its humor with the stubborn motto drawn from tyrants, tortures and tragedy: If they beat you in one life, come back and beat them in the next!

Portrait of Francis Bacon, engraved by W. C. Edwards, after a Paul van Somer painting, c. 1616

Britain's greatest intellect, Francis Bacon fathered inductive reasoning and the modern scientific method, conducted experiments of his own, shepherded a group of the Elizabethan era's greatest writers, oversaw the translation of the King James Version of the Bible, supported the colonization of the New World and New-foundland and even, some say, authored the Shakespearean plays.

Francis Bacon is known as the father of inductive reasoning and the scientific method which, more than any other contributions, are responsible for the age of technology in which we now live. He foreknew that only applied science could free the masses from human misery and the drudgery of sheer survival in order that they might seek a higher spirituality they once knew. Thus, science and technology were essential to Saint Germain's plan for the liberation of his lightbearers and through them all mankind.

His next step was to be nothing less bold than universal enlightenment!

"The Great Instauration" (restoration after decay, lapse, or dilapidation) was his formula to change "the whole wide world." First conceived when Bacon was a boy of 12 or 13 and later crystallized in 1607 in his book by the same name, it did indeed launch the English Renaissance with the help of Francis' tender, caring person. For over the years, he gathered around himself a group of illuminati who were responsible among other things for almost all of the Elizabethan literature—Ben Jonson, John Davies, George Herbert, John Selden, Edmund Spenser, Sir Walter Raleigh, Gabriel Harvey, Robert Greene, Sir Philip Sidney, Christopher Marlowe, John Lyly, George Peele, and Lancelot Andrewes.

Some of these were part of a "secret society" that Francis had formed with his brother, Anthony, when the two were law students at Gray's Inn. This fledgling group, called "The Knights of the Helmet," had as its goal the advancement of learning by expanding the English language and by creating a new literature written not in Latin but in words which Englishmen could understand.

Francis also organized the translation of the King James Version of the Bible, determined that the common people should have the benefit of reading God's Word for themselves. Furthermore, as was discovered in the 1890s in two separate ciphers—a word-cipher and a bi-literal cipher embedded in the type of the original printings of the Shakespearean Folios[14]—Francis Bacon *was* the author of the plays attributed to the actor from the squalid village of Stratford-on-Avon. He *was* the greatest literary genius of the Western world.

So, too, was Bacon behind many of the political ideas on which Western civilization is based. Thomas Hobbes, John Locke and Jeremy Bentham took Bacon as their ideological starting point. His revolutionary principles are the engine that has driven our nation. They are the very essence of the can-do spirit. "Men are not animals erect," Bacon averred, "but immortal Gods. The Creator has given us souls equal to all the world, and yet satiable not even with a world."[15]

Francis Bacon also continued the task he had begun as Christopher Columbus, promoting the colonization of the New World, for he knew that it was there that his ideas could take deepest root and come to fullest flower. He convinced James I to charter Newfoundland and was an officer in the Virginia Company, which sponsored the settlement of Jamestown, England's first permanent colony in America. And he founded Freemasonry, dedicated to the freedom and enlightenment of mankind, whose members played a large part in founding the new nation.

Yet he could have been an even greater boon to England and the whole world had he been allowed to fulfill his destiny. The same ciphers which run throughout the Shakespearean plays also run through Francis Bacon's own works and those of many of his circle of friends. Both ciphers contain his true life story, the musings of his soul, and anything he wished to bequeath to future generations but could not publish openly for fear of the queen.[16]

Its secrets reveal that he should have been Francis I, King of England. He was the son of Queen Elizabeth I and Robert Dudley, Lord Leicester, born four months after a secret wedding ceremony. But she, wishing to retain her "Virgin Queen" status and afraid that if she acknowledged her marriage, she must give power to the ambitious Leicester, also lest the people prefer her male heir to herself and demand the queen's premature withdrawal from the throne, refused to allow Francis, on pain of death, to assume his true identity.

The queen kept him dangling all his life, never giving him public office, never proclaiming him her son, never allowing him to fulfill his goals for England. No, she would not allow her son to bring in the golden age of Britannia that was meant to be but never was. What cruel fate—a queen mother unbending, contemptuous before her golden age prince!

He was raised the foster son of Sir Nicholas and Lady Anne Bacon and at age fifteen heard the truth of his birth from his own mother's lips in the same breath with which she barred him forever from the succession. In one night his world was in a shambles. Like young Hamlet, he pondered over and over the question, "To be or not to be?" That was *his* question.

In the end, he determined not to rebel against his mother or later, against her ill-fitted successor, James I. This despite the great good he knew he could bring to England, despite his vision of the land "as she might be, if wisely governed."[17] He knew he had within himself the power to be a monarch such as the land had never known, a true father of the nation. He wrote of the "impulses of the godlike patriarchal care for his own people" he would exercise[18]—shades of the golden age emperor of the Sahara.

Fortunately for the world, Francis determined to pursue his goal of universal enlightenment in the avenues of literature and science, as adviser to the throne, supporter of colonization, and founder of secret societies, thereby reestablishing the thread of contact with the ancient mystery schools. The outlet of his wounded spirit was his cipher writing in which he poured out his longings to a future age.

By the time of his death in 1626, persecuted and unrecognized for his manifold talents, Francis Bacon had triumphed over circumstances which would have destroyed lesser men, but which for him proved the true making of an Ascended Master.

May 1, 1684, was Saint Germain's Ascension Day. From heights of power well earned and beyond this world's, he still stands to turn back all attempts to thwart his 'Great Instauration' here below.

Desiring above all else to liberate God's people, whether they would or no, Saint Germain sought a dispensation from the Lords of Karma to return to earth in a physical body. They granted it and he appeared as the Comte de Saint Germain, a "miraculous" gentleman who dazzled the courts of eighteenth- and nineteenth-century Europe as "The Wonderman." His goal: to prevent the French Revolution, effect a smooth tran-

The Count Saint Germain, Wonderman of Europe, 18th century

sition from monarchy to a republican form of government, establish a United States of Europe, and enshrine the fleur-de-lis as threefold flame of God-identity in every heart.

Though admired throughout the courts of Europe for his adeptship—removing the flaws in diamonds, disappearing into thin air, writing the same verses of poetry simultaneously with both hands, accomplished in many languages, fluent in any subject, recounting any history as an eyewitness—he failed to secure the anticipated response. Though willing to be entertained, the royalty were not easily prodded to relinquish their power and move with the winds of democratic change. They and their jealous ministers ignored his counsel and the French Revolution ensued.

In a final attempt to unite Europe, Saint Germain backed Napoleon, who misused the Master's power to his own demise. The opportunity to set aside the retribution due an age thus passed, Saint Germain was once again forced to withdraw from a karmic situation. In this episode, though clearly visible as the mediator, Saint Germain with his miracles *en main* and his prophecies fulfilled could still be ignored! What would it take to turn people's hearts?

The Ascended Master abandoned his sponsorship of Europe, turning instead to the New World, upon which he had kept a watchful eye for several centuries. Even as Francis Bacon, he had seen America as his last hope. He wrote in cipher, "I trusteth all to the future and a land that is very far towards the sunset gate.... I keep the future ever in my plan, looking for my reward, not to my times and countrymen, but to a people very far off, and an age not like our own, but a second golden age of learning."[19]

Having discovered the continent and encouraged its colonization, he must also insure a proper foundation for the new nation. Saint Germain stood by George Washington throughout the Revolution and during the winter at Valley Forge. His past efforts in initiating the society of Freemasons had enfired many of the key figures of the Revolution. General Washington, Alexander Hamilton, James Madison, John Hancock, Benjamin Franklin and as many as fifty-three out of the fifty-six signers of the Declaration of Independence were all members of the Masonic order,[20] whose principles had guided them in founding the new nation. Further, Saint Germain called for the signing of the Declaration of Independence, directed the writing of the Constitution and anointed Washington first President of the United States.

America was secured as the land of opportunity and Saint Germain devoted himself to the raising of the consciousness of her people.

In the twentieth century, the Master went before the Lords of Karma to plead the cause of freedom for and on behalf of the original 576 he had sponsored, expanding that circle to include the lightbearers of all centuries—the original Keepers of the Flame who had come with Sanat Kumara as well as the children of God who had been evolving unto the spiritual gifts and graces through earth's numerous ages.

However, as the decades have passed, the rate of increase in the return of mankind's karma has precipitated what is known as the Dark Cycle—the era of Chaos and old Night whose signs are foretold in Revelation, even as the hoofbeats of the Four Horsemen can be heard throughout the land.

Let us listen to the prophet Samuel—dubbed Uncle Sam by his people—who has indeed begun to sound his prophecy to the chosen. He has warned that the I AM Race—those who have the seed of the name I AM THAT I AM within their hearts—"have not hearkened unto the LORD, nor have they fulfilled the wholeness of the Law."

Therefore, the Master says:

> Some among this people must be and become direct initiates of Sanat Kumara, for always there has been the requirement of the ransom. Let those who are the inner circle of the devotees, those who are the firstfruits who come and stand as the ensign of the people, raise up the banner of Christ as the one whom they serve, the one who by his very Communion promise at the Last Supper designated each and every son and daughter of God for the internalization of the Word….

Unfortunately, and this word is mild, but it is unfortunate indeed that the laws of Christ and his Teachings, so meticulously brought forth to the close initiates, are not fully known today, having been taken even from the holy people. Therefore, to obey Christ becomes the challenge of the hour—to find the Person of that Christ, to find the Way and the Teachings.

You have received the lost Word and the lost Teachings of Jesus Christ through our effort.... As a result of this, you have been strengthened and protected in that Word and Teaching. And some from among you have taken their leave at the conclusion of their embodiment and gone on in the full resurrection with Jesus Christ.... Thus, the proof of the Teaching and the Path is that it leads one successively to that higher and higher consciousness whereunto the individual is assumed into the very heart of the I AM Presence [becoming indeed the pure Person of that Christ].

Today, as we see the cycles of earth's returning karma reach a mounting crescendo wherein even the four sacred freedoms are threatened, the Brotherhood has set aside a place in America's Rocky Mountains for the pursuit of the Lost Teachings of Christ to their fullest expression.

Saint Germain spoke of it in 1983 when he said that we have come "to a similar moment to that of that final hour of the golden age when I presided where the Sahara now is. My family is much larger than it was then, for I include every one of you who love me as my very own family…. In that hour, our family was taken to the golden etheric city of light. In this hour, we have summoned you to a higher place in the mountains of the north."

As the outpost of the Royal Teton Retreat, it is called the Royal Teton Ranch. Beloved Jesus announced on May 31, 1984, that to this Inner Retreat in southwestern Montana, to this "Place Prepared," Lord Maitreya had come again to reopen his Mystery School, which had been withdrawn from the physical octave just prior to the sinking of Lemuria.

Let us see what we may accomplish for our beloved Terra and our brothers and sisters on earth with the renewed opportunity the Hierarchs of the Aquarian Age, our beloved Saint Germain and his twin flame, the Ascended Lady Master Portia, have given to us.

Let us study to show ourselves worthy of the gifts of prophecy and of the working of miracles which he brings. And most importantly, let us strive to the utmost to overcome personal and planetary karma through those invocations to the violet flame and Seventh Ray rituals of transmutation we once knew, that the prophecy of Saint Germain's Great Golden Age may be fulfilled.

The Keepers of the Flame have vowed to be victorious in this age. And they shall!

Saint Germain, The Knight Commander,
Keepers of the Flame Fraternity, Norman Thomas Miller

The Chart of
Your Divine Self

There are three figures represented in the Chart of Your Divine Self. We refer to them as the upper figure, the middle figure and the lower figure. These three correspond to the Christian Trinity: The upper corresponds to the Father, who is one with the Mother, the middle to the Son, and the lower to the temple of the Holy Spirit.

We address our Father-Mother God as the I AM Presence. This is the I AM THAT I AM, whom God revealed to Moses and individualized for every son and daughter of God. Your I AM Presence is surrounded by seven concentric spheres of rainbow light. These make up your Causal Body, the biding place of your I AM Presence. In Buddhism it is called the Dharmakaya—the body of the Lawgiver (the I AM Presence) and the Law (the Causal Body).

The spheres of your Causal Body are successive planes of God's consciousness that make up your heaven-world. They are the "many mansions" of your Father's house, where you lay up your "treasures in heaven." Your treasures are your words and works worthy of your Creator, constructive thoughts and feelings, your victories for the right, and the virtues you have embodied to the glory of God. When you judiciously exercise your free will to daily use the energies of God in love and in harmony, these energies automatically ascend to your Causal Body. They accrue to your soul as "talents," which you may then multiply as you put them to good use lifetime after lifetime.

The middle figure in the Chart represents the "only begotten Son" of the Father-Mother God, the Universal Christ. He is your personal Mediator and your soul's Advocate before God. He is your Higher Self, whom you appropriately address as your beloved Holy Christ Self. John spoke of this individualized presence of the Son of God as "the true light, which lighteth every man that cometh into the world." He is your Inner Teacher, your Divine Spouse, your dearest Friend and is most often recognized as the Guardian Angel. He overshadows you every hour of the day and night. Draw nigh to him and he will draw nigh to you.

The lower figure in the Chart is a representation of yourself as a disciple on the path of reunion with God. It is your soul evolving through the planes of Matter using the vehicles of the four lower bodies to balance karma and fulfill her divine plan. The four lower bodies are the etheric, or memory, body; the mental body; the desire, or emotional, body; and the physical body.

The lower figure is surrounded by a tube of light, which is projected from the heart of the I AM Presence in answer to your call. It is a cylinder of white light that sustains a forcefield of protection 24 hours a day, so long as you maintain your harmony in thought, feeling, word and deed.

Sealed in the secret chamber of your heart is the threefold flame of Life. It is your divine spark, the gift of life, consciousness and free will from your beloved I AM Presence. Through the Love, Wisdom and Power of the Godhead anchored in your threefold flame, your soul can fulfill her reason for being on earth. Also called the Christ flame and the liberty flame, or fleur-de-lis, the threefold flame is the spark of the soul's Divinity, her potential for Christhood.

The silver (or crystal) cord is the stream of life, or "lifestream," which descends from the heart of the I AM Presence through the Holy Christ Self to nourish and sustain (through the seven chakras and the secret chamber of the heart) the soul and her four lower bodies. It is over this 'umbilical' cord that the light of the Presence flows, entering the being of man at the crown chakra and giving impetus for the pulsation of the threefold flame in the secret chamber of the heart.

The lower figure represents the son of man or child of the light evolving beneath his own 'Tree of Life'. The lower figure corresponds to the Holy Spirit, for the soul and the four lower bodies are intended to be the temple of the Holy Spirit. The violet flame, the spiritual fire of the Holy Spirit, envelops the soul as it purifies. This is how you should visualize yourself standing in the violet flame. You can invoke the violet flame daily in the name of your I AM Presence and Holy Christ Self to purify your four lower bodies and consume negative thoughts, negative feelings and negative karma in preparation for the ritual of the alchemical marriage—your soul's union with the Beloved, your Holy Christ Self.

Shown just above the head of the Christ is the dove of the Holy Spirit descending in the benediction of the Father-Mother God. When your soul has achieved the alchemical marriage, she is ready for the baptism of the Holy Spirit. And she may hear the Father-Mother God pronounce the approbation: "This is my beloved Son in whom I AM well pleased."

When your soul concludes a lifetime on earth, the I AM Presence withdraws the silver cord, whereupon your threefold flame returns to the heart of your Holy Christ Self. Your soul, clothed in her etheric garment, gravitates to the highest level of consciousness to which she has attained in all of her past incarnations. Between embodiments she is schooled in the etheric retreats until her final incarnation when the great law decrees she shall return to the Great God Source to go out no more.

Your soul is the nonpermanent aspect of your being, which you make permanent through the ascension process. By this process your soul balances her karma, bonds to her Holy Christ Self, fulfills her divine plan and returns at last to the living Presence of the I AM THAT I AM. Thus the cycles of her going out into the Matter Cosmos are completed. In attaining union with God she has become the Incorruptible One, a permanent atom in the Body of God. The Chart of Your Divine Self is therefore a diagram of yourself—past, present and future.

Book Two

DICTATIONS
OF THE
LORDS OF THE SEVEN RAYS
AND
THE MAHA CHOHAN

INTRODUCTION

Lives of Great Men All Remind Us...

In studying the dictations as well as the past lives of the Lords of the Rays and the Great Lord, not only those lives which culminated in their ascension but also those which went before, we come to understand in the sine wave of their accomplishments and setbacks what is that unique path of Christhood we must forge and win on the seven rays that lead us Home at last to the primordial light of the Sun behind the sun.

Come, let us join hands as we form a solar ring here below and love and learn together from these wayshowers the most joyous calling of our Lord—how we can be victorious overcomers in earth's schoolroom and do it not for ourselves alone but for the blessing of all life!

Let us sit by their fire a while and learn of them. For we should learn to use the world, not to abuse it. So the saints tell us. And these Ascended Masters are not mere visionaries who have lived hypocritically. These are extraordinary intellects who have known the Mind of Christ, people of spiritual ingenuity from whom our age can learn.

Yes, we can learn from the activities of Saint Francis of Assisi. We can learn from the activities of Prince Mori Wong of Koko Nor and Akbar the Great as well as other luminaries and revolutionaries whose names, by device, have not landed in the forefront of world thought.

We can learn from the activities of our Brother Christ Jesus—in his lifetimes which he spent in Israel preparing for the final one—when he was Elisha (ninth century B.C.) apprenticed to the alchemist, healer and prophet Elijah; or when he was Joseph (seventeenth or nineteenth century B.C.?) with his coat of many colors, favorite son of Jacob, the envy of all the rest, whose seed, reincarnated in the nations of the English-speaking peoples, are still the envy of all the other tribes reborn.

Were we also there with him? And did we help or hinder him while he yet wrestled with his soul or ours?

These things we wonder in the silent musings of our souls and well we should, for what we have done or left undone tells much about what we are doing or should be today. And ever-present karma, through the hand of Opportunity, is an interval of time and space. And these, too, are the spiritual graces, kal-desh, given to us to set the record straight.

And the Lords of the Seven Rays are called of God and his Christ to answer our questions and meet our specific needs as these fall into the categories of each of the seven rays and the attainment of their seven hierarchs.

Thus, while acquainting us with the Chohans, Jesus also told us of his endearment to Saint Germain when the Lord of the Seventh Ray was embodied as his father, Joseph. He spoke of their profound love for one another and of their service together in the sponsorship of the true seed of Abraham, the Hebrew lineage of Sanat Kumara's lightbearers.

Moreover, he spoke tenderly of their close association when Saint Germain was the prophet Samuel and he anointed the soul of David—Jesus himself—as King of Israel (c. 1000 B.C.), and together they challenged the mad King Saul, seed of the Evil One, who fell on his sword in battle for fear of the spirit of the departed Samuel.

He said that under Saint Germain's Seventh Ray dispensation in Aquarius we could accelerate the balancing of our karma of many lifetimes by using his violet flame decrees—and that with their continued use and our reliable progress on the Path, Saint Germain and his beloved Portia would sponsor the reuniting of twin flames first on inner levels and then on outer levels— karmic circumstances permitting.

Yes, we can learn from the dictations of the blessed Chohans because they are so real. Then and now these were and are people like ourselves. Endowed with the God spark, they creatively exploited its splendor and reflected the inner radiance to a world through the mirror of consciousness. And it shone through the mortal form. And when the form was no more, the soul—enlivened by its own star fire—stepped forth from the coil of mortality to transcend the law of rebirth, having outlived its usefulness.

Sic transit gloria mundi. Thus passes the glory of the world. Enter the glory of the next.

Let us therefore enter the world of the Chohans. Let us enter their Cosmic Consciousness and become a part of their God Self-awareness through the intimacy of their dictations which follow.

EL MORYA 1
Lord of the First Ray

Initiation of the Throat Chakra

Retreat: Darjeeling, India

Vibration: Blue, White

Gemstone: Diamond, Sapphire, Star Sapphire, Lapis Lazuli

Quality: POWER GOODWILL FAITH

Gift: Faith in God's Will, Word of Wisdom

Day: Tuesday

El Morya, Lord of the First Ray

Message to America on the Mission of Jesus Christ

Greetings, beloved of my heart. I welcome you into the fervor of the will of God that has been the best part of my life for centuries.

Oh, as I contemplate the vast mysteries of Cosmos, were it not for the sustaining power of that will divine in my life and myriad angels who also succored me in my hours of travail, I should not have reached the goal or been able therefore to assist you to attain your own.

I am grateful to welcome you to the Heart of the Inner Retreat, the place consecrated for our worship of the one God. I am grateful for your sustaining grace and a momentum worldwide of these devotees who have seen that star of the will of God and are determined to bring its fruits to their families, communities, and states.

I would tell you that if there were a moment in history when I should choose to embody and live for the betterment of mankind, it would be in this hour of 1984. I come to encourage you in the way of standing for the light and assisting the progress and the *healing* of nations and hearts.

I would give you, then, a morsel of my own—my sense of compassion not alone for people everywhere but in fact and indeed for the individual. As I once wrote, "The orphans of the Spirit are our concern"[1]— those who have not been tutored in the inner light and know not the way to go.

Many of you understand the journey of Jesus our Lord to the Far East, and you understand the purpose of his journey taken when a teenager, as many of you who are here today are. It was in pursuit of the teachers of the Far East and a teaching itself. It was preparatory to his final years in Palestine.[2]

And so he did meet the great lights of India, and he did take the teachings of Hinduism and Buddhism and make them come alive. And he did challenge, therefore, the priesthood, the classes who denied to the poor the full flowering of that Spirit. And he preached to the poor and he gave them back the dignity of life. And for this, they who held the reins of power in religion sought to take his life as they did later in Palestine.

Beloved ones, I point out to you one of the most pernicious errors of orthodoxy this day, and it is the lie that Jesus is the only Son of God, and furthermore that Jesus came into embodiment in the full mastery of Christhood and did not himself have to follow the Path and realize his own inner God-potential before beginning his mission.

These things are plain in scripture, but the scriptures have been read and reread so many times that the true intent is no longer heard by the soul. The layers of misinterpretation and then the removal of the very keys themselves have given to Christianity today a watered-down religion that does not have the fervor or the fire to meet the challengers of civilization—whether it be in World Communism or in pornography or all manner of perversion or immorality that does steal the light of the soul.

Beloved ones, I tell you, nothing can move forward in life unless the individual has a true understanding of God and his relationship to that eternal Spirit. Therefore, realize that Jesus did not come from God a new soul, born for the first time in his incarnation in Nazareth. Nay, I tell you! He was embodied as Joshua, the military hero of the Hebrew people. He was embodied as Joseph and wore his coat of many colors as the favorite son and did go through all manner of trial and persecution by his own brothers who were jealous of him; and yet he found favor in the sight of Pharaoh.

Beloved hearts of light, you know the soul of Jesus in Elisha, the disciple of the prophet Elijah. And you know that Elijah came again in the person of John the Baptist as was prophesied and as it is written. Jesus gave to his own disciples the confirmation that this John the Baptist was Elias come again, thereby ratifying the teaching of reincarnation. Yet it is still denied by those Bible-quoting Christians who have determined to say it is not so.

And I will tell you *why* they say it is not so: it is because they do not want to accept their accountability for their own past karma!

You cannot *believe* in reincarnation unless you will also stand, face, and conquer the deeds of the past. Thus, the nonaccountability, due to the upbringing of children in the West today, does not prepare warriors of the Spirit to meet the inroads that are being made by all forces of lust and greed after this nation's light and after this citadel of freedom.

Understand, then, that your understanding of the one God and the one Christ enables you to see that that one God and one Christ has vouchsafed to you the I AM Presence and Christ Self as the manifestation of pure Divinity—not many gods, but one God. And the pure Son of God is the Universal Christ whose Body and bread are broken for you. And therefore, as partakers of the light, as one with the Holy Christ Self, you also may pass through the initiations of discipleship as Jesus did. And you ought to look forward to and expect the fullness of that Christ dwelling in you bodily.

Wherefore evolution of a spiritual nature? Why have the prophets come? Why have the avatars appeared? Because they are favorite sons and all the rest are sinners? I tell you, *no!* And it is the most pernicious lie, as I have said, for it stops *all* short of the mark of that high calling in Christ Jesus of which the apostle spoke. And none dare become heroes or leaders or examples. And those who do are set on a pedestal of idolatry rather than seen as the example!

What one can do, all can do. And this is the philosophy of the Darjeeling Council that we would impart. We would quicken and enliven you, as God has empowered the saints to do, to unlock that potential of your heart, that divine spark, and to show you that lifetime after lifetime you have been moving toward that point of the courage to *be* who you really are and not to accept the philosophy that you are evolved from animals and that you cannot exceed the matrix of the animal creation.

Beloved ones, what shall be left of a planet?—a scientific humanism? What shall be left?—world socialism and all shall become drones in a planetary movement controlled by moguls of power East and West?

Beloved hearts, this is the goal of sinister forces. And let none deny that there is an Antichrist. For the Antichrist is every force within and without the psyche of man that would put down that true and living God within you. Realize that this is not of necessity a person who will appear at a certain time, but it is the decision on the part of many to embody the destructive forces of the universe to put out the light of freedom, nation by nation.

Without the understanding of the equation of Armageddon, without the understanding of free will, it is impossible to realize that some have chosen the left-handed path of destruction, of the Lie, and of the Murderer. And without accepting this, it is impossible to understand so-called human behavior, which is not human at all, but it is *devil* behavior and the behavior of devils incarnate.

Do I sound like a fundamentalist Christian? *Well, I am!* [applause] Remember well: I came first to adore.[3] I was transformed. I was transfigured. I was, if it need be said, the first "born-again Christian."

Beloved hearts, I say it only that you realize that saints East and West, whether or not they have contacted Jesus the man in his life or since, have had the conversion to Christ. And they have perceived that Christ in Buddha. They have perceived that Christ in Krishna. And let none deny it, for when you deny the Son of God in one who has outpictured that virtue and love, you effectively close the door to that light coming into your own temple.

Thus, you see, a religious teaching that denies the calling of the individual to embody the living Christ is, in fact, calculated by dark forces to deny the open door to divinity to every son of God. John said, "Beloved, now are we the sons of God...," and this he learned with his head upon the breast of Jesus.

Therefore, understand the meaning of the trek to the Himalayas by the teenager Jesus. Those lost years— eighteen in number—show the great preparation of this soul of light, this Son of man, this one who truly embodied the full effulgence of our God. It shows that by his example he left for you a record of the path of discipleship—that it is true, that it is legitimate.

And in the ancient texts of the Vedas and the teachers of India, stored in the Himalayas and held in the heart of unascended masters, there is that living record—the Law written in the very body temples of those who have kept the vigil of that which was held in the ancient temples of Lemuria. For those teachings of the law of God that were there were transported to the caves and retreats of the Himalayas before the sinking of that continent. Thus, going back, far back beyond all recorded history, you find the lineal descent of those who have come to earth for a single purpose: to seek and find the thread of contact with Almighty God and to demonstrate by their lives a living Truth.

Men may tamper with scripture. They may rewrite the codes of law to suit themselves and their lowered and lowering standards. But they may *never* change the records of akasha. In akasha—as the subtle energy and force that permeates the planet and your auras—you will find the record of all past incarnations of yourself, of all previous incarnations of masses of lifewaves who have come here from other planetary homes. You will find the records of civilizations.

You will find that today those who write the stories of motion pictures and books—such as Taylor Caldwell, who wrote as a child of the story of Atlantis[4]—have been given the gift of tying into these akashic records. And they have sat down and written about subjects concerning which they knew nothing. And not only have they recorded for people all sorts of invaluable information that would give keys to the past and past glories of civilizations of great light and scientific achievement, such as in the Edgar Cayce readings—but they have also shown a teaching and a path and an understanding for each individual soul to find his true roots all the way back to the birth in the heart of the Great Central Sun and the descent to incarnation here.

What for incarnation in a darkened world and a darkened star? Why put on veils of flesh? It is because the soul demanded free will and the right to experiment in the universe of God, and the Father accorded the request. And they went forth as from the bosom of Abraham, from the Great Causal Body, and evolved into denser and denser spheres. And, alas, came those hours when the fallen angels did tempt them away from their first love and that of the God Most Holy. And there began to be the densification of the flesh and the mind, and people lost the contact with their God. They forgot the name I AM THAT I AM.

And God sent the knowledge of the true monotheism in the midst of pagan cultures, even to Ikhnaton and then to Moses. And once again the great I AM became the focal point as the sun—symbol of the Presence of God—the many hands extending as Ikhnaton saw it, the power to move a nation as Moses perceived it, and today the source of your strength and your healing as you perceive the same Presence.

They may attempt to divide the Body of God upon earth by religious schism and argumentation, by placing the emphasis on the letter of the law. We have seen enough of inquisition in our time!

We have seen enough of the wars of Protestant and Catholic! What is the net gain? The only true gain on the path of religion is the Spirit, the Holy Ghost with the individual and then moving nations—Yahweh moving among his people, who is still able to draw out of America those servant-sons of God who will truly manifest an example of the path of freedom and discipleship with Saint Germain, the beloved Joseph.

Beloved hearts of light, you see that the return to discipleship is necessary, for a people have forgotten their God. They have not understood the true coming of Jesus and therefore they do not understand why the saints have lived, why they have sacrificed, why they have left a record—because the emphasis is not on *you*, but upon Christ nailed to a cross.

This will afford you nothing unless you yourself realize that all that was in this Son of God can be yours. And the imitation of the path of Jesus Christ is surely our calling and our teaching. It is the fundamental teachings of the Spirit. It is the teachings given to the apostles. It is the anointing of the apostles. It is the transfer of fire, heart to heart! It is a leaping and a speaking in tongues. It is the power of our God with us unto healing. And yes, it is poring over the ancient scriptures. John the Beloved himself took from the Vedas: "In the beginning was the Word, and the Word was with Brahman." Blessed hearts, such fragments, such husks are left.

And thus, where does a nation stand when challenged by the taunting of a Kaddafi or terrorists or Cubans or Communists? It is divided and weak. Where does it stand when there are those who tamper with the money supply and the economy? Where does it stand when the children cannot read and write and cannot rise up to become leaders and representatives of still the greatest nation on earth?

Where do a people stand when they do not have recourse to Almighty God and his Spirit in them? What can they do when their bodies are beset by drugs, when they are caught up in violence, when all manner of pleasure and entertainment is the first thing they think of when their jobs are through? I tell you, if America is to be saved from that which is plotted by the dark ones on this planet, there must be a rising fervor and a return to first principles both in Church and State.

How shall we tell them? How shall they be God-taught when the false pastors have invaded the temples and denounced even the very communion of saints which we enjoy with you and you with us in this Spirit of the Great White Brotherhood? Brothers and sisters of light on earth have a right ordained by Jesus Christ to commune with brothers and sisters in heaven, not by psychic or astral means, but by the true Holy Ghost. And the Holy Ghost is the Comforter and the Teacher who has come to you to bring all those things to your remembrance which Jesus taught you.

When did he teach you those things that you are

now reminded of? *When?* Were you all there in Galilee? It is not quite possible for the tens of thousands and millions who ascribe to the path of the Brotherhood on this planet to have all been there in the flesh. And thus, Jesus spake to all of you to whom he preached in all octaves of being in that hour and mission. For the Son of God truly spoke from the etheric retreats, and all the world heard him.

Do you think his fame spread only by the apostles or only by the grapevine, as they say in India? I tell you, no. The power of the presence of Jesus Christ in the earth has been the power to contact every living soul these two thousand years with the inner knowledge and the sense of the honor of Christ's presence in them. And that teaching is ongoing no matter what is said in their mosques or synagogues or temples.

For the living Christ does shepherd his own, nation by nation, and for this reason: People understand right and wrong, they know what ought to be and ought not to be, they know what is evil if they will allow themselves to perceive it. And therefore, the Standard lives. The honor code is present with the comings and the goings of philosophers and psychologists and all the rest who now say, "this is right," and then say, "this is wrong."

Relative good and evil is not the story of your life. Put that aside and recognize that it is the Absolute Good of God present with you that is the power to devour the forces of Absolute Evil, first and foremost being that tyranny over the soul and the spirit and the heart of man.

We, the Darjeeling Council, assembled in this hour of summer solstice, do address our chelas worldwide here and in the Spirit. And we summon you (as has been said before but we say it again) to a new birth of freedom—this time to a spiritual birth of freedom.

I commend you to the seeking of the presence with you of the Holy Spirit. I commend you to a path of devotion. I commend you to the path that has always worked for those who have truly and sincerely applied it just as Jesus taught it: prayer and fasting, sacrifice and devotions, prayers to God and service to the poor and the meek. This is the path of the balancing of karma, putting on the consciousness of God day by day, being the instrument of the flow of the mighty River of Life.

This is the message of the discipleship of the teenager Jesus who went to find his teacher Maitreya, who went to sit at the feet of Buddha who had come and gone five hundred years before his journey. He came to sit at the feet of those masters who had gone on before him. And he stopped at Luxor to be initiated in the first steps of the initiation temple, when he could have been accorded the full mantle of the Master of that temple.[5]

Jesus gave obeisance and deference to the order of Hierarchy. And this you see well-recorded in scripture in the hour of his transfiguration—the Father and the Son ordaining the presence of the Ascended Master Moses, the presence of the Ascended Master Elijah. They talked with Jesus, they spoke with him! Ascended

Masters spoke with the unascended Son of God; and his disciples Peter, James, and John were witnesses and they wrote of it.[6] And it is set forth in the Gospels.

This is the example that is unmistakable of the chain of Hierarchy. It illustrates that there were some who ascended and were in heaven with God before Jesus—such as Enoch, who walked with God and was not, for God took him.

Thus, the ancients who went before were taken up by God. Thus you realize that the path Jesus followed was never an exception, was not something unique and exceptional where one life should forever atone for the sins of the many, but the example of what had been done again and again and again—always the avatar coming to give to the disciples on earth the example that there is a way out of Death and Hell and the round of suffering. There is a way of self-transcendence. Death is not the end of life.

And in the parting of the veil in that hour it is well to be prepared, to have woven the Deathless Solar Body which is referred to by Jesus as the wedding garment. And he said to that one who came into the marriage feast, "Friend, how camest thou in without the wedding garment? Bind him, hand and foot, and cast him into outer darkness!"

The wedding garment is the spiritual body that you weave with the Word and the Work of God. It is the fiery aura of the saints, and it is the means of transporting the soul to those octaves of light whence you descended into this lowly estate of flesh, as it is put—and to which you shall return.

Beloved ones, the prayer "Thy kingdom come on earth as it is in heaven" is the prayer of the saints who would bring that rarefied light of the etheric octave into the physical, who would bring to this earth plane a Utopia perhaps—a new world, a New Atlantis, a way of life that can exceed this one, where people can be free from pain and terminal diseases caused not alone by their karma but caused by the chemicals, the impure foods, the substances they take in—a world free from war and the eruption of violence from the bowels of those whose free will has been used to commit them to a path of error.

And error leads to unreality. And unreality leads to insanity. Thus, the insane stalk the earth taking innocent life. The insane take the life of the unborn and call it woman's right. Woman's right to murder her child! Is she liberated? No! She is enslaved to a pain that gnaws within her for the rest of her life and in future incarnations until it is resolved.

Offering liberty, they sow corruption—corruption of the spirit and the soul and not of the body. And this is why the dangers of this age are so great. And this is why I say it is the greatest moment in all history for each and every one of you to make your statement and to establish that contact with God which all who have gone before you have made, and thereby become instruments of light and spiritual power and healing and the holding of the balance of nations.

The overwhelming proof is on the side of the path of discipleship. It has a consistency over tens and thousands of years. You will not find any difference, save perhaps in a slight manner of form or ritual, in the paths of the saints East or West. There is no difference in the light of the eye or the shining of the aura or the power of the chakras or the beginning ability of transmutation and alchemy that comes into your life when you begin to invoke the violet flame.

The consistency of this path, side by side with the absolute *inconsistency* of the factions of Protestantism, of Catholicism, of Judaism, or of the Moslems who argue perpetually one with the other and remain separated and divided because they cannot agree on the letter! And they have left off from the true Spirit. And even in that spirit of ecumenism, beloved ones, you find that they have not come to the resolution of their doctrine nor have they given to their flocks the power of God to turn the tide of world conditions.

One and all, understand the great joy as a child rejoices in his first step, the first word he can spell or read or identify on a sign, the first piece he can play on the piano, or a laurel wreath given at graduation. Understand that the path of achievement—striving, running in the race, winning the gold cup—is a path that mirrors the path of discipleship to all. It is the sense internally: "I have worked, I have mastered—God with me and by his grace. And because I know who I AM and God is with me, I can do these things."

It's like having it in your pocket. It is something you have done. When and if it should ever be the case that a master do for the disciple what the disciple can only do for himself, the disciple will be just like the child or any of you. The person for whom something is given without responsibility, without effort and work, without inner achievement resents the individual who gives to him that reward without effort.

Thus, the false pastors who preach create in fact a servile relationship of sinners to a favorite son, and internally and subconsciously it is actually the hatred of Christ that is at work. It is a psychological maneuver of the fallen angels, preaching hellfire and brimstone and enormous fear and an angry God and the promise of everlasting hell and damnation to those who do not repent. These are the preachments of the Devil who has created an alternative religion to the true teaching of Jesus Christ.

Realize this: that many pastors who are thus indoctrinated are not of an evil bent but have simply followed the party line they have been given and that has been carried on for generations. The proof is in the pudding. The proof is in the action. *Where* are the results? *Where are the results?*

When Billy Graham goes to the Communist world and declares that all is well and Baptists have freedom and they ought to submit to their governments, how is all well—when, not having the power to challenge Communism, they decide to give in and recommend that true Christians submit to the brutality that is going on yet today and the persecutions?

Who will cry out to the living God and take a stand and be willing to be a fool for Christ? ["We will!"]

Beloved hearts, we look here and there over the face of the earth and truly we declare that those isolated individuals such as Reverend Wurmbrand who are determined to tell the true story of torture and torment of Christians—these are they whose voice of Truth will never be denied. The flame of freedom cannot be put out! It speaks in many, many hearts. We are here, summoning the mighty archangels to go forth with their legions of light to cut free those souls who are bound, to cut them free from astral nightmares of demons and discarnates that prey upon the mind and the body.

Who will take a stand and cry, "Outrage!"? Where are the Christian nations who ought to be standing in defense of the freedom-fighters in Afghanistan? Who of the most liberal and left-wing bent can justify Soviet takeover and destruction in Afghanistan? Who can approve the dropping of toys which when picked up by children maim them for life? Who can defend the system (in the name of Jesus, mind you) that results in the destruction of souls and nations one by one? Who can claim himself a Christian who does not run to their aid and provide that aid that must be had if that nation is to endure?

What is transpiring upon this planet, I tell you, is the result of the softness of religion itself and a dearth of religious leadership! Thus, we come to give to you our momentum—and the momentum of the Holy Ghost with us—that your fervor for freedom and for the will of God might take you into those avenues of your own choosing and of the leading of your inner self where you can champion human rights wherever *you* can draw the line, wherever you *must* draw the line.

For surely *somewhere, some* injustice must say to your heart: "I cannot live in the honor and integrity of my soul and allow this injustice to continue! I must take my stand. I must speak. I must inform. I must show that mankind need not go down into this degradation of the denial of the dignity of *any* man or woman or child *anywhere* on earth and his freedom to be and to find God!"

The entire purpose of life is finding God—finding God in yourself and your talents and your calling and your sacred labor—and endowing anything that you do with his Spirit. They may say otherwise, but when it comes down to the depths of the soul, no one in this world is happy until he has made his peace with his God, his I AM Presence. There are many who would deny this, yet are they truly happy? They say they are happy but they have not known the joy of Reality. Many are insane, many are bound, and yet do they take up the path toward God?

Why don't they take up the Path? Is it because it has been given to them from childhood with such distaste, with such obvious flaw that they have become atheists and agnostics rather than hear the same old bromide

Sunday after Sunday? Many people have learned to hate God in the churches because they have never been told that there is an exciting path waiting—the Homeward path that enables you day by day to know the joy of doing more for those in need because more of God is in you.

Have you ever thought about that—that the churches turn more people away from God, the true and living God, the reality of the way of the cross, the reality of life as it ought to be? I can tell you without equivocation that the doctrines taught in America today in the mainline religions will never afford the people the ability to save this nation!

Do I preach a particular brand of religion? Nay. The Teachings of the Ascended Masters incorporate the path that the Mystical Body of God has walked through all eternity. It is not even unique to this planetary system. It is the same descent of the soul unto the grand experiment in freedom and free will, meeting all forces that pretend to be the adversary when the only true enemy is within. And that is the ultimate knowledge: Man, know thyself and know thyself as God, and know that the only foe that can ever overcome in thy life is thine own fear or internal schism or compromise or failure to surrender truly to God.

Is this a church? I tell you, nay, it is more. It is a movement. It is a revolution back to the fundamentals of every avatar who has launched a path of freedom, developed specifically for the lifewaves or nations or times when they have come. Thus, you find nothing peculiar about saying a Buddhist chant or a Hail Mary or an Our Father or communing with Archangel Michael or speaking to Gabriel—nothing peculiar at all. Well, it was spoken of the Hebrews that they were a *peculiar* people, and what was unique about them was that they knew their God.

I pray that this trek that you have made as a pilgrimage to our shrine of light, dedicated as the Western Shamballa, will afford you the opportunity for soul searching and that perhaps something we have said or written will be the spark to connect you to that God-potential that has been dormant for aeons.

It is the quickening that we would convey. It is the native power of God unto you. And it is especially the love of our bands and hosts for you personally as our brothers and sisters. We tarry on earth on behalf of you and millions of others who truly would do better if they knew better, who truly desire to know the Truth, and who persecute many righteous men thinking that they do God service.

The path of the violet flame and the spoken Word, beloved, is certainly the path that can lift the accumulated debris of density of the centuries—the covering over of the chakras, the limiting of the human brain because it has lost the impulse of the crystal cord and the flow of light. Mankind do not need to wed the computer to gain superhuman powers, but only to unite with the living Christ.

I pray every day that this nation and all peoples on

earth will not have to come to the knowledge of Truth through adversity, through nuclear war, through economic collapse. I trust you will also pray with me in this wise, for, beloved, the prayer of the righteous—those who use the righteous law, the right use of the law of the Science of the Spoken Word—availeth much.

And thus, let us say:

Our heavenly Father, we beseech thee in the name of the saints who have gone before and the precious people of this earth that enlightenment shall come by the might of the archangels, by the interactions of angels and men, and by the Holy Comforter.

Our Father, we ask you today and every day to bring healing, light, and comfort—peace and the awareness of the enemy of their souls.

O God, send thy Angel of Faith, Archangel Michael, to their aid! Send that holy one of God that they be not plucked from the screen of life in an untimely manner and therefore miss the opportunity to fulfill their divine plan and to glorify thee.

Our heavenly Father, make us stewards of thy grace and thy abundant Life. Make us responsible in caring for the sick and the needy. Give us the understanding heart to walk many miles with our brother.

Our heavenly Father, we pray for every soul of Jesus on earth—all who are the lovers of his heart, all who truly worship thee through him even though they have been limited by orthodoxy in some form.

I call to legions of Truth, and in the name of the Son of God, I, El Morya, call to the twelve legions of angels of the Lord Christ to descend for the rescue of the churches this day that they may be infilled with thy true Spirit and not the spirits of the night that seize their bodies and their chakras, causing them to writhe or dance or jump or scream or weep.

I demand, as the Chohan of the First Ray, the exorcism of the churches of those foul spirits and the exorcism of every form of demon taunting them away from the true and living Spirit of the Holy Ghost!

Maha Chohan, enter them now and purge them and let the living fire of true freedom and true worship be upon them. For these are thy hearts, our Father. Cut them free and let them become fierce disciples, taking the true stand for defense instead of advocating the pacifism of the Devil.

O living Word, as thou hast written, I, too, have taken my pen this day and I have written my coded message in the hearts of my own. It is my forget-me-not.

Precious chelas of the will of God, in fervor and faith, fight the good fight and win ground for Reality.

Bind unreality and illusion and set the captives free! For it is your calling and your desiring and all of your love fulfilled.

I remain with you as a mentor on the Path, ever desirous of assisting you, especially in your calls for God-government and the abundant Life in the economy.

In the name of my teacher and friend of light, the Great Divine Director, in the joy of my co-worker Saint Germain, I AM El Morya Khan.

July 2, 1984
Royal Teton Ranch
Montana

Keepers of the Flame in the Heart of the Inner Retreat, 1982,
Royal Teton Ranch, Montana

The holy mountain Kanchenjunga, seen from Darjeeling, India

You can journey in your finer bodies to attend classes at El Morya's Temple of Good Will at Darjeeling, India. The Lord of the First Ray suggests that those who wish to attune with the vibration of his retreat concentrate upon a photograph of Darjeeling and listen to the keynote music of the retreat, which was set down in part by Sir Edward Elgar in his "Pomp and Circumstance."

To Awaken America
to a Vital Purpose

Good evening, chelas and would-be chelas of the sacred fire. I am Morya of the First Ray of the dawn. And the golden light of the morning is already upon the evolutions of a portion of Terra. And I have traversed the lines of longitude, and I have watched as the golden light releases the first rays upon the people of Terra. And I have come here to the City of the Angels to address you tonight on the golden light of the dawn of the will of God within your consciousness.

How many aeons ago did I become a chela of the will of God before I even knew the meaning of the word *chela* or of the concept of the Guru? But God to me was the golden light of the dawn. And I sensed in the first rays of the dawn the will of a cosmic purpose—the will of a Life and of a Creator beyond myself.

And for a number of incarnations the focal point of my observation of the Deity was the morning light of the sun. And by and by through that contact, unbeknownst to me, with Helios and Vesta, there was established an arc—an arc of flow over the arc of my own attention. And I began to feel the response of my own God flame within to the God of very gods in that Sun behind the sun.

The observation of this attunement with Life continued for several more embodiments until I was not able to even begin the day of my life without this contact and this flow of energy—a literal infusion of my consciousness with ideas, with the understanding of the work that I should do. Almost, as it were, at subconscious levels I would move into and out of the sun as my point of contact.

And so it came to pass as my devotions increased and the concentration of energies increased within my chakras, that after succeeding embodiments I contacted a teacher—a teacher of the ancient science of astrology. It was the science of the study of heavenly bodies and their influences upon the evolutions in time and space. And that teacher gave me insight into the energy and the contact that I had made with the very core of creation.

And so it was by will, not my own yet which I made my own, that the contact with Life was established, that it grew and expanded. And the light of Helios and Vesta that glowed within my heart became a magnet— a magnet of the pursuit of God through the application of science.

I have always, then, followed the path of science, whether on Mercury or on Earth or other planetary homes of this system and other systems of worlds. The LORD God has permitted me to understand the law of the heavenly bodies and the earthly bodies and of the flow of energies in time and space.

And I have found myself becoming one with the cycles of Matter for the mastery of those cycles, almost, as it were, going within—within the heart of Matter before going to the outside of Matter. Growing from within—from within the sun within the earth and the Sun behind the sun—I learned the way of God and God's laws by the inner geometry of the molecule, the atom, the Cosmos.

And my appreciation of that which I did not at first call God came through the humble awareness, the awesome awareness of this thing—this thing that is Life, this thing that is energy, this thing which is the harmony, this thing that I now behold as the will of God.

Through countless incarnations and services rendered to the Hierarchy, learning the ways of the world and the ways of the Cosmos, I came to the place where I could follow the ray of my own God Presence back to the heart of the flaming One. And so at the conclusion of the last century, I followed that ray to the white-fire core, and I did not return with the dawn of the morning light to Mater. But I accepted the ritual of the ascension for one purpose—to serve the will of God in a greater capacity than I was able while in embodiment.

My service, then, continues from the Darjeeling retreat of the Brotherhood where I am counseling with other brothers of the will of God so many of the evolutions of earth who serve in the governments of the nations, who serve as teachers and scientists and musicians and those who control the flow of the will of God that is power, that is the abundance of supply.

The will of God is applied in all levels of human endeavor. For the will of God is the blueprint of every project. It is the foundation of every task. It is the skeleton of your body. It is physical energy. It is etheric fire. The will of God is the fiery diamond in your heart. The will of God is your will to be God in manifestation. And without that will, you would not have taken incarnation as you are now.

And so the scope of the work of the brothers in Darjeeling, both ascended and unascended, is to continue to endow lifestreams following the cultures of both East and West with the appreciation of that first ray of the dawn—the ray that is the quickening of consciousness at birth, the ray that is the quickening of the chakras in the process of enlightenment, the ray that is the quickening of the divine plan as the child comes of age at the age of twelve ready to take the responsibilities of karma and the duty to fulfill the inner blueprint.

My purpose in coming is to etch a fiery will within you that is the product of my meditation upon the will of God and the sun of your own I AM Presence. For I perceive that there is a cancerous substance moving across the mass unconscious. It is a substance that I call anti-will.

It is a substance so subtle that most among mankind do not even perceive that by this substance there is a denial of freedom, a denial not only of the will to be but of the ability to will to be. Like the weakening of the form, like the drawing away of the very strength of the body, so is this substance moving against the flame, the fiery flame of the will to purpose, the will to perfection, the will to Life itself.

This is the plight of the evolutions of Terra. Both in East and West there is that hypnosis, that manipulation of consciousness at sublevels by the substance of selfishness itself, by the substance of lesser wills of desire—willing for pleasure and phenomena and the psychic, willing for power and manipulation, willing for everything but the will of God which is sufficient to meet all aspects of life within the soul.

The plight of modern man is the plight of a false will—a will not to Life but to Death, a will to be unconscious, not to face the issues, not to take the responsibility, but to become drunk by the media, by the chemicals in the food, by the dissipation of individuality through a mass mesmerism, a collective consciousness of the crowd instead of the individual rising, rising to a self-awareness carved out of the will of God.

I come to wake you up. I come to shake you to a larger purpose, a larger destiny to which you were born. I come to let the decibels quiver, to let the frequencies and the vibrations of your beings be attuned now. Let them be struck as the tuning fork. So let the body and the temple and the spirit and the soul of man and woman be shaken by the winds of Darjeeling, by the great quivering of the movement of the will of God.

Let the diamond of Morya, let the diamond of the devotion of the chelas of the will of God be the rallying point to awaken mankind from the lethargy and the sleep of the ages, to awaken America to a vital purpose, to awaken the individual to that first ray of the dawn which is strength and courage and self-discipline and the will to sacrifice this deathlike mesmerism whereby the people give in so easily to sloth and sleep and sensuality and every form of pleasure while the world, the world of the energy of God, instead of a spiraling into a cosmic purpose, unwinds down and down and down until there is nothing left but the inertia of the rest of death.

Do you not see how this substance, this pall, this pollution that is the very core of the pollution of the elements of your beings, how it is taking from you your very life so that you wander willy-nilly from pillar to post, accepting what the day brings as though it were the will of God?

I will not stand for the chelas of the light to call their own karma the will of God! Let us put karma where it is. It is the will of man. It is your free will. You have made it. Now undo it if you will. But do not blame God for that which you have created.

Let us not consider that cataclysm is an act of God. Let us not consider that the rise and fall of civilization is the will of God. Let us consider how man has failed to implement the will of God, has failed to contact the very core of being as the fiery sun.

Let us consider, then, life beginning right where you are. I am here. But I am not where you are. For I have ascended into the presence of God. If you would rather be where I am, then be where I am! Who is holding you back? Who is stopping you from the path of self-mastery? Shame on you for blaming your parents, your teachers, your culture, your civilization! God is in you. And God is sufficient to your attainment if you will to sacrifice all lesser manifestations.

It is better to choose another word, for sacrifice has the implication of pain. There is no pain in carving away the fat of the mortal so that the lean soul of the spirit can fly. There is no pain in entering the bliss of the will of God. There is no pain. There is the awakening from a pain that you have endured for centuries. Your souls are in agony and you have not even made contact with the soul in this life to know its agony.

Yet you would be a chela (student) of the Lords of the Seven Rays. What would be a chela then? Is it your ego? Is it your human will? Is it your pride? Is it your desperation with failure and repeated failure?

We have requirements, you know. We demand the exercise of a will and a discipline and that you bring a discipline to our retreat. If you would be disciplined, we demand that you first be self-disciplined.

Yes, I like the yogi Milarepa. I like sacrifice to the

nth degree. We are not pushing our chelas to that total self-denial. But if there are those who would deny themselves year in and year out as he did, I can promise you the very same rewards. For not by chance but by law and by science has every overcomer in the flame won the gift of the will of God—the will to be lo, here, lo, there, lo, everywhere in the consciousness of God.

This is the willing of your mind to be in conformity to the Mind of God. And then you will see how you will learn to transform the water into wine, how to levitate, how to project ten or a hundred or a thousand bodies of yourself across the earth.

And when you have had the attainment of this mastery of Matter, you will come to the same conclusion that the great yogis have reached—that it is better to quietly meditate on the Mind of God and to release the pulsations of the Mind of God to a cosmos than to impress anyone with these acts.

It is good to demonstrate mastery. But there comes a time when mankind must not follow those who show phenomena as the way, whether legitimately or illegitimately, whether as the white or the black magician. The time must come when mankind follow the Teacher for the very sake of the flame of the Teaching itself, for the very sake of the vibration of the will of God.

How do you know what is the vibration of the will of God? Well, it is high time you knew! And if you do not, I will tell you. You must fast away your own human will. You must allow your mind and your emotions to become emaciated, deprived of all the indulgences of the human will and of stubbornness against the inner Law of Life.

You must fix your concentration right there at that point of God-free vision. And then you must count your indulgences as though you had a time clock, counting the moments and the seconds and the minutes and the hours.

And you will watch yourself like steel, like a sword, a two-edged sword. You will watch yourself from the moment you awaken to the moment you close your eyes. You will watch your thoughts and feelings. You will see how you respond to this or that stimulus. You will see how you respond to the will of God.

You will stop on the line of your God-determination to be free. You will stop the indulgences of this and that, especially the wandering all about of the mental body and of the feelings. You will obey the injunction "Man, know thyself." And you will keep a log of your manifestations.

And I can assure you that everyone who has determined to be free from the density and the subjugation of mortality, every saint on the Path—out of desperation with the paltriness of the vibration of a certain level of existence—has taken this step of self-discipline.

The will to sacrifice is the will to train the body and the mind and the desires and the memory to go where God goes because you have disciplined yourself by free will. That is the making of a chela. That is the making of the strength of the overcomer who will walk the way of the stations of the cross and who will be found with Christ in the flame of the resurrection on the morning of the third day.

I am Morya. I am always in search of a chela. And I always find the chelas of the will of God. I scan the nations and the continents.

I scan Australia and Africa and New Zealand. I scan even the North and the South Pole. And I identify the chela by the blue halo and by the sparkling of the diamond of the heart. And I am magnetized to that chela who takes that step of determination that is total responsibility for action, for word, for desire.

Like attracts like. I go where the chela is. I go where the vibration of the will of God is. And I am there and my presence is felt. And there is not one soul on earth who has ever been neglected during the period of my Chohanship who has first placed himself in that position of doing the will of God. Not one living soul who has given preeminence to the will of God has escaped my eye since the hour of my ascension.

And I have sent the legions of the angels of goodwill to minister unto these individual souls until they were found worthy in their self-discipline to come (in their finer bodies) to the etheric retreat of the Brotherhood in Darjeeling to be trained of the Masters of the will of God. And there are many Ascended Masters whom you know on the inner planes who are not known to you in your outer consciousness. And they come to Darjeeling, and they teach the reinforcement of that will.

Therefore, let all know that the piercing eye of God is penetrating souls in this room, souls on Terra. And I am measuring your attainment and your will to attain. And if you feel naked before the eye of God, it is good. For naked you will stand before your God at the conclusion of this incarnation, and naked you will stand before the world in the initiation of the crucifixion when you are stripped of your outer garments.

Do not be disturbed. For all individuals who come within our gaze for the first time (they think) have that feeling of uncomfortability when they consider that an Ascended Master can know all of their actions, all of their involvements, all of their petty indulgences.

I can assure you that I have seen it all before.

I have seen it all because it is repeated over and over and over again in the mass consciousness ad nauseam. I have seen this world and its folly. And I have seen the same old plots cued up by the fallen ones, the same old tapes played again and again until they are so old that those tapes of the fallen ones played in the inner ear of the children of God actually sound worn like a record that has been played a thousand times.

And yet the children of God do not even think for a moment that they are being subjected to the same old conditioning that they heard in their last incarnation and the one before that and the one before that and the one before that.

The plots are the same. Very little new literature has

been written in thousands of years. If you were among the fallen ones, you would not have to be creative because the same few plots work again and again.

How long will the Ascended Masters wait while the chelas who could make lightning progress in the Mind of God go here and there for entertainment, to this and that teacher and this and that course for the aggrandizement of the ego?

We have aeons to wait. The question is, how long do you have to wait? We know the hour of our going and our coming in the white-fire core of God. Do you know the hour of your coming and your going, of your aborning in the womb of time and your moving again through space to other shores?

Are you certain that you will reincarnate in another embodiment? Are you not concerned with the problem of abortion? Are you not concerned that if you do not attain on the Path in this life that you may very well be aborted again and again and again as the race spirals into greater and greater selfishness and the denial of the birth of the Divine Manchild—the image of God in the soul of every child born of woman?

And where will you go to balance your karma? Where will you go to fulfill your inner blueprint when you are bound to reincarnate on earth because all of the evolutions with whom you have that integration of karma are here also?

As the decades pass and mankind enter into new lows of insanity, is it any wonder that we are concerned from our level how the chelas and how the sons and daughters of God will conclude the path of initiation? We are concerned. We are concerned! And our only hope of clearing the way for evolution is to contact those in embodiment, to contact you who will listen to the word of Hierarchy and of the Great White Brotherhood.

You who have come to hear, are you like those who have gone out into the desert to see John the Baptist, to see this one who is called a madman, a prophet, a messenger of God? Do you go here and there to be entertained, to look for a reed in the wind? Or are you really responding to the call of the soul for that wholeness, for that harmony and for that light which is your very Life, your very sustenance?

We contact the chela on the Path. And we contact those who are on the verge of becoming chelas on the Path.

You are people of goodwill. This is a land of goodwill, a land of abundance that has been shared with the nations of the world. The people of goodwill have also been infiltrated by those who have come to steal the light of the Christ and of the Mother and of Hierarchy and to twist and to turn and to torture the children of God until they even come to the place of the denial of the light and the goodwill and the God-government that was intended to be manifest in this nation.

I perceive in you that ray of hope that is contact with Hierarchy. My presence here fully in my light body is given to you this night that I might anchor within you that awareness that God in you is real and that sons and daughters of God have walked the way of overcoming, have attained to a reality in the ascended state and can now contact those who are following in the evolutionary chain.

I have come to convince you by the very essence of my presence, my life, my radiation that the Ascended Masters are real. To doubt in their existence is to doubt the existence of your own Reality. To doubt the Path is to close the door to Life. To doubt the way of initiation is death itself.

The Christ in you declares evermore, "I AM the open door which no man can shut." Do not give the power to anyone on any plane of existence to open and close the door of your consciousness. Give that power to no one, for God gave it to you to keep unto yourself, unto your Real Self, your own Christ Presence. Do not relinquish it to anyone, and thereby you will not lose time in the detour of the personality-cult consciousness that is filled with maya and selfishness and manipulation.

I contact you for a cosmic purpose—to right the wrongs of civilization, to clear the way again in the marts of education and culture for the recognition that life itself is a path of initiation, that all of government and all of industry and all of learning must serve this end, this end to which Christ was born, to which Christ came into the world, to bear witness to the Truth.

Let us see, then, one by one how you will eliminate from your life that which does not serve the cosmic purpose of bearing witness to the Truth of your own inner reality and your own inner being. Let us see how you will eliminate those factors and conditionings that rob you of your sleep, rob you of your energy, and keep you on the treadmill of economic survival. You had better consider the survival of your soul and be less concerned with your status in society. For this society will crumble unless it be infused by the will of God.

Let us see how you strip yourself, then, day by day from those impediments to the will of God. Let us see how you mark the way of the overcomer. Let us see how you become prepared to manifest the sacred labor that will be the proof of your witness of the Truth, that will be the infusion of Matter with the flame of Spirit and that is the only salvation for America and for every nation on earth.

Yes, civilization will crumble unless some among mankind respond with the fervor of the devotees of the will of God to hold the balance for America, South and North America, and for all evolutions of this world. Some will make the supreme sacrifice—a sacrifice that is not death but of total living unto God and the God flame.

That supreme sacrifice and only that supreme sacrifice by those in embodiment will bring this world into a golden age. I assure you by all that I am that the responsibility is totally upon you who have life in physical embodiment. It is totally upon your free will what will be the determination of this age.

Cast your superstition into the flame of fairy god-mothers and the like. There is no way of the "miracle" that will bring in a golden age. It is the miracle of hard work, of application of the law and of the science of initiation. That is the great miracle. And when the sons and daughters of God demonstrate that law and that science, the children say, "A miracle has occurred this day." It is not so. It is the alchemy of the overcomers—always.

May I also add that when you work the works of God, the Ascended Masters multiply your effort by the alchemy of the Holy Spirit. But this too is law and you can expect your investment in life to return to you with interest. It is the law of the abundant Life. But if you sow a narrow field, you will reap a narrow harvest.

The will to sacrifice is in your hands, for I have already made my determination. You will give answer this night and every night, for the guardian angel of your Presence takes note of the increments of the will. The increments of the will are the all-determining factors of who you will become, whether or not you will succeed in the material or the spiritual universe. Increments of will determine whether you will live or you will not live in the consciousness of God.

Chelas of the sacred fire and those who would be, I ask you this question: Are you ready to will to sacrifice? ["Yes!"]

April 16, 1976
Los Angeles

A White Paper from the Darjeeling Council Table

The orphans of the Spirit are our concern—those who, without the thread of contact with Deity, remain wedded to an unwholesome environment, those to whom the real purpose of Life is never revealed; for the crystallization of their intellectual concepts and the hardness of their hearts, rooted in selfishness, do not open the cosmic doorway to our domain.

So many are the mysteries of Life, so many are the powers of Love. Yet the dust seems to be more their choice than the destiny God ordained.

Now there is a remnant, and the remnant is one of hope; and these are responsive hearts, but the great cosmic net must reach into the deep and find them out.

We must draw many to the higher pilaster. We must amplify the filaments of light in the body-bulbs of those who are the true seed of God. We must protect and direct. Yet the veil of obscurity is very, very heavy.

While man's concern for his ecology mounts, what

shall I say is happening to the soul within? The moral standard, recognition of the plane of Spirit, listening to the music of the stars and the spheres, creating that tie of cosmic identity which is the forte of the will of God— these are the strong banners we raise.

Now we compliment those who have assisted in the expansion of the light beams from The Summit Lighthouse: those who perceive our reality standing behind the printed word, those who understand that the Messengers and staff are glad servants, a veil of flesh through which we indicate strands of the holy pattern.

Expansion goeth on. Many things have been done of God-direction for the general improvement of the organization; and now in the very envelope of physical manifestation, the spirit of light and movement is stirring. Progress is the order of the day; and one day all that is now being prepared will break forth its own melody, and many shall sing a new song because of it.

Noting the widening schisms, the deliberately maneuvered divisions being created through the dichotomies of mind and spirit in the total world order today, it is my desire to speak from our level concerning our viewpoint and our intent. Those who would set nation against nation, those who would set people against people, those who would point the accusing finger of one religion at another, by so doing create that fracture in consciousness which is a destructive negative spiral.

May I, then, set forth so that all may hear me once and for all, the policy of The Summit Lighthouse, sponsored by the Great White Brotherhood. As the brother of humble service who assisted in the pangs of birth, may I now order the promulgation of our statement of policy and see that this shall reflect our thoughts both now and in the future.

It is well known that there are in the world millions who are labeled "left wing." There are other millions labeled "right wing." There are others who choose, in some degree of human pride I might add, the position of the middle of the road. May I say that we do not espouse any of these causes, and may I tell you why.

The magnitude of Cosmic Christ service is such that we cannot identify ourselves or our movement with one confined to a secular slice of opportunism.

Those who desire to sell many copies of their magazine espouse controversial subjects, knowing that half of the people in the world will probably subscribe to their view. They play the percentages, and to them life is a wheel of roulette.

From our level we can scarcely engage in such conduct. We choose, then, not to favor any of these positions, but rather to recognize the whole spectrum from right to left, including the middle of the road, as the valley of reality where truth may appear mingled with error.

Ours is not to create division, and The Summit Lighthouse, our organization, reflects those goals which are sound and strengthening to the human spirit.

May I say in all cosmic honor that there are

virtuous causes across the whole range of human endeavor, but there are many that are unvirtuous, unrighteous, deceptive and wrongly motivated. We cannot identify with any; for our purpose is not to be popular, but to be truthful and to embrace those spiritual causes which will enable the soul itself to expand its life.

I have not denied that the poor, as Jesus said, are with you always. I have not denied man's right to fulfill those social needs which to some have become a way of spiritual service. Likewise, we clearly see that among the traditions of men there are many of virtue, albeit sometimes sagging, that ought to be upheld; but where shall we position the timbers? We cannot identify with the right or the left, and we cannot identify with the middle of the road.

As I speak, truth and error slide, and the human jackal of division has man in derision. The powers of darkness laugh as people espouse this cause and that cause in a radical way. Others are at the center of lukewarmness. They would not wax hot and they would not wax cold. So be it. The salvation of the soul is not served by social reform, nor is it served by opposing social reform. The progress of man can best be accented if it is first set in the right direction. May I point out how this can be done and what our perspective is.

It is reasonable to suppose that there are many things of a spiritual nature unknown to men, and divine revelation has not yet closed its mouth of uttering the great fiat of the Word. There are those who think religious tradition is complete and that man has but to go about the gentle and yet sometimes not so gentle business of attaching labels to various people and to various groups. These labels are intended not to liberate, but to confine.

When the man of honor sees clearly, he will realize that both social reform and opposition to social reform have their own way of sapping his total energy. People feel the need to espouse one cause or the other, and those who are of a radical nature find niches of comfortable radicalism in varying degrees to the right or to the left of center. How one radical can condemn the other is difficult to understand in the light of spiritual knowledge.

Yet spiritual knowledge is the highest knowledge and takes into account the total compass of the brotherhood of man. For example, when we make a pronouncement that seems to sanction one or the other—and as I have said before, the garment of righteousness must run the whole spectrum—we find ourselves being labeled and our outer voice of cosmic reason, The Summit Lighthouse, being labeled also.

The choice we make, then, is to render the greatest service to all men and women upon the planet wherever they appear on the social scale, from the poorest to the wealthiest, from the weakest to the strongest, from the most unspiritual to the most spiritual, from the foolish to the wise. We must serve them all; and unless we do, we have fallen short of our divine office.

When human reform is needed, let us be about our

Father's business; but let us put the brakes on those unfortunate situations which literally tear from man the vital energies of his life, leaving him a profitless servant.

As the spokesman for the will of God, I do not believe that division is the divine intent. I do not believe that manipulators do not exist in the world. I know that they exist, and that they exist to the total degradation of man.

What we need most is honor; and those who espouse that honor should see to it that the textbooks of the world, the magazines, the radio and television programs, and all media should honestly present to man all sides of the question.

Man should not become so enamored with his environment that he loses his soul in the process of egotistically molding his environment. Rather he should understand that the opportunity for life, which he sometimes wears solemnly and then again unceremoniously, is his God-given right, one through which he may, if he will, attain enough self-control to become the master of his own destiny.

In truth, may I say that man *can* be the God of his own universe. He can supplement his desires with holy reason. He can transmute and direct the total course of his being.

The purpose of our weekly newsletter, the *Pearls of Wisdom*, is to assist men upon the planetary body in the business of mastering their environment. Therein is the way of initiation made plain. It is not grasped in a moment. It can be understood by application to the heart of God and to the cosmic Hierarchy.

But man must be patient with himself; for our words, albeit directed to all, are not always understood by all, but more often are understood in part. From day to day we can increase the fountain of knowledge vouchsafed to man if he will faithfully pursue the reading of those words and thoughts and the communing with that spirit which we send earthward.

We are concerned primarily with the little children, that they be given the opportunity of expanding the richness of the universe, the abundant life. As the flame of knowledge increases within them, new dimensions of the Spirit appear from day to day.

But when religion becomes a gambit to be used by one religious group against another, with jealousy increasing rather than decreasing, we think of the fable of the fox and the crow and of how the crow held the cheese in its beak. Then, with flattery the fox induced the crow to speak, the cheese fell out and was devoured, and the crow did not partake of its meat.

So let men realize that often by their greediness and grasping, the very things they want most are driven from them. But by humility and a reaching-out for knowledge, their lifespan is extended; and with it comes an accretion of practical knowledge enhancing the business of living.

I am known as a practical Master. My teachings are gladly given, but they are more gladly given when implemented through the armor of action. What a pity it is that men do not appreciate the depths of their connection with us. The Great White Brotherhood—an intensity of magnanimity, a flash of divine grace as the holy brothers contemplate the welfare of man—is truly an organization of service and grace.

Little do men dream, when first coming in contact with us, of the extent of our holy order. Through the bonds of The Summit Lighthouse and the *Pearls of Wisdom* men can expand their knowledge beyond their farthest dreams; but they must, from the very tenderest beginning, understand that what they are reading is not ordinary material.

If they find it difficult at first to consider its content simply because it is printed by human agencies, let them think again; for while functioning through human agency, it is not of human levels. It possesses light and it is charged with the radiation of cosmic intent. Witness that in more than one instance during the California earthquake, focuses of our holy brothers and of the organization remained fixed to the walls, while other pictures crashed to the floor.

So let men understand that each word, each sentence is a repository of great knowledge. Many have told our Messengers that when at first they began to read, they did not fathom the depths of the work. Later, in reviewing the extent of the virtue of the Teachings, thousands of new ideas were revealed that they had not seen at first.

By study combined with meditation, contemplation, and holy prayer—if he is not too proud to engage in silent communion—man can in reading our words enhance his opportunities until at last he will come to understand the depth of our service. And then nothing can stop him from moving toward the divine magnet.

By the divine magnet man is drawn Godward. And this is truly the fastening of the abundant life, of cosmic delight upon his soul, upon his mind, upon his feelings. His very heart of hearts becomes the chalice of spiritual opportunity, extending its light rays of strength into every act of the individual. Ultimately, sometimes slowly, sometimes swiftly, man passes those milestones representative of the higher goal.

Above all, let men understand that negative spirals must not be their lot, that positive upreach must stand before them. They must not engage in dalliance and, above all, they must not fail to hear our messages when spoken in their vicinity or made available by electronic recording; for thereby the spirit of new joy will ultimately be theirs. The old saying "If at first you don't succeed, try, try again" applies to the will of Spirit.

Those whose psyches have been conditioned by the monsters of human creation should understand that the repudiation of these forcefields of misfortune lodging in their own auras must be swift and sudden; yet, like unto a great cosmic sheet of white fire let down from heaven, the buoyant treasures of new devotion are manifold. By these the consciousness can become so imbued with new strength as to literally create the spirit of eternal youth in man.

Nevertheless, the world order does not provide for the proper training of its young. There is too much recklessness and wild abandon, too much deceit and personal motivation devoid of honor.

Our Brotherhood often finds itself under attack by the dark ones, simply because they wish to avoid that cosmic confluence or spiritual union which truly wipes away all tears from the eyes of men and brings them such a measure of divine comfort as they have never experienced before.

When the sacred fires are left to do their work of burning away old barriers and opening up new vistas in the world of man, then men will understand that our purposes are not the material purposes of men, but rather that they are the spiritual purposes of God. These are to extend those cosmic traditions to man by which the saints and sages of all ages have found their greatest peace and attainment.

Will you view our every act from this position of thought and cease to attach to us or to our movement those labels of your own making which can, if persisted in, successfully mar the cosmic image we seek to place before you?

If you will do this, putting away childish things, you will become a man of God, destined for cosmic mastery. If you will do this, maturing in spirit and waiting upon the proffered word, you will find that each week and each opportunity we bring to you will be a Christ-renewal of God-magnificence; for these are the jewels of your own crown you are gathering. They are the pearls of great price whose wearing will make you worthy of service to God and love to man.

From the tall pines of Darjeeling we waft our message of eternal strength and goodwill to men. May our Father who is in heaven magnify that Christ-unity and reality born of no winds of delusion and fanned by no fanatic fires, but clearly indicative of the whole spectrum of the consciousness of the Great White Brotherhood, which holds the Banner of Truth above all.

Valiantly in His service, I remain

Morya El

Chief, the Darjeeling Council
of the Great White Brotherhood

1971
Colorado Springs

LANTO 2
Lord of the Second Ray

Initiation of the Crown Chakra

Retreat:	Grand Teton, Wyoming, U.S.A.
Vibration:	Yellow, Gold
Gemstone:	Yellow Diamond, Yellow Sapphire, Topaz
Quality:	WISDOM UNDERSTANDING JUDGMENT
Gift:	Word of Wisdom, Word of Knowledge
Day:	Sunday

A scene reminiscent of the friendship of Lord Lanto
and his disciple, Confucius

Possibilities in New Dimensions

Greetings from the heart of the Royal Teton Retreat. Greetings from the hosts of the LORD and the brothers who serve with us. An emerald light is magnetized in this hour by illumination's flame. And as you have sent forth the call of freedom, so freedom answers.

I would bring to you a chapter from the Book of Life—your life. I would read to you a poem of the soul. I would share with you the deliberations from the minds of the Chohans and those who gather in celebration of your gathering here [in the heart of the Inner Retreat]. In this case, it is man who proposes. And so, God disposes himself to be moved from his throne and to regard once again possibilities in new dimensions.

I come, then, on a ray of light that touches now every heart from out the crystal fire. Illumination's flame is upon each one as you are extensions of the hand of God in form, so envisioned by Amenhotep IV. And this ray of light does activate now the hidden man of the heart and the voice of one who within you knows the hour of birth, the hour of immortality, the hour of the coming and the going of your soul.

You contemplate in wonder the question of the unknown future. You say, "How can forces pitted against one another, how can a reeling economy or hatred that remains in the hearts of some be tamed or tested? How can one know the temperature of earth? How can one predict the future?"

With the quicksilver quality of human nature, millions of people make decisions in every hour, but key individuals decide the destiny of nations. We see clearly the hand of God writing—not only in the sky but in the human heart. But we also see free will as choices yet to be taken and sand that has not yet fallen in the hourglass of life.

Therefore, my beloved, consider then with me as the hour strikes and opportunity is at hand: The only certainty in the cup is your own will to be. Reduce the entire equation to yourself seated here. All that you can trust is God, and all that you can hope is that your will tethered to his, your hand reaching out and reaching again for Christ, will take the right step and make the decision—not for life or death, for these are not thine own, but the decision of the securing of the soul wherever it may be found.

Since last I addressed you, I have received some from among this Community who have made the transition and been taken to our retreat. Theirs was not the expectancy of transition, and yet they found themselves in a new dimension with other opportunities and new life. As the prophet was wont to say, "Death comes unexpectedly!" Therefore, I say to each and every one: It is not life and death in this octave, but the onward movement of the soul toward the goal of permanency in the very Being of God that ought to be your concern.

Looking beyond earth's future, we contemplate the future of the stars—your star, the causal body of your life. Therefore, decisions wisely taken in confirmation of the Word, in praise of God, and in sweet love for his tender vines—these things so precious, these interchanges with brother and brother, the witness unto Truth are of paramount importance.

I have seen individuals in the very final week of a given embodiment make such heroic stand for Truth, be so outspoken in the pronouncement of the Word by the very impulse of their own Christ flame, as to set a stream of fire that could be seen in the next galaxy! And swiftly the sands would fly, and that one would find himself before the bar and receiving the commendation of "a word well done"—not necessarily for a life fulfilled, but surely for a mark of valor that will count and set the sail for a new beginning and thrust the soul into another plane where angels, too, bear witness to his coming.

I like to think in terms of eternity, for only eternity is real! And the mark we make upon the face of earth must surely be that others may follow and find the stronger path, the courage, and a buoyancy because our step was light and sure as the deer that leaps and lights upon a higher rock.

You have moved to higher ground.
For what purpose therefore
Does the soul abound?
Again we contemplate the philosophers' stone
And we realize that in life
There is much for to atone.
The atonement, then,
Is the balancing of every wrong.
Let us not lose the song
Of the bird within the heart
That sings and sings again,
Even when bowed down — its earthly wings —
By soot and chemical warfare
And the burdening of the toil of earth.

Your souls would fly,
Yet you are also encased in form
That binds you to a mortal coil
And a gravitational pull.
Yet it is the will, the perception,
The set of the sail and the heart!

My point: As the blacksmith,
Let us strike a blow —
A strong blow for the LORD!
Let us provide for others
Who will follow after.
Let us rid ourselves
Of the stifling of a pleasure cult
That has as its goal no tomorrow
But the surfeiting of today

And lacks the vision.
And men wear spectacles
While they themselves are a spectacle
Across the board of life,
As we who count ourselves among the wise
Wonder when they will face
The inevitable demise
Of an ego long spent
And the realization that
Only the soul can fly!
But it cannot fly unless it test its wings
And form those wings as pinions of light.

Without the wings of prayer and hope,
Without a destiny and a concern,
Where may the soul fly
When the body has no more heart
Or nerve or verve to continue in this octave?

Let us use this land to the full cup of our potential! Let us understand that illumination and its flame must not be snuffed out in this land—as youth are in delirium and their senses dulled by drugs and rock, and think of no other thing but lyrics that take them down and down again to a lower level and therefore deprive them of the blossoming of the yellow fire of the crown! Let us realize that there is a movement, a force—and I must say, it is the tremendous force of 'hell' itself moving across the land to take a stand against the light—against the wisdom of the heart!

I AM Lanto in the Royal Teton, and here is a blazing fire of wisdom!

Who shall pursue the fount of wisdom? Who shall be able to rise and mount the ladder of the chakras when these drugs and the downward-spiraling beat does take the youth even beneath their feet to subterranean levels of hellish fires of fallen ones—who themselves long lost their wings, blackened now with other things, and therefore dwell in places of insects' origins and biting and stinging things that ought to be no more but are—fed as they are by mass ignorance?

I come to pierce the veil of ignorance! And if it were up to me, I say: I would dedicate this land to learning, to education of the heart and every level—and the divine art! I would secure the culture of the nations ere they fall! I would bring from one and all the mementos of the past—of artisans and handicraft and those things that souls did work in Matter as a mighty work of the ages before they lost the will or the desire or the love to bring out from within some beautiful, noble thing.

Therefore, let it be the gathering place. Let us see here the fruits of Tibetan monks and their scrolls and records of pilgrims of the ages and of Saint Issa and his journey to the East. Let us see some memory of the architecture of those lamaseries on the rock, of the Buddhist stupa, of the places of prayer that have been destroyed even in this century—without a protest from the West[1] and those who say they love Christ best but honor him not in Buddha or in the great and noble Confucius, who has never been truly appreciated for the fervor of his mind.

Hear the one from ancient China. Hear the one who now serves you as the hierarch of our retreat. For he is come also with me, bearing a scroll—the lovable, noteworthy one whom you all have known.

The practical side of the culture of America comes from the causal body of Confucius. Now and then banned and then popular again, the fallen ones seek to use him in China. But here in America, his dream of God-government is a flame of illumination that lights the way of those who follow Saint Germain in a buoyant freedom.

If I, then, were to have my say (as you have so graciously allowed me this day), it would be, my beloved, to dedicate this land and a portion thereof to the noble goal of the light of Confucius. Had he been heeded, so China should never have fallen.

The sealing of the family and its love, the purity and honor, the grace of interchange and, above all, the wisdom of Buddhic learning before its time was his bequeathing to a race—a yellow race so named, for they pursued the Second Ray. And all of these and many more are embodied in North America in this age, as another race has taken their place and not always carried the pure lamp of the Goddess of Liberty.

Truly this land is the land where the eagles gather. Truly it is a place where the Ascended Masters have come, where Glastonbury and the place of the ancient Druids and the sign of the seasons recorded at Stonehenge and the work and light of Francis Bacon and

Thomas More may be sealed and protected in the fire of the rock, in the heart of the mountain.

There are so many secret places of the Most High for you to find and see and know. Why, have you considered that each and every one of you could be hidden in these hills, never to be found again? It is like playing hide-and-seek with fairies and star-fire beings—and realizing that the greatest secrets of God are hidden in the human heart, the divine heart made so by the spark of Life!

Yes, if I had my say, I would tell you that unless the flame of illumination be understood as the apex and culmination of all of life and the key to immortality, unless it be revered, all else must go down.

Think upon it, blessed hearts. One may tell you the law; but without the understanding, did you always obey it? Nay. It requires a teaching, a reasoning of the heart, a motive that comes through understanding and understanding alone. You may know the truth, but the truth that sets you free is the truth that is understood by illumination's flame.

I encourage the refinement of the heart by the secret rays,* the nobility of the path of discipleship, and the pursuit of the highest culture of the soul. This is not a place of escape. This is a place of building! This is a place for the rescue of the great books of the world and the great teachings of all time.

This is a place to begin once again the library of

---

*The five secret rays are hidden rays whose colors have not been released to us. They bring initiations of purifying and refining to the senses of the soul.

Alexandria, where those immortal tomes were burned and then retrieved again in the heart of our retreat. This is a place for the gathering of the artifacts of Atlantis and the lore of Lemuria and the music that has not been heard on earth for a quarter of a million years!

I challenge you, son of light, to write that music of the ancient temple and to know the true rhythm of the heart that is for the healing of a world—yea, the creating of a new world! I challenge you to defeat this lower beat of fallen ones that intrigues the mind for a season but can never, never, never deliver the soul-satisfying nectar of the Buddha whereby that enlightenment of all-knowing does come!

> There is a music *you* can write thereby,
> And so allow each one to hear
> The ringing of the sacred tone
> For the unfoldment of the crown!
> There is a science of sound
> Waiting to be born—
> Waiting to be heard!
> For sound is the creation of worlds
> And sound is the uncreation of worlds.
> And therefore, only to the highest sound
> Does the highest unfoldment
> Of divinity take place.
> Without the sound, no creation will occur.
> And if you do not write,
> Another may come and steal thy light
> And write not the highest but a lesser melody!

Alas, for each and every one, a noble task
From the Book of Life I read.
If you do not succeed
According to the plan,
Look again, for another man
Will stand in your place,
Sit in your seat,
And take the pen that you ought
And write a book that you could have.
Writing, then, thy destiny out of fire
Demands the certainty of will.

You see, then, there are things to be built whose construction, begun on earth, continues in etheric octaves. For some of you, transition will be a mere breath and then a new breath and a sigh, and on again with the work at hand, with scarcely a break in the measured beat of the artisan or the heart!

You are so close to the start and then the end of life. And in the etheric retreats the onward movement of the building of celestial cities is ongoing and there are places where all these things that you contemplate can indeed be contemplated, and more! because we are free of war, free of hate, free of the rolling tides of energy that must always and always be transmuted by violet flame in these lower octaves before you can begin the day again to strike some noble purpose for the LORD.

Why, can you scarcely begin to realize
How immortality is such a guise

That in its folds, this garment wise,
You yourself can create
And continue to create with certainty
After the Master Architect's plan
With scarcely being troubled
By a gnat or Nephilim god?

Think, O where the saints have trod,
My beloved,
Think where they have walked
And how you have here talked with God.
Think how your footsteps can be light,
No more pulled by earth,
And your soul take flight
Into the fiery domain of the Sun.
Think of your longing
And your inward soaring
And your heart's devotion!

Think again, for just above you
The saints are playing games of life and joy
And instruments of music.
Saints are wooing you to a higher octave.
And here in the openness of life,
Here in God's own beauty,
You may contemplate
The immortality of the soul.

August 26, 1982
Royal Teton Ranch
Montana

Confucius (c. 551–479 B.C.) was born in the feudal state of Lu, the modern Shantung province. Observations of perpetual warfare between Chinese states and the tyranny of the overlords led Confucius to formulate a new moral system and statecraft that would give the people an equitable government and restore peace to the nation. Believing he had a personal mission to spread his doctrine, he began, at the age of 55, a ten-year tour of neighboring states, visiting rulers and trying to convince them to appoint him to a high office so that he could introduce his reforms. Meeting with no success, he was attacked at the town of Kwang, but responded: "Heaven has appointed me to teach this doctrine, and until I have done so, what can the people of Kwang do to me?" Confucianism has been described as a "social order in communion and collaboration with a cosmic order." It depicts man as a member of a social order who is bound to others in his community by *jen*, "human-heartedness." Jen governs the interpersonal relationships and is expressed through five primary relations—ruler and subject, parent and child, elder and younger brother, husband and wife, and friend and friend. Each one of these relationships is harmonized by adherence to li, a defined system of etiquette and ritual; for Confucius believed that true respect in filial relationships would lead to right conduct in all things. Although Confucius was primarily concerned with principles of conduct and morality, later adherents of his teachings became preoccupied with the detail of ritual, devoid of his pioneering spirit.

The Duke of Chou [joh] (d. 1105 B.C.), regarded as one of the greatest statesmen in Chinese history, was considered to be the architect of the Chou dynasty (1122–256 B.C.) and the true founder of the Confucian tradition. Confucius looked to the Duke as his model and believed it was his mission to reestablish the principles and culture of the early Chou era, which was thought to have been a golden age. Confucius often dreamt about the Duke of Chou in his early life. In the Analects he lamented, "Extreme indeed is my decline. It is a long time since I dreamed that I saw the Duke of Chou." It has been said that Lanto was the Duke of Chou and that Confucius was at one time embodied as his son or a close servant.

Huang Ti, illustration from *Li-tai ku-jen hsiang-tsan*
(1498 edition); in the collection of the University of Hong Kong

The legendary Yellow Emperor (Huang Ti, born c. 2704 B.C.),
also called the Yellow Ancestor, ruled a golden age in ancient
China and is considered to be the ancestor of all Chinese people.
He is also known as the God of Architecture, the patron of alchemy
and the originator of Taoism. According to Chinese tradition, his
teachings of Taoism were transmitted orally from generation to
generation until Lao Tzu (6th century B.C.) wrote them down in
the *Tao Te Ching*. Taoism, then, is often referred to as the "teachings of Huang-Lao" (Huang Ti and Lao Tzu). Huang Ti taught his
people how to make fire and is believed to have invented wheeled
vehicles, weapons, bronze casting, writing and wooden houses.
His wife discovered and taught sericulture (silk production).
His capital was in a southern area of present-day Inner Mongolia.
In his lifetime, he was held to be a "paragon of wisdom" and is
believed to now be an Immortal. That there is a connection between
the Yellow Emperor and Lord Lanto is more than a speculation.

The Great Synthesis of the Mother Flame

I am come from the Royal Teton Retreat to place my flame within this city of San Francisco, a flame of Cosmic Christ illumination, the distillation of the path of East and West—the path of illumined action fostered by enlightenment, the ennoblement of deeds, and the love, the light of hearts one in that love.

I say to you, Rule your circumstance and be not ruled by that circumstance. Many who may be praised for virtue would not be altogether virtuous when placed in other circumstances. This is why the edict went forth, Judge not lest ye be judged.

Many of you find yourselves today in certain circumstances solely because in another life you have criticized the action of another who was beset by similar circumstances. And therefore, the Great Law, in its infinite mercy and kindness, has given to you the opportunity to walk in the moccasins, as they say, of the one upon whom you placed that judgment.

Now, then, if you are not satisfied with your circumstance or your dealing with those circumstances of life, remember that you have recourse—recourse to your own Great God Flame and Christ Self who responds instantaneously to your call.

The instantaneous response of Almighty God is not always the immediate change of circumstance. It is rather a release of light, a coil of infinite energy that begins to cycle from the plane of the I AM Presence to your Christ Self through the lines of your etheric, mental, emotional, and physical bodies.

And therefore, the answer to the call may seem a long time manifesting to those souls who look only to the physical to know God's will or God's life.

We are not so much concerned with the physical as we are with the revolution of consciousness beginning at the very core of being, the inner blueprint.

When you ask for healing, God always releases a sacred fire sphere of healing light. It is deposited deep within your subconscious. As this light begins to flow and cycle through the planes of being, it pushes out to the surface unwanted conditions. It is an electrode that is a focus of God's wholeness. Therefore, all unlike itself must be uprooted, must be exposed.

And therefore, many times when you come in contact with the Great White Brotherhood and begin the experiment as the alchemist of the sacred fire, you find for a season more problems than you had before you even began, and then you wonder why you are on this path in the first place.

Beloved ones, if you want outer wholeness, then go to other sources. There are faith healers. There are psychic healers. There are medicine men, witch doctors, voodoo specialists, and medical scientists. In every society they hold the position of prominence. It is not our intent to in any way disparage souls of light who pursue to the best of their ability the healing of the bodies of mankind. In fact, we have inspired upon many the very healing arts which are practiced.

But I tell you, it is often better to suffer pain than to take the aspirin or the painkillers that give you the false sense of security that all is well. Pain is a signal like the red light on the dashboard of life. It tells you that you are not whole and that you had better learn the alchemy of wholeness. Suffering in itself is neither good nor evil, but it is the use that is made of suffering to bring the soul nearer to God that is telling.

Understand, then, the answer to the call. Understand the depositing of light within you. It is God's intent, as God lives and as I am his servant, to bring you into the reunion with the One. And therefore, when you are on the path of initiation, do not be so concerned as to your success or failure as a metaphysician measured by the index of the outer sign.

The Lord Christ said that a wicked and an adulterous generation seeketh after a sign, but there shall be no sign given, save the sign of the coming of the prophet Jonah. Jonah in the whale's belly is the symbol of your soul—your soul entering into the subconscious of your own being, working out the formula of that being not only in the level of the mental plane by a scientific alchemy and the affirmation and denial of prayer and fasting but also in the working out of the problem of energy, energy forcefields, the law of cause and effect, and ultimately the responsibility for life.

There is much more to the Path than a miracle here or there. We could bring forth the miracles. We could bring forth the multitudes who always run after the miracles. But we are here that you might be made real by reunion with God. As for us, we prefer a road that is a bit rough, a bit steep, a bit lonely for ourselves and for our chelas than the easy way that gives the false security.

There are many who have mastery of this plane. They use hypnosis, autohypnosis, all forms of mental science and psychic probing. And they can show you miles of testimonies of altered conditions of consciousness and all sorts of phenomena. Well, beloved ones, the rearrangement of energy within this octave will in a few short decades be the first-grade program on the path of life. There is nothing that is simpler.

But many are caught up for years and years and think that they have a certain attainment because, by some spiritual or other process of mental cogitation or meditation, they are able to bring about change—a change that is never the alchemy of the Holy Spirit reforming the mind, the soul, and the being, that is not the alchemy whereby the soul experiences the rebirth, but a change that is the rearrangement of dust, the rearrangement of matter molecules.

What is sickness? What is health? What is poverty? What is riches? Simply the yin, the yang of a relative condition that is yet illusion, except the individual so manifesting may see beyond that manifestation to the reality of the New Day.

From the Ascended Masters' octave, then, I come to speak to you.

Whether the condition of life be happiness, whether the condition of life be suffering, I say, seek the goodness of God. Seek the happiness of God. And if the happiness of God be suffering, then seek suffering. Do not judge good and evil, light and darkness by the state of your comfortability, but judge by the state of your oneness with God—a oneness that is not a verbalization, a oneness that is a Be-ness.

Be-ness stripped of all else—this is the path to reunion. Be-ness. I AM. Not to know about it, think about it, feel about it, but simply To Be. And in being, *be* the perpetual action of Life becoming Life. Be the sword of Kali. Be the scepter of Christ authority. Be the Buddha and let the Holy Spirit live in you.

What is love? Love is whatever brings you to the feet of God, be it cataclysm, be it the perfume of a rose, be it the raindrop upon your nose. Whatever will shake you to the remembrance of me, saith the LORD, *that* is love.

Be not, then, interpreters of the Word. *Be the Word!* And let the interpretation be the judgment of the action that proceeds. By their fruits ye shall know them. Be the Tree of Life. Let the earth evolutions come and pluck the fruit of your tree, eat of it and enter samadhi.

There is a shortcut to God. It is surrender. There is a shortcut to immortality. It is the death of the ego. There is a way to purity. It is bathing in Mother Ganges. Let the flow of Mother now be unto you purification for a purpose. If purification had not the purpose of the salvation of the soul, then what need of purification?

I come, then, not with a doctrine of pain and punishment, but a doctrine of merging into the fire without the pain of fire, merging into the fire without the punishment of the depths of darkness.

Beloved ones, I speak to you of an altered state of awareness whereby you enter into a flow where there is no longer resistance to the God I know. For the God I know is the God that I AM, and that God in you is ready to absorb, to assimilate, and to become yourself.

See, then, there is a step-by-step process of salvation as the process is a coil of energy. And the coil is the scroll of life, a golden scroll upon which is written the sacred alchemical formula of Being, in order that day by day you may pass through the process. We call the process *ritual.* Ritual is the walking of the Path, the assimilation of the sacred fire without the burn—without the pain of the burn.

I am Lanto. I come to show you that the goal of life is Sacred Self, that there is no struggle to become that Self but the stepping out of the uniform of humanism, the stepping out of the masquerade of the carnal mind. All that is not yourself cannot bind you unless you give it the power to bind you.

Walk away from the old habits, the old patterns, the old man, the old associations. Stand in the center of the white-fire core of your Being. Command that that circumstance that surrounds you now submit to the Great God Flame within your heart. Command by the authority of Almighty God and be free.

Do not submit to darkness but submit in humility to the light of God that affords every trial, every tribulation. Be the obedient servant of the Law but not of the demons who would mock your humility and call you servile in that fear which is only the fear of the demons because they have not the salvation of God.

I tell you, the only fear there is is to know that you in your soul—in your soul potential to be God—have never taken a moment in this life to ratify your oneness, have never gone to the Holy of Holies to submit your case to Almighty God, have never said, "LORD, I would be washed by the waters of the Word. I would come into alignment. Show me what I must do to inherit eternal Life." In other words, in the good old-fashioned evangelism, make your peace with God—"Prepare to meet thy God."

Earth is a schoolroom. You must not pass from this life in that vulnerable state whereby you become caught in the astral plane, defending yourself against the vultures, the fallen ones who would eat your very flesh and blood because you have not the cylinder of light around you to carry you to immortal heights.

Secure, then, your soul's opportunity to live in eternity in this very moment. Secure it, beloved ones. For I tell you, many are the sudden transitions, and they come in every walk of life among all types of people. And once the transition is made, the soul, then, must reap the consequences of this life on earth. And many spend hundreds of years in the astral plane because they fail to take the opportunity on earth to secure that identity in God.

You may not be ready for the ascension in this hour. But you are ready for your commitment to the eternal covenant. You are ready for the conversion to be God within your heart. You are ready to go forth as a conqueror in life, to command all circumstance to come into the subjection of the one Great Law. You are ready to enter the age of Reality—realism, whereby you do not turn your back but face with the calm certitude of inner knowing all that has been less than Christ perfection.

Let the little mechanisms of the subconscious mind that have been instituted to protect a weak consciousness from Reality now be set aside in part. I call it forth for the lightbearers of this band across the earth. I call it forth that you might see the debt to Life you owe, that you might command Life and be free, that you might invoke the sacred fire and know that day by day you are transmuting the causes and cores of those conditions which heretofore you have denied.

When you deny these conditions, declaring them

unreal, whether from the standpoint of the Buddhist or the metaphysician or the intellectual or the moron, I say to you, beloved ones, you turn aside the opportunity to redeem energy.

Energy is God. Every erg of energy that has passed through the nexus of your consciousness through thousands upon thousands of years of incarnation must now be passed through the flame of the sacred fire, be stripped of the outer coating of human consciousness, and sent back into your causal body of Life. This is the real challenge of life on earth—not creature comforts, not the attributing of success to those who have become adept at the manipulations of matter.

Beloved hearts of fire, I have one great longing. It is to see you free in the real sense of the term. And because of that longing, I long ago espoused the flame of illumination. For to extend illumination is to remove the screen of maya whereby the soul may see light, may see darkness, may understand the equation, may know that in the ultimate sense all wrong is unreal.

But in order to be unreal—to be rendered unreal in the physical octave where illusions have the appearance and concreteness of a quasi-reality—it must pass through the fires of transmutation. Therefore, affirm the unreality of sin, disease, and death even while you invoke the violet flame to transmute the effect of a condition of consciousness whereby in former times and spaces you accepted and qualified the "reality" of that sin, disease, and death.

Thus molecules of light are stripped of false belief

and systems of error by this ritual of transmutation. And healing is complete. And the inner man is made whole.

Do you understand that this is the Science of the Immaculate Concept whereby you behold the true geometry of Life—and that that Life beholding itself in you is the quickening power of the true scientist of Christ? And that in that quickening power, you invoke the Holy Spirit and the cause, effect, record, and memory of illusion must also submit?

Therefore, in each chakra there is a practice of the sacred law and the science of Being. In some of your chakras you may decree, in others you meditate, in others you visualize wholeness, in others the science of the Word is the confirmation of health. Then realize, beloved ones, that every path of every religion is intended to supply the Body of God upon earth with a component of this cosmic science—of this way and that so that when you play the seven notes of your chakras and the five notes of the secret rays, you begin to have the full expression of the divine complement of harmony whereby you are the instrument of the total consciousness of God on earth as in heaven.

When you find the thread—the precious thread of contact—which connects each one of these levels of mastery, you will enter into the great synthesis of the Mother flame. This great synthesis is the white light, and out of the white light is born that religion true, undefiled.

And therefore, we have no argument nor do we come in condemnation of any faith, but we come to bring light, illumination, and understanding of every faith, that those who are divided in the separate churches might see that each way is a key; and the understanding of the blending of the keys of life will enable all humanity to contact the very core of white fire.

Let this Church Universal and Triumphant, let each devotee within and without realize himself an electrode for the vast understanding of "I AM the Way, the Truth, and the Life."

I am Lanto. I seal you now in the fires of understanding. Let all drink of the eternal fount of the Mother flame and live.

November 13, 1977
San Francisco

The Grand Teton, Wyoming

Château Borély, Esprit-Joseph Brun, architect, c. 1770

Paul the Venetian's retreat, the Château de Liberté, is located in southern France on the Rhône River. Château Borély, situated near the mouth of the Rhône River on the outskirts of Marseilles, recalls Paul's retreat, which has been described as possessing graceful marble columns, fountains and fragrant rose gardens.

PAUL THE VENETIAN 3
Lord of the Third Ray

Initiation of the Heart Chakra

Retreat:	Château de Liberté, Southern France Temple of the Sun, New York
Vibration:	Pink, Rose
Gemstone:	Ruby, Diamond, Garnet, Rose Quartz, Pink Beryl
Quality:	LOVE CREATIVITY BEAUTY
Gift:	Discerning of Spirits
Day:	Monday

A tribute to Paul the Venetian, Lord of the Third Ray,
painted by his twin flame, Ruth Hawkins (now ascended)

The Art of Living Love

Good evening, ladies and gentlemen. I come in the flame of Love to adorn you with the sacred adornments of the God of Love.

> As fires of creativity flow
> From this sacred God I know,
> I bring to you an impartation of the soul—
> 'Tis the fragrance of Alpha and Omega
> That will make you Whole.

As Love is the flowing essence, the ephemeral quality of God, as it is the movement of the wind and the flowing of water, it requires the greatest of discipline to be able to retain—to have and to hold that Love that is so tender, so gentle, and yet the ultimate expression of creative fires. Those who are the greatest artists, poets, and musicians who use the flame of Love to implement an idea of God are those who have the greatest discipline—discipline of self, energies of self, of life, even of time and space.

I come, then, to bring to you an understanding of this discipline so that you will understand that discipline is not something to be feared, but discipline is the Law, the fulfillment of Love. Discipline is a grid, a forcefield that is necessary in order to have the flow of Love and to retain the flow of Love.

You notice all around you where there are undisciplined lives how Love flies out the window, how Love is compromised and perverted and then lost. Where energies in motion are undisciplined, where there is not a chalice that can contain the liquid fire of Love, mankind lose that Love.

And so they are happy for a day or for a week or for a year, but to be happy for eternity means that Love must be ensconced in a discipline that requires self-sacrifice. To continue to receive Love you must give Love. But Love is given in rhythm, in measured harmony, in increments of gratitude and a bursting forth of joy—a bursting forth that seems uncontrolled yet that proceeds from the bubbling fountain of the heart, the heart that knows that it is in that God-control of energy flow.

Understand, then, that when you discipline your energy, your supply, your expression, the hours of your day, your service to life, you are increasing your capacity to release Love. The more you are disciplined the stronger are the grids of consciousness. And to have a strong consciousness, as strong sinews, enables you to balance megatons of the light-force that you call Love.

Alas, so many are destined to carry the pink flame.

So many have incarnated on the Third Ray who are my chelas although they know it not. And they are in walks of life where they are expressing that creativity of Love in various ways.

But because on Terra there is such difficulty on the part of lifestreams in their handling of the currents of Love, many who should be masters of the flame are now in states of degradation, having perverted that flame. Thus their bodies are in states of disintegration and their minds are filled with foul spirits and the mutterings of those spirits.

Because Love is such a powerful force, precious ones, its abuse results in a very severe karma and a deprivation of life and the life-force. Therefore, you see, all of the science of the Aquarian age, given at the hand of the alchemist Saint Germain, is channeled to mankind as the flame of God-Love. For out of Love is the fulfillment of the Mother flame of every invention, every aspect of Divine Reality that is waiting to be lowered into manifestation through the creative genius of many among you and many among mankind.

Unfortunately, due to the educational systems of the world and the equation of certain mass concepts and certain omissions of concepts that ought to be taught from childhood, mankind have a misunderstanding of native genius and they are not taught of the talents of the LORD given to each one, nor are they taught how to release those talents and those flames of their innate God reality. People feel a sense of worthlessness and that only the few have the ability to invent and to create.

But I am here to tell you that locked in the heart of every one of you is a unique idea of Love that you can bring forth for the benefit of your fellow man and the progress of the culture of the Divine Mother. It may be an invention, it may be a poem, it may be a geometric design, but it is a gift which only you can bring forth. Unfortunately, many of you have held that gift in your heart for a succession of embodiments simply because no one has told you that you could release it, that you could bring it forth, that you are beings of ultimate creativity.

Why, creativity is the nature of God—your Father, your Mother! If God be creative, then you are creative. In your hands, in your eyes, in the movement of energies through you there is creative flow. And if you have the discipline here below you can realize beautiful thoughtforms in Mater [Matter]. You can release those things that are not for profit nor for the trade and merchandising in the world that are here today and gone tomorrow. But you can release something of enduring worth, a pearl of great price, something that will transcend the fads of the times and move across the centuries as a permanent contribution to the race of mankind.

And so, as I looked upon you in analyzing what my message should be, it was first of all to tell you that the art of living Love is to be creative. And the art of being creative is to be self-disciplined. And so now I have given you an entirely new reason to be self-disciplined—not because if you sin you will die, not if you sin you will be punished, but simply because if you are disorganized (and this is a sin against the order of the cosmos), if you are slovenly in your personal habits, if you allow yourself to be moved by every little current and every little sway, you will lose the fires of Love that will give you the greatest enjoyment of your life, the fulfillment of your creative destiny.

Now self-discipline becomes a point of enlightened self-interest. To move toward the fulfillment of your divine blueprint and your divine plan can be accomplished in the greatest beauty and joy of the fire of Love if you will only take me into your daily invocations and give generously of the "Introit to the Holy Christ Flame" so that you can receive directly from your Christ Self the impartations of genius that are native to the "droplet of identity"—and this is what you are in this vast ocean of God's being.

To come into union with the Christ flame is to move with Love.

Why cannot you walk the earth as Christed ones? What is hindering your manifestation of the Christ? Only the ignorance, the banality, and the sleep of the ages; only because your billboards and your media are not constantly telling you that you can become the Christ. They tell you other things and you fulfill them out of the hypnotism of the mass consciousness.

Well, I tell you, the media were given to mankind as a means of disciplining self, selfhood, and of releasing to mankind the messages of the Ascended Masters, the Elohim, and the angelic hosts.

Can you imagine if every time you turned on the television set the announcer said, "You can become the Christ"! You would begin to believe it. It would become a common fact—no longer startling or astounding. Well, turn on the television set of your inner being, of your etheric body, tune in to the teachers in the retreats of the Ascended Masters and hear these teachers as they teach classes in Ascended Master law.

Here I am releasing an opportunity for you to realize that there is an invention right within you already functioning, a means of contacting through the etheric body—by a mechanism and an electronic frequency far above the physical plane—the octaves of the Ascended Masters.

The Ascended Masters have retreats on the etheric plane, do they not? This you know. You also know that you have an etheric body. You also know things equal to the same thing are equal to each other. If you have an etheric body, you have a body that is functioning at the frequency of the Ascended Masters and their retreats. You have been told that your soul, using the vehicle of the etheric body, can journey to those retreats while your physical temple is at rest.

Well, then, since there is in reality no time and space, realize that you can be at any moment of the hour or day in the presence of your teacher. You can be in that retreat through your etheric body because there is no time or space at that plane. And you are where you will to be, where you think you are, where you feel you are.

It simply takes the practice of projecting the mind's eye to that physical point, that geographical location in time and space that is the coordinate of the retreat which is on the etheric plane. And then, by an inner key which I will allow you to receive from your own Christ Self, you can be transported in frequency, in consciousness, through the ear and the eye and a congruency of your chakras with the Ascended Masters to their inner retreats. And so, you see, creativity can flow, flow, and flow through you.

There are so many simple truths that ought to be broadcast across the radio waves. I am delighted to hear the "Hail Mary" coming forth, entering the atmosphere. And do you know that the elementals (Nature spirits, beings of fire, air, water, and earth) are tuning in their radio sets to play that "Hail Mary" and to give it with the Mother of the Flame and the sons and daughters of the flame as that recording is played each morning?

Do you know, then, that the elementals rejoice to see the media, the airwaves, used by the frequencies of the Ascended Masters, for they know that this will lead to their freedom, to the resurrection and the life within them whereby one day there will be imparted to them that threefold flame which will be the gift of immortal Life?

And so, let the waves of the air, let the plane of the mind conduct now that which is in the Mind of God that is transferred to and through your mind.

So let us have an experiment, for do you know that my pink cape is lined in green? And I am a scientist of the first order, and you need not relegate me to the exclusive corner of being an artist. For I am a scientist as well as an artist, and I rejoice that both faculties have been given into my hand by the Great Logos.

And so, let our experiment be the transfer of frequencies through the lobes of the brain and through the mental body. Let there be a transfer through your minds by the momentum of my Love that is God's Love, by the momentum of the emerald ray of precipitation—yes, let there be a transfer of energy of God's Mind to all minds on the planet and to the mental belt. And let there be a permanent recording in that belt this hour of the geometry of Love.

The geometry of Love is the art of living Love according to the sacred science, the science that was taught by Melchizedek, king of Salem and priest of The Most High God—the science that is practiced by artists and artisans of the Spirit.

So let the chalice that was released many years ago as a thoughtform now be given here below as a chalice for the mental body, as a chalice for the mental belt. And let that chalice be for the elixir of Love. Let the chalice be a disciplined forcefield given to you at my hand and yet which you yourself must fashion. For this chalice will not remain with you unless you reinforce it by daily application to the discipline of the flame, specifically with calls to the white-fire core made with Serapis Bey and the ascension flame. For this chalice is composed of ascension fire.

As water seeks its own level, so the flame of perfection seeks its own level. And since the level of mankind's consciousness is at the level of imperfection, all that is perfect that is lowered into form must either be reinforced each twenty-four hours by those in embodiment or, if it is not, it will return to the higher octaves.

You might say, then, that this is a decay rate in reverse, for, of course, perfection does not decay, it simply withdraws. Particle by particle, then, the chalice will return to the level of your Christ flame unless by invocations to that Christ flame you continually reinforce in the physical octave the atoms and molecules of fiery light that compose the chalice.

Now isn't this an interesting experiment? It's almost like going the opposite way on a moving conveyer belt. If you don't keep moving and keep decreeing, you will lose the ground that you have gained. And that is almost how it is prior to your ascension, as though you were on an uphill climb and as though that belt were continually moving, so that once you get on the belt you can never stop, for to stop is to move backwards with the automatic reverse trends of civilization that move down, down, down the Mount of Attainment.

And that is why progress is the Law of Being in infinity. Unless you are forever transcending yourself, you are not coming into the perfection of the Christ flame that is continually gathering more of itself, more of God's Self-awareness, continually becoming more and more of God until God in you is the All-in-all.

So I come to release creative fires. I could release much more. But I am limited, not by the laws of Cosmos but by karmic law—the law of your own being. For your own being has a law of its own, and each individual has made that law of himself according to himself and his own self-discipline.

And therefore, where there is the presence of sin, impurity, human consciousness, past records of karma that remain untransmuted, the law of your being is written that the ascended hosts cannot pour an increase of Love into your forcefield until you show that the Love which you have already received, albeit it is now misqualified energy, is or shall be in short order returned to the flame, purified, multiplied as an offering on the altar of the LORD.

In reality you are chalices filled with Love. But you have inverted those chalices and made of them the entire complement of the electronic belt—the record, the memory of all past misdoings contained in the subconscious at the level of the astral plane.

Now, then, if you think about it, all you have to do is turn that chalice that is upside down right-side up: let the sacred fire pour in, let the misuses be consumed, and you will have megatons of cosmic Love at your disposal and a new law of your being, the law of infinity won here below as you become the electrode for the sendings, not only of angels and elementals, but of mighty cosmic beings, Elohim, Mighty Victory, and the very God of very gods himself.

See, then, karma as the opportunity of God's own Love to fulfill his science and to learn the art of living Love.

Will you not think of me as you come across those jagged patterns and emotions in your world? Think of the rose of my heart and the delicate petals. Think, then, of taking that energy and fashioning the beautiful rose, even as the lotus grows in the swampland and out of the mud comes forth the beauty of the light of living fire.

So, you see, you can plant a garden that grows from the energies of the electronic belt. You can sow Love continuously. You have a reservoir of light on high in your causal body. It has been told to you. But I would remind you that every erg of energy that is transmuted in answer to your call is 'money' in your cosmic bank account. It is 'money' that can be drawn forth and multiplied for the bringing in of the kingdom of God.

Therefore, accept the challenge of the hour to go back and undo those misqualified energies that you left behind on the trail of life. Where you have walked away from karma, go back and fulfill that karma. Be the one who has dominion. Accept the challenge of life to liberate God's energy, to use that supply for the bringing into manifestation of the city foursquare.

If you have walked away from a situation, a karma, a marriage, a family, a job, a business where you should have fulfilled the transmutation of Love, you still have time in this life to go back and be the living presence of the Christ. And then you will see that to "go back" does not mean to compromise, but to go back means to take your stand with the sacred fire, to compel all human creation to move into that flame. And let the flame take that energy and place it upon the altar of the LORD. This is the cosmic honor flame as it is outlived in Love.

As I have watched and seen among mankind how there are some of such endurance and such long-suffering who take upon themselves perhaps the brutality, perhaps the insanity of another part of Life, uttering not a word of complaint nor having a feeling of self-pity— I have said these are they among mankind who are counted among the saints, for their way is the way of transmutation by Love. And they almost allow themselves, as it were, to be flagellated for the LORD. And this is not a disturbance of the psyche nor anything to do with masochism. It is in many cases a legitimate expression of selflessness.

And often in the outer consciousness these souls have not the least understanding except an inner conviction to remain. They have the staying power of Love. And by allowing themselves to be the forcefield on which there is outworked certain energies of the mass consciousness, they win their immortal freedom by the flame of Love. And so, then, I would give you this understanding of a path—a path that is won through sacrifice, through selflessness.

There is also the path of God-Justice and the flame that refuses to allow itself to be trampled upon by the human consciousness. This, too, is the legitimate stand. You see, when you are a pillar of fire and it appears to the world that injustice is being practiced against you, it is not always injustice from the level of the eye of God in the inner flame. For mankind do not see the action of transmutation whereby the flame infolding itself, involuting within, is drawing into itself that substance, even as your body is the buffer for that energy as it returns to God for its freedom in Love.

And therefore, you must weigh in the balance of the scales of Libra each decision of your life and you must come to know that the flame of God-Justice is the flame of God-Mastery that is a gift to you because you have conquered in Love and in the art of living Love.

Let the pyramid of Life now be upon you. And let the flame in the heart of the pyramid as the resurrection fire resurrect within you the full complement of Divine Love.

So I am your Chohan of the heart. And as the pink flame of the heart is the frequency of Love to the world, may I come into your heart at least on Monday to be received there in the chamber of the heart so that I might release to you at the hand of your Christ Self the energies of Love so necessary to reverse the course of the cancer that is eating away at the body of the world?

Do you not understand that all of the problems of the planet on a planetary scale can be transmuted in the flame of Love? This will take place more and more as you bring your consciousness into congruity with your Christ Self. In some of you that Christ Self is hovering perhaps an eighth of an inch or a hundredth of an inch from full congruency with all of your chakras and your mind and heart.

Call, then, for the transmutation of the blockages to the meshing of your consciousness with the consciousness of the Christ. Call for that Christ flame to press in and through you. Call for that Christ consciousness to take over your life, to purge you of all darkness.

I want your hands to be the hands of your Christ Self. I want your very skin to pulsate with the frequencies of the fire of that transparent one, that image of Life. I want you to be, through and through, the frequency of the Christ. For by that Love, the planet will be transformed and mankind will know that Love has returned. For your own Logos, your own self-awareness in the Christ consciousness is the fulfilling of Law as Above, so below. It is healing. It is science. It is victory. Love is the All-in-all.

As we have communed in Love, as we are one in Love, we cannot be separated. And therefore, consider your life a continuation of the flame that we have shared this day and know that I am aware of you, each one, intimately—of your problems, of your past, and of the potential of your future. No matter what you have been you can be better and life can be better and fuller from this moment on because you have accepted my Love.

Do not, then, be ashamed, for in actuality sin is not real. It is a forcefield of energy that must be consumed. But you have the flame of the sacred fire that is real, that is all of your reality. You have but to consign the past to that flame, your will to that flame, and let that flame reveal the firing of God's will within you.

So I am your Chohan of Love. Remember, I live in Love and I have, by the grace of God, at my command the energies of Love from the Great Central Sun for the healing of your heart, for the healing of your soul and your mind.

Won't you prepare yourself to receive more Love? Won't you invoke the fires of transmutation and come to my retreat and knock on the door and say, "O beloved Paul, here, I have transmuted another sphere of energy. I give it to you that I might receive God's Love"?

And I will take you by the hand and show you my castle. I will show you the works of art that have been brought forth by chelas unascended and ascended. And we will go through many rooms, and lastly I will take you to the room where there is that frame that hangs. In some cases it will be an empty frame, in some cases it will have a canvas in it. It will be your frame, the frame of your identity waiting for you to bring forth the genius of your soul. And when you see that frame, if it is empty, you will want to fill it.

And so I will take you to that place, "The Atelier," where you can work with other artisans who are learning the art of living Love by the discipline of the hand

and the discipline of expression so that you can draw the image of your own Christ-perfection. And when it is the best that you have to offer, it will be placed in your frame.

And when you come again before that frame after many months of purging and self-purification, you will say undoubtedly, "Beloved Paul, may I have another opportunity to express my Christhood, to draw the image of myself? For I have perceived a new aspect of that image, and I would like to have this, my best offering, now placed in my frame." And, of course, you will have the opportunity.

Of course, those who come for the first time and find the canvas in the frame are those who have come before in other lifetimes or perhaps in this one. And you do have a record of your self-awareness there, and you may or may not be pleased with that record.

A certain few among you have been artists in other civilizations on Atlantis and in South America, and you do have in your frame an expression truly worthy of the Christ. In some cases, you have lost that memory. In other cases, you have retained it. And so you will rejoice to see the continuity of your soul's expression and how you have been fulfilling a path of destiny for so, so many incarnations. And you will say, "I am grateful for these many opportunities to perceive the Christ, but now I would enter the wholeness of immortal spheres."

And so, your time is coming to an end when time and space will be no more of your experience, but only infinity here and now, eternally the expression of your soul's creativity.

I am, then, the discipline of the white fire. I am the science of the emerald ray. And I am the filling of the cup of consciousness with Love's creative fires. I am the fulfillment of the law of your Divine Being.

I am Paul, a teacher of Love.

October 14, 1974
Los Angeles

Ensouling Frédéric Bartholdi's statue is a Cosmic Being who so exemplifies the God-quality of Liberty that she is called the Goddess of Liberty. Last embodied on Atlantis where she erected her retreat, the Temple of the Sun, in the area where Manhattan Island now is, she is the Spokesman for the Karmic Board, better known as the Mother of Exiles. Once the western gate of teeming Atla, Manhattan is today the "golden door" for thousands who would yet immigrate to the land of the western Sun. Upon the sinking of Atlantis, the physical Temple of the Sun was destroyed. Its etheric counterpart remains a major world center focusing the flames of the Twelve Hierarchies of the Sun. Mother of Paul the Venetian, Lady Liberty is the Keeper of the Flame of Liberty on behalf of America and the "I AM" Race. Her motto "I AM Gratitude in Action," she says, is the true meaning of immigration.

She is also the guardian of Paul's focus of the Threefold Flame of Liberty transferred from his retreat in southern France to the Washington Monument, September 30, 1962.

The Beauty and Truth of Love

O Lord, thou who art the author and the finisher of our faith, I am come in the flame of Love to address thy sons and daughters. I am come to infuse them with the love of my heart that is the foundation and the culmination of the beauty of Life.

O Lord, I pray to thee that thou wilt place within this message thy message of the beauty of Love. I place upon the altar the beauty of my heart, the beauty of my soul and of my ascension and of all that I am. Almighty One, let it be transferred by thy Love to these chelas of Love this night.

Most gracious ladies and gentlemen, I greet you in my love for your life and for the evolution of your soul on the path of Love. The initiations of Love and all that it entails are taught at my retreat, the Château de Liberté. And I call you to my retreat to be representatives of Love to earth. I call the students of Summit University, all Keepers of the Flame, and all who love Love just for the sake of loving Love.

I call you because of my concern for the little children and the distortions of Love which are being placed upon them even from the moment of conception and certainly from the hour of birth. I am concerned for the disregard of the science of Love which God himself has formulated in the vast panorama of Nature and in all with which he has surrounded man and woman for the fulfillment of their love.

I am concerned with the distortion of both form and formlessness. For instance, the work of many modern artists is an attempt to portray on canvas formlessness. Indeed, God embodies the quality of formlessness. And it is true that a transfer of the flame of formlessness can be made to the canvas.

But, precious ones, the lowering into manifestation of this dispensation of art, which ought to be the art of the new age, has been set aside by the coming into manifestation of the false hierarchs of the Third Ray. These false prophets of Love have infused the consciousness of today's artists, for the most part, with an awareness of the astral plane and the endless miasma of portrayal of the imitation of formlessness, which is not an imitation at all but a counterfeit of that creation out of the Mind of God.

The fascination with horror and with the ugly is a symptom of the psychology of the age and the devastation of the soul that lives in separation from the Mother and in rebellion against the Mother.

With the forcing of the chakras by the taking of violent drugs, the Holy Spirit energies of Love have been taken by force, and the forcefield of the Holy Spirit—as Alpha and Omega (the plus, the minus polarity of the sacred fire) within the chakras—has in many cases been torn or shattered.

And thus, Pandora's box has been opened, and the open door is through the chakras of those whose consciousness is half within the physical plane and half within the astral. And the juxtaposition of these planes at obtuse angles has created a warping of Life that is not the warp and woof of creation but the absolute distortion of the flame of living Love.

I trust that you well realize that I know that I am risking my popularity in being truthful this night. But did you know that the brothers of our retreat wear the emerald band and that our understanding of Truth is that it is the other side of Beauty? For to us, art must convey the truth of God and the truth of Life, and this is true realism. For realism is the Reality of God and not the unreality that is continually changing and that passes away as transient.

That which is portrayed on canvas today is in many instances no better than the sewer itself. The sewers of life and of the astral plane are being poured out from the palette to the canvas and from the canvas to homes of all classes. Hanging on the walls of the American home, such paintings are the foundation for the perver-

sion of the consciousness of the Christ and the Buddha
within the Holy Child.

As you well know, the fallen ones who perverted the
great civilizations which once existed on the continent
of Africa did so through the perversion of the art form,
through the perversion of the Love Ray.

It seems that the children of light and even the sons
and daughters of God have neglected this one great
truth—that beauty is in the eye of the beholder and that
as a man thinketh, so is he. And as a man thinketh *in his
heart,* so is the transfer of that thought to the canvas of
life through the vision of the All-Seeing Eye of God
(focused through the third-eye 'chakra' at the brow).

In order to portray beauty, one must have a vision
of beauty. And so, you see, we use the emerald ray—first
the vision, then the transfer of the vision to the canvas
by the technique of the Master Artist himself.

I am a chela of Almighty God. And Almighty God
has tutored me, heart and head and hand, in the way of
transferring to the canvas, even in the ascended octaves,
the most magnificent manifestations of himself.

Therefore, for the clearing of the stream of the
flame of Love within the heart, we must work backwards
and forwards. We must clear the vision, for the vision is
polluted. And the polluted stream comes from impure
motive and the perversion of Love. And so, we work
from the without to the within and from the within to
the without.

We must mop up the mud of mankind's misqualified substance in all of the chakras. And I tell you, precious ones, you can get along fairly well without the functioning of a number of your chakras, for instance, when you perform tasks such as driving your car. But if your windshield is covered with mud or ice or snow, you can go nowhere before clearing your windshield. And so you carry implements with you and you use your windshield wipers.

But I tell you that the sons and daughters of God are not using their windshield wipers for the clearing of the third eye and the seat-of-the-soul chakra for the penetration of that which is real. And if they did, they would be here by the tens of thousands, for they would see clearly the great work of light and the release of light of the Great White Brotherhood.

But the false prophets of Love have seen to it that the windshields of the children of the light have remained muddied. And therefore, the vision of their souls is retained inside of a very narrow room and a narrow space. And they cannot see beyond that narrow space or beyond the immediate presence of the false prophet of the arts of Love.

It is important, then, that you become the ones who clean the windshields for mankind in order that this magnificent focus of the All-Seeing Eye of God,* which I myself have guarded for you and for the Mother and her children, shall now become the focal point for the

---

*A large painting of the All-Seeing Eye of God by Charles Sindelar secured as a most beautiful and powerful focus of God's abiding Vision for the creation.

most glorious equalization and manifestation in form of that God-Vision which is the foundation of victory. For right within the very eye of God is the vision of the fullness of his manifestation within the City Foursquare.

Therefore, intensify the calls to Cyclopea. And include in your calls to Cyclopea a call to me that with that vision will come the joy of beholding the beauty of God.

How sordid life is when mankind prefer the ugly to the beautiful. It is because they are uncomfortable in the presence of true Divine Beauty—because their very auras are the ugly manifestation of ugly thoughts and feelings. And the heavenly patterns and the Divine Image are an offense to their lesser sense of selfhood.

Let us educate them and elevate them to the inner standard of the Universal Christ. And let us pray, then, for the little children. For the fallen ones know that these little children will grow up and come into their own to take their place where they will be called of God to carry the torch of freedom which you now carry. And if their perception of the Love flame within them is warped by all of these distortions of Truth and Beauty, then I tell you, they will not have in mind and heart the necessary chalice or grid or forcefield to be the instrument of the arts of Love in the day at hand, expressing Truth and the inner symmetry of Beauty in design, architecture, fashion and that symbolism which is embedded in advertising and the communications media.

The children of earth are being mercilessly sub-jected to a completely thought-out plot of the fallen angels in their midst to hypnotize their minds, to hyp-notize the subconscious. And they combine the distor-tion of art with the distortion of music—music, the God-intended manifestation of the All-Seeing Eye and that which carries the flame of Beauty in formulas of sound and rhythm or mantras of the soul—yantras of the Spirit.

Combining music, then, with true art as formulas of the Word, there is the double stimulus to the soul to go back to the white-fire core of the Central Sun and to contact the very heart of Beauty itself. And so, you see, as you combine music and art in your own meditations, you find the inspiration of worlds within worlds which you once knew but which have been cut off from you by the outer appearance world and senses dulled thereby—undiscriminating, untutored.

Let us proclaim, then, once and for all, that for the purpose of the geometry and the mathematics of build-ing the intricate patterns of the soul and the conscious-ness, there is nothing that can replace classical art and classical music of the highest order.

The days are long gone when the chelas of the Ascended Masters were concerned with popularity. Let your homes be filled, then, with the music that has been brought forth by the chelas of the Ascended Masters in all past ages. And let your children be filled with the sound of this music which transfers to them in the Mat-ter flame inner keys of their own causal bodies—fohatic keys that release the sacred fire to heart and cell and chakra and every brain molecule by sound and imagery.

Do you know, precious ones, that the great musicians have actually tapped the causal bodies of the saints and the lightbearers to bring forth that "music of the spheres"? And the "spheres" of which they are speaking are the spheres of the causal bodies of ascended beings and of unascended souls of light. And so, in the great symphonies and piano concertos, the little children often hear music which they heard when their souls were cradled in their causal bodies of light. Now, it is this Beauty and this Truth of the higher octaves that must be before the children from infancy so that they will know the voice of inner conscience and of the Almighty and of their mentors, the Ascended Masters, when they come of age.

As there is a dearth in the land of souls who will give their life for Beauty and Truth, for Love itself that is unselfed, I ask you to come into the awareness of the living flame of Love as it was set forth in poetry and in prose by Saint John of the Cross.[1]

Learn what it means to pursue the Beloved—the Holy Christ Self who is the "hidden man of the heart." Learn what it means to be empassioned with the freedom of the soul to love God and to love him in every part of Life. Let the Holy Spirit that comes to your heart through the Third Ray be for the refinement of your appreciation of the deeper mysteries sealed, until you love enough, in the secret chamber of the heart. As you learn to appreciate Beauty, precious ones, you become sensitive to fine detail, to workmanship, to the crafts, and to the culture of the Mother.

Life is not intended to be gross or crude or dull or dense. But it is intended to be in Power, in Wisdom, and in Love—and in the delicate flame of the zephyrs and the strong winds of winter—the most magnificent release of light whereby the thousand strings of the harp of your soul might be played in order that your inner ear might appreciate a thousand chords of God's Cosmic Consciousness.

When children have placed before them from birth the images of lesser or incomplete forms, animals having human traits and sympathies, or gross features, comic strips, cartoons, and films which are made in a distorted (sometimes hideous) portrayal of life that is unreal, they do not develop an appreciation for the qualities of the saints—qualities that build character and self-esteem, opening channels for independent, creative thought stimulating new solutions to old problems.

Do you know that when little children gaze upon the paintings of the saints, of Jesus and his lambs, that their souls see beyond the painting into the inner octaves of light? For the little ones do retain that connection with the inner spheres whence they descended into form. And the inner world is so real to them that they do not often speak of it because they think, in their innocence, that everyone around them has the same perception. And it is only after three or four years of incarnation that they begin to lose that ability to see through the eyes of the soul beyond the veil.

But alas, in this hour we are finding that that soul faculty of perception and penetration beyond the veil is being destroyed from the earliest months of life and the physical senses are not being developed in conjunction with the development of the inner senses of the soul. When the physical senses are not developed and the spiritual sensitivities are not stimulated, then the relationship between the inner and the outer development is practically nil.

The inner development of the soul must parallel the outer, and vice versa. And therefore, if there are not manifestations surrounding the child that key the inner development of the spiritual centers called chakras, then that development will be bypassed, and it may not take place in that given lifetime—the cycles missed may be beyond recall.

And so, you see, the keys to Cosmic Consciousness must surround the child in the earliest years. The period of gestation through the age of seven affords the most creative hours of the child's entire incarnation. It is during this period that the life patterns are set.

And so, beloved ones, although you know this law, I repeat it tonight because I desire to bring to the very fore of your attention the fact that civilization in America and in every nation on earth is being destroyed in this day and age by the fallen ones' manipulation of art forms from their positions of power both in and out of embodiment. *I say it is being destroyed and I mean every word of it!*

The downward spirals of darkness come from that which contacts the eye of every single individual in embodiment. Look at the billboards. Look at the newspapers. Look at the magazines. Look at the use of motion pictures and tell me how often you see a pure, undiluted, unperverted thoughtform of the Ascended Masters' octave. So often there is beauty portrayed. But that beauty in Nature or in man and woman is perverted because it is used to sell sex and death and cigarettes and liquor and every form of violation of the chakras.

And therefore, as the souls of individuals cry out to drink in Beauty and the only Beauty they see is in association with perversion, they therefore take in both. And thus, there is the magnetism of Beauty to which the soul is receptive, and upon the tail of it comes the trigger of the thoughtform of black magic which, as you know, is the misuse of the science of imaging, or projecting upon the screen of life through visualization a desired manifestation.

People do this all the time. They simply see themselves accomplishing their goals and then they set about realizing them in a practical manner. This is "eye-magic" as the "I" images the will or intent of the soul.

The misuse of this science for factors of control and the manipulation of people's tastes, preferences and decision-making through advertising or any means becomes, as you can see, a violation of the All-Seeing

Eye of God, who holds the immaculate concept for the whole of creation. This violation affects everyone at the level of the third eye and seat-of-the-soul chakra—even as the malpractice of this science of imaging involves the misuse of these chakras by its practitioners.

This misuse of the fundamental principles of the law of precipitation, or alchemy, is indeed a form of black magic which individuals unwittingly practice upon themselves even as they are the hapless, unsuspecting victims of such abuses through the media.

How long can this continue? It is gaining momentum. It is a downward-moving spiral. And today the art culture that was born out of the drug culture has become a style and a way of life that has left its mark on everything, even to the clothes and accessories you wear.

And that which was once shocking is no longer shocking because the senses are dulled, the ears are dulled. Even the physical ears are no longer as perceptive of sound as they were a decade ago. And thus, the inner ear listening to the inner voice is also burdened, even as it is stunted, by the absence of proper stimuli in early development.

Precious ones, I could go on and on. But I come upon the sweep of love of Lady Venus, of Chamuel and Charity and the great love which you have brought to this conference.

As the Lord of the Third Ray, I desire to make practical to you the science of Love, which is connected with the science of vision, in order to make you understand that living the way of Love is going out and taking the action of the Holy Spirit and moving into society and challenging those conditions that are the very destruction of souls and that are making inroads into a way of life that even in this hour of the Dark Cycle (noted for the accelerated return of personal and planetary karma) could be a way of light and beauty.

I appeal to you, then, on behalf of the children of earth and on behalf of souls of light whose vision is being tampered with in this very hour. Will you not, then, make the fiats of Love with me that there be the shattering of the forcefields of darkness and of the veils of illusion and of the membrane of density's distortions that cover the all-seeing eye, the third eye, of the beloved souls of light on earth?

I call, then, in the name of Almighty God, to the entire Spirit of the Great White Brotherhood. I call to Saint Germain for assistance.

I call to Freedom for assistance. And I, Paul, stand before the Lords of Karma this day and I make my plea for freedom—freedom for the souls of lightbearers from the perversions of Vision, of Beauty and of Truth, freedom from the perversions of the beauty of the chakras of God in their body temples.

In the name of the Mother, I send forth the lightning of the Mind of God to shatter the forcefield of human bondage! And in the name JESUS CHRIST I say: Shatter the forcefield! Shatter the forcefield of human bondage!

In the name of the Christ, I, Paul, demand the binding of the false hierarchs of Love by the Archangels of Love, Chamuel and Charity! Let them be bound this hour. Let blue lightning from the Great Central Sun explode as the fireworks of the Fourth of July. And let the exploding and the imploding of light be for the shattering of forcefields out of the depths of Death and Hell that are spawned by sinister forces of anti-Beauty, anti-Love, and anti-Truth.

Blaze forth the light! (repeated 20 times)

Beloved ones, I would explain to you this element of the Science of the Spoken Word. When you give a series of decrees or fiats for a specific purpose and you are tackling the entrenched forcefields of darkness that have existed for thousands of years as an astral belt of effluvia surrounding planet Earth created by the mass consciousness of human hate and hate miscreations, you need a more than ordinary science and expression of that Word of the LORD for the protection of your soul as you ascend Bethany's hill with Jesus.

When you give a concentrated series of fiats such as this action of "Blaze forth the light!" or any short decree for a specific action, if you will give it in rhythm and continue to give it and visualize the Holy Spirit moving against the entrenched darkness of the earth in all areas where Love is perverted, even in the areas of pornography, prostitution, gambling, organized crime, drug trafficking, child molestation and child abuse, you will do much to assist the hosts of light to alleviate the suffering and burdens of the planet and the children of light.

All of these areas, through the perversion of Vision, are become the perversion of the culture of the Mother, the body of the Mother, the innocence of the Mother and the Child. To tackle them you must be prepared to grapple with the most vicious forces of the astral plane. I tell you, precious ones, to defend Love is to take on the sinister force itself. Do not marvel, then, when you are met with opposition. For the greatest of saints have described that opposition to Love and the coming of demons and discarnates moving against this mighty work of the ages—the restoration of Divine Love to a planet and her people.

It is time, then, for those who have learned of the armour of Archangel Michael and the use of his flaming blue sword and of the action of the Great Blue Causal Body to stand forth in the flame of wisdom and wise dominion and call upon the Trinity to tackle now all that is pitted by Death and Hell against the pure Love of Father-Mother God, of twin flames, of Mother and Child, of Guru and chela and the youth of the world.

So, before you begin, give this call to the Captain of the Lord's Hosts at home or in your car:

Lord Michael before, Lord Michael behind,
Lord Michael to the right, Lord Michael to the left,
Lord Michael above, Lord Michael below,
Lord Michael, Lord Michael wherever I go!

I AM his Love protecting here!
I AM his Love protecting here!
I AM his Love protecting here! (3x)

Precious hearts, the attack is on Love—Divine Love blazing from the hearts of God's people as the nucleus of the new age. Therefore, say with me, in the name of Almighty God, and visualize the great blue sphere from Alpha and Omega—

Blaze forth the Love! (repeated 22 times)

Use this technique, precious ones. It is for the transmutation of energy fields of darkness. By the rhythm of the sphere of Love, from your causal body you will invoke an action of the blue lightning angels of the First Ray serving under Archangel Michael who, by the power of the will of God, will break down forcefields of misqualified substance so that the violet flame angels and the legions of Astrea* can come back again and again for a whirling action of the sacred fire as they hold the balance for your soul's liberation from all evil on the First and the Seventh Rays.

You have been told of the blue lightning wielded by the Lord's hosts and its shattering effect upon negative forcefields most dangerous to society—even toxic waste and radioactive fallout. And indeed, the cosmic blue lightning of purity is an action of sacred fire incomparable. Now, coupled with the sphere of Love and the

*the Starry Mother who wields her circle and sword of blue flame for the exorcism of possessing demons of addictions of every kind including the suicide entity

relentless Love of the decreers of the Word, you will see a magnificence of Love never known before and a breaking down of all of those vortices of darkness spawned by the fallen angels which are pitted against the souls who are making their way to the light of their Mighty I AM Presence.

I am Paul. I seal you now in the third eye. It is a seal of Beauty, a kiss of Love. And it is my hand cleaning the windshield of your consciousness.

AUM… Ma Ray.

July 3, 1977
Pasadena, California

Temple of Luxor, eastern Thebes

Superimposed upon the physical temple at Luxor is Serapis' etheric retreat. Here initiates pursue the ascension disciplines under the tutelage of Serapis and the 144 instructors who work with him in preparing candidates for the alchemical marriage. When the adept has passed the last of the rituals of immortality, he is led to the flame room where the ascension flame pulsates in the rhythm of Life. Surrounded by ascended brothers and attending seraphim in a wide circle, he takes his place in the center of the temple as the flame of Alpha descends from the ceiling and the flame of Omega rises from the floor, freeing him forever from the round of rebirth.

Lord of the Fourth Ray

Initiation of the
Base-of-the-Spine Chakra

Retreat:	Luxor, Egypt
Vibration:	White, Crystal
Gemstone:	Diamond, Pearl, Zircon, Quartz Crystal
Quality:	PURITY DISCIPLINE JOY
Gift:	Working of Miracles
Day:	Friday

Serapis Bey Receives a Neophyte into His Mystery School

The Path of the Ascension
Is the Path of Love

The path of the ascension is the path of Love. It is love and the dream of love fulfilled. The disciplines for the initiations of the ascension into Higher Consciousness can be borne only by love—by the heart and the soul so filled with love for God, the Great Guru, that it will endure unto the end, the end of the cycles of human consciousness. The Path is straight and narrow, as you have heard. The climb is over rigid heights, scaling cliffs jagged, over precipice and abyss into the high road, into the mountains of the Himalayas.

Souls are called and impelled by Love—the love of the mountaineers, the love of the Elohim who have anchored their focuses in the heights of the mountains of the earth. Love and Love alone is the key to overcoming. For God is Love. And where selfishness lurks, there will be compromise, there will be the moment's hesitation and the battle is lost, the moment of indecision when the idling of energy creates a gap in the spiraling and in the flow and the movement of God.

Therefore, in the hour of decision, in the moment when the question arises out of that human questioning to be or not to be on the path of initiation, we ask a question. For we are the hierarchs of Luxor, of the Retreat of the Ascension Flame. We guard the steely white, intense sacred fire that can be contained only by those who live in the purity of Love. And therefore, while you are engaged in your human questioning of the Guru, we ask the supreme question: How much do you love, how great is your love?

Is your love great enough to make the sacrifice for the overcoming, for the Path, for the cause of the Great White Brotherhood in order that others among mankind might also receive the Teachings, the Law, and the understanding of the fulfillment of the promise of Love? Faced with this question, the individual must either retreat into his old ways of the self-centered existence or come forth from that cocoon of selfishness and fly with the wings of the Spirit, the wings of Love that are the certain victory.

There is a key in the disciplines to Higher Consciousness. The key is not to become entangled in the labyrinth of human questioning and the fears and the doubts and specters of the night that haunt that labyrinth. You do not have to trace the meanderings of the carnal mind and the human consciousness through all of the levels of the subconscious in order to come to the knowledge of Truth, in order to come to Reality or to overcome in Love.

The key is not to be drawn by curiosity or a fascination with horror or a gluttony for the things of the senses, drawing you down into more and more astral experiences and psychic phenomena. The key—instead of taking a thousand steps through the astral plane—is to take one step into the arms of the I AM Presence, into the plane of the Christ Mind where the oneness and the wholeness of that Great Pyramid, the oneness and the wholeness, is the dissolving action.

Transcend your cycles! Do not follow those negative spirals round and round and round, down and down unto the death manifestation in the very crypt of the electronic belt. But with one invocation to the ascension fire, let that flame leap and arc from spiral to spiral, consuming on contact the debris. The flame is not linear; it need not travel over the lines of human creation. And so your soul, enveloped in the flame, also need not remain any longer in the consciousness that the only way out is through the labyrinth.

I say, transcend it! This means that in the moment when you would indulge your pettiness, your argumentation, your human nonsense, your dalliance in childishness, in that moment you instantly let go and you let God be the light that swallows you up in the victory of Love. And the Love that is your victory is your own love that is God made manifest within you.

And our God *is* the all-consuming fire of Love.

Love God enough so that you do not need to satisfy human desire. You do not have to appease the carnal mind and give it what it wants so that you will have a moment's peace, an hour's peace. You do not have to engage your energies in imperfection. As much as you think that it is sometimes necessary, I tell you that by meditating within—within the heart and upon the threefold flame of Life—by meditating upon the Presence and keeping that steady flow of energy of loving God arcing to him and his love returning, completing the whole of the two arcs as the two halves of the circle, *you can transcend the former cycles.*

If you can sustain your attention upon your I AM Presence and upon the light, you will receive the energy necessary to deal with all outer circumstances (karma) and that without traveling through them in your emotions, in your mental concepts, in your memory, and in physical labor. Think, then, upon this. The disciplines for Higher Consciousness demand that you prove how it is that you can be in the world and yet not of this world.

And how is it so? To be the disciplined one, astute in the understanding of the Law and its counterfeit creation, the first step is to become as a little child. You must become the child of innocence before you can mature to the Christed man and the Christed woman. Do not, then, try to become the full Master of Galilee before you have traced the coils of God consciousness and of Christ consciousness which are lawfully yours to trace—not the labyrinth of the carnal mind, but the blueprint of the etheric path of initiation. And therefore, become as the little child.

I will now regress you in your soul awareness to that point of embryonic life of your consciousness of innocence, entering into that form of the tiny babe. Total trust and faith and hope and charity are yours. You have not hardened your heart, you have not hardened yourself to become a cynic in the world. Your skin is tender; it is not toughened by the failures of others. And so in the sweet perfume of your love of Mother and the Mother's love for you, you remember wholeness in God and this is all of your identity.

You are a babe in Christ. You are calm and serene, with the absolute conviction that your life is in God, that God is caring for you. And the most essential quality of becoming this tiny babe is to understand the quality of helplessness. When you are totally helpless, then you must allow God to work his work within you. You can truly say, as the child of Christ: "I of mine own self can do nothing. It is the Father in me which doeth the work."

You have a clear transparency, purity from the immaculate vision of the Cosmic Virgin. Immaculately conceived, you know no sin, you know no separation from God. You are in the womb of the Mother. You are surrounded by the waters of the living Word. You are at peace, and life is yours to conquer because you are God in manifestation.

Now you are ready for the disciplines whereby the babe will become the child, and the child as the Manchild will grow and wax strong in the teaching of the Lord. And by the time he is twelve, he will know the doctrine of the Ascended Masters and he will be discoursing in the temples.

And so you come out into outer manifestation, out of the inner womb into the outer womb. Now your habitation is a cosmos, a brave new world, a world filled with light and yet with shadows and darkness somehow as yet undefined to your precious soul. You come forth and you travel the cycles of your individual Cosmic Clock and you bow before the great initiators of Life, the solar hierarchies.

And each one gives to you the disciplines of the sacred fire: of God-power, God-love, and God-mastery, of God-control, God-obedience, God-wisdom, God-harmony, God-gratitude, God-justice, God-reality, God-vision, and God-victory. Your soul within those four lower bodies knows all of this teaching of the Cosmic Clock.[1] You have been close, so very close to the heartbeat of Mother, and through her heartbeat you have learned the cycles of the Father.

The little child in innocence begins to learn the ways of the world—a little fall and scrape, tears, and demands that cannot be fulfilled. And therefore, you learn to fulfill your own demands: the shaping of the feelings and of the mental body, the shaping of the mind, the memory, and the noble form—the form that is to house the spiritual fire of Life.

This little child—this little child born to be God.

As the veils of innocence are parted one by one and you mature in the understanding of the world as well as in the understanding of the Law, take care. Take care that you do not forget your Source and the fairies and the undines and the gnomes with whom you frolicked as a little one.[2] Take care that you do not forget the faces of angels who have tended your crib, who have watched over you. Take care that you do not forget that there are masterful beings who took you by the hand and walked with you safely through the places of danger.

There are few who will remind you, there are few who will know, for they have all been deprogrammed away from God into the ways of the world. And thus, if you retain your innocence of the little child, you will become the little child who leads all of the aspects of the creation into the knowledge of the Christ.

The little child is the leader of the Aquarian age— the little child within you, the little child now coming of age, not forgetting the Source, but coming into that oneness of balance, of discrimination, of learning, of mastering the studies necessary to function in this world and to be of service and to have the sacred labor.

You must not only become the little child to have the disciplines of Higher Consciousness, but you must also remain the little child. Better to be hurt again and again than to have the cynicism of the existentialists. Better to be taken advantage of than to mistrust your fellowman.

Better to live in Him and have your being in Christ and let the world have its ways than for you to steel your-self with a false set of armor that is not the tube of light, the holy innocence of white fire, but that is the mastering of deceit and intrigue, the mastering of a carnal ego, the mastering of all of its defenses, its indulgences, and all of its experiences which the fallen ones tell you you must have in order to distinguish light and darkness.

This is the first and fundamental Lie that is told to the child to take the child from the path of initiation: "Come and experience this, come and experience that. Taste and see, taste and know for yourself whether or not this is for you."

God has said that the little child in all innocence need not taste of the energy veil [temptations of illusory evil], need not partake of it or absorb it or become contaminated by it in order to know the Truth. And there are many saints, such as Saint Thérèse of Lisieux, who from early childhood, like Mother Mary and Jesus, have entered into the Holy of Holies and who have found the satisfactions of love in God and in his holy angels.

And those who have accepted that Lie and entered into the compromises of all of the things that are offered in the marts of the world are burdened today by a cross of their own making, a cross of their own karma, a cross that is the hatred of the Divine Mother in whose womb they live and move and have that being of light.

And therefore, the little child maturing to become the master in the way, to carry the cross of world karma, cannot take upon himself that cross of world karma because he is too busy carrying his own cross of selfishness and self-indulgence. And so, many are not equipped to enter into the age of responsibility of the sons and daughters of God, to bear the sins of the world as Christ did when he hung upon that cross—the cross, not of his own human karma, mind you, but the cross of the karma of the race.

In every age there must be souls who are willing to bear a certain portion of the weight of world karma. In these times it is by and large elemental life who bear that weight, for those among mankind who care at all to carry a little extra baggage are few and far between.

Those who love are the disciplined ones who can walk through the narrow streets of the cities of the Middle East where every form of temptation lurks and every aspect of the sins of human consciousness is displayed in these marts.

To walk through or to tarry and explore?

It is one thing to enjoy a shopping trip; it is another to become addicted to going shopping and to examining the manifestations of human consciousness when you ought to be meditating upon the light that burns within the shops of your very own chakras—the shops of the Buddha and the jewels of the Buddha that are in the jewel shop.

Precious ones of fire, discipline means to withdraw energy (and with it your attention) from its encasement in the tomb of Matter. It means to sacrifice the flow of energy into lesser creations and to consecrate it to the one flame of Life. You have the pearl of great price! The pearl is the symbol of your causal body, and the layer upon layer of the pearl are the spheres of consciousness that you have built layer upon layer around the central core of the I AM Presence.

This iridescent mother-of-pearl is worth all; and therefore the wise man will go and sell all that he has for the one pearl, the one pearl of Cosmic Consciousness. Its discipline demands that you let go—let go of all of these involvements and realize that from day to day you never know when your soul (bereft of the physical body) will find itself cast on another shore in the mental plane, in the astral plane (God forbid), or in the etheric octave.

If you were the Messenger, you would be in the position to observe day by day those who are born and those who are dying, those who come into the physical plane and those who leave. It is a vast parade of souls taking incarnation and moving on. But the disciplines for Higher Consciousness, if it is to be retained, must be proven in the physical plane. And therefore it is the admonishment of the hierarchy of Luxor to make time and space count, for they are the crucible whereby you prove your God-mastery and the alchemy thereof.

You require that bowl. You require that matrix that you might fill it with fire. Little progress is made in other planes; for here in Matter—in the physical aspect of Matter—you made your karma, and here you must balance it. And therefore, let none think that they will live forever and forever in these four lower bodies. They are but vehicles of consciousness which are loaned to you, as all of the energy of God is on loan to you, that you might prove the mastery of free will.

I come to you, then, to give you the concept of discipline. You can read in the *Ascension Dossier* and in other documents and dictations from the flame of purity what are the testings of the soul. You can read what are these disciplines. You can read the life of Jesus and Gautama and perceive very clearly the path to the ascension on the seven and the five rays.*

But I would come in the mystery of Love. I would come in the mystery of the cross of Love that is a cross of obedience to the inner law of Life. It is a cross of fire. It is the cross of the monstrance that was used by Clare, holding it up as that sacred vessel of the eucharistic Body of Christ to turn back the Saracens who came warlike in their hatred to tear down the city. And you remember other accounts of saints who have held the Host before the oncoming hordes and armies, who have held up the image of the Virgin Mary.

And so your cross of Love is a cross of white fire. It is a cross of energy which, when it is exalted in consciousness by consecration, reverses the tide of human hatred, reverses the darkness of the night, and is your certain protection on the path of Love.

Let your burden be light! Let the cross of your karma become a cross of intense devotion and love. And let your burden be light, moment by moment. May you sense that the victory of Love is in correct seeing. And if you have

*See note on the cosmic clock, page 559, col. 2.

the vision of the diamond of the All-Seeing Eye of God, the fiery core of Truth, you will see and know that each succeeding burden is yours in your hand to place in the crucible that it might be transmuted and refined as the gold of Love, and gold as God consciousness.

Let the cross be transmuted daily. Let your cross be a cross of light so that even while you are balancing your karma, you may carry the weight of world karma in this Dark Cycle which is manifesting now under the hierarchy of Leo, causing mankind to enter into new lows of selfishness, thoughtlessness, carelessness, a spirit of ingratitude that is actually spiritual/material blindness, a failure to see the gifts and the joys and the abundance of the Creator. And carelessness is a failure to love as He loves, as Mother loves, as the innocent child loves while it is yet in the womb.

I ask you, then, as you make your petitions to the Lords of Karma during this conference, as you write your letters for dispensations, preparing to receive the dispensations that will be written from the Royal Teton Retreat that will be read to you by the Goddess of Liberty on the Fourth of July—as you write your petitions asking for dispensations, asking for light, will you also tell the Lords of Karma, in the name of your own Christ Self, that you are applying to carry a portion of world karma, a portion of the substance of the Dark Cycle, so that earth can have a reprieve, so that mankind, especially the people of America, can have an opportunity to know the Law and to fortify themselves for the victory?

I tell you, as I survey the world scene in all of the dreadfulness of that which is taking place—so much of it unknown to you—that it is pathetic how your leaders have deprived you of the knowledge of what is actually happening in secret diplomacy, in international politics, and even in your state legislatures.

As I survey all of this, I see as the one hope that path of initiation that leads to the ascension and the teachings necessary for the Path—the teachings of the Great White Brotherhood. I see as the one hope the white-fire core of the Keepers of the Flame who will carry the teaching and go near and far to disseminate that teaching, to talk and walk with mankind in the way until they awake from their sleep and begin the path of enlightenment in Buddha.

The one hope, then, is that somehow in a cosmic interval, a cosmic dispensation of the holding of karma and the holding of time and space, that millions will come into a new devotion to Christ and Buddha, will come into a devotion to meditation and the invocations given in the knowledge of the Science of the Spoken Word, that by this action of understanding and vision and a demonstration of the Law, nations and peoples and continents will be saved from a downward planetary spiral of death, destruction, and disintegration.

Let it be, then! For this is my call to the Lords of Karma ere the final decisions are made during this cycle of the year. My call and my petition is, then, for "a cosmic interval," an opportunity for Keepers of the Flame and people of light everywhere to demonstrate the Law and the disciplines thereof, to set the example, to radiate the crown of wisdom, to raise up the energies (i.e., Kundalini) of Mother.

This is my petition, and I am also volunteering to carry a portion of world karma. And yet I know that that request cannot be granted because an Ascended Master cannot bear that world karma which only those who are unascended can bear as the causes and effects in this world. But I ask it nevertheless, for I ask it hoping that my chelas will observe my petition and that the chelas of the ascension flame will likewise make that call and, having made that call, stand fast and be ready to receive all manifestations less than the Christ which might begin to appear in their worlds.

For you see, that burden can become light and be transmuted before it ever cycles through your four lower bodies. And therefore, the bearing of the weight of world karma need not be a *via dolorosa* but a way of joy, a way of victory and overcoming. For as soon as that energy of world karma is given to you, you consecrate it to the Holy Spirit and the sacred fire. It is transmuted, and lo, your burden is light! This is the calling. You may make it your election if you will.

Let the blessed saints and the devotees of the Catholic Church hear my words. For they do carry in their bodies much of the momentum of the death spirals, and this is why the priests and the nuns have worn black for so long. They are bearing the weight of the momentum of planetary death in the name of their Lord. They are bearing the energy so that mankind can pass through the initiation of the crucifixion.

And those who have not understood their path and their calling have ridiculed that they have the crucifix everywhere, for others who are engaged in other initiations would prefer to see Christ resurrected from the tomb in the garb of the resurrection and the ascension.

Well, all initiations are valid. And therefore, let us have tolerance; for the entire body of God must carry in manifestation these initiations. And therefore, the great religions of the world were founded so that each group mandala might work out that specific way and calling as an example to all. And now you have come to the place of responsibility where you can stand in the center of the sun—the Sun of Righteousness who is your Holy Christ Self—and all of the rays of all of the teachings of all of the religions going out from the center converge in your heart chakra.

And now you have this synthesis of the teaching of the Mother, and so you can be a member of a world religion that is not controlled by the World Council of Churches or the fallen angels who seek to possess mankind. It is a world religion of the Great White Brotherhood and its teachings. It is a world religion of the converging of souls in the flame of the Christ consciousness. It is a world religion of Love, of all who have loved enough to surrender those portions of the self that are out of the way with Christ.

And so I say, let us have our cosmic interval! Let us have our cosmic moment and allow the Divine Mother to show the world the Teaching of teachings, the Great Synthesis of all of the great Gurus—the Gurus who are now the Ascended Masters who come to claim their own.

In the victory of ascension fires, I AM Serapis Bey! I welcome you to Luxor! But I say, if you come to study in our retreat, if you come to prepare for the ascension, if you come, if you come to our retreat, then I say, *Come to stay!*

July 2, 1976
Washington, D.C.

The Sphinx and the Pyramid of Chephren

Love That Has the Courage to Be

Out of the cycles of God, Elohim—light descends! And I am come joyously in the white flame, in the white fire, in the whiteness of His glory, to seal you in ascension's flame.

I am the hierarch of Luxor come again to magnetize you to the very fire of the heart! Thus I have given to you, through the Messenger, some of the instruction which I give in the retreat of Luxor concerning the entering into the point of the heart before releasing the sound of the Word.

Necessity is the mother of invention. And truly necessity is the mother of ascension's flame.

Blessed hearts, the hour is come. This class has been a great boon to increase your own God-capacity for God's awareness of purity anointed by wisdom—and wisdom anointed by purity.

The wisdom of the Christed ones, coming under the sign of the Piscean conquerors, is symbolized in the beautiful feet of the Saviour and the preacher of the

Word of righteousness. The anointing of the feet of the Master by the would-be disciple is the acknowledgment "How precious are thy feet, O LORD! I would anoint, by the purity of my heart's devotion, the wisdom of thy Word."

Thus, upon the foundation of wisdom do men stand. And some stand not so tall at all, for their wisdom is not founded on the Rock.

Feet firmly planted upon the wisdom of Christ, I bid you—Go *forward!* Follow in his footsteps. And when you press your feet into his own footprints in the sands of time and space, you may hear the groan of a heart burdened by the planetary momentums of sin or by the betrayal of a close disciple. But you will also hear the fiat of light that dispels all of that and pushes it back spherically.

> Let there be Light!
> And there is Light where I AM.
> And I AM THAT I AM!
> So long as I AM in the world,
> I AM the Light of the world.

Pressing your precious feet—disciple's feet—within the master blueprint of the inner walk with God, you can attune to the meditations of the Saviour's heart, to his communion with angels, their songs of comfort and praise when no praise or comfort were forthcoming, even from his own.

Would you learn to listen with the sole of your feet?

Blessed hearts, every part of the mystical body of God within you contains the elements of every other part. Yes, you can listen to the heartbeat of Mother Earth through the sole of the feet. Yes, you can sense the Homeward path and follow it—blindfolded, if necessary—because of the sensitivity of the points of the five secret rays within you: the precious hands that extend healing, love, comfort; and the sign of the Word incarnate, the precious feet; and the eighth chakra of the secret chamber of the heart where thou art, I pray, with thy God as Father, Mother, Son, and Holy Spirit.

Thus, we step into the spiral of Love and Love's Ray expressed as charity, compassion, chastening, purest Love, and the Holy Spirit as the highest manifestation of Love which is the dissolution by Love's purest, wisest judgment of all that is anti-Love.

Thus, we press through the first and the second spheres of the causal body and enter the pink sphere of this unfolding rose! And thus, the circle of petals of this spherical chamber move from the most delicate pink of sensitivity to the heart of the babe newly born, the throbbing of the bird in spring, sensitivity to the whispering of the sun, the delicate breezes, the burden of heart upon the loved one. Delicate shades of pink and golden pink glow-ray enfolding within move, then, to the more intense manifestations of the ruby light and the Ruby Ray which, as the laser beam, must go forth in defense of Love!

Blessed hearts, unless Love had the built-in self-defense of its own self-preservation, the fallen ones would long ago have swallowed it up. But it was not to be. And it could not be. And it cannot. For you see, the Ruby Ray itself is the essential, I say, *essential* element of Love whereby all anti-Love, as hatred, is turned in upon itself and self-consumed.

Therefore, by the right hand of Serapis I send the Ruby Ray as radiating light, as the corona of this sphere of our causal body, even the causal body of the entire Spirit of the Great White Brotherhood! Enter into our Love and realize the protection of Love as the Ruby Ray *siddhi** that goeth forth.

Siddhi! Thus, fearlessness flame is born out of the Ruby Ray.

> A love that is love at all has the courage to be!
> It has the courage to be,
> Else it is self-denied.
>
> A love that is worthy of the name
> Claims this hallowed ground for love
> And will not retreat.
> A love that is worthy of life
> Holds the line of life itself
> And does not permit death to enter
> Nor death's vibration to steal in the night
> Within the garden of God.

---

siddhi (Sanskrit): power of the Self; a power that is equally effective in the spiritual as in the material world; accomplishment, fulfillment, complete attainment. The supreme siddhi is enlightenment.

Love that is worthy of the name
Will have none other
Save the fullest expression of Being—
Will not withhold the full flowering
Of the calla lily.

Love that is love will give
The biggest, the best, the mostest,
And even the rest
Of all that is blest
Of the good things of life.

Love that is real is the full opening of the heart
And the giving of self *fearlessly in love!*

Blessed ones, in this fourteen-month cycle abuilding from the spiral of our heart, there is the opportunity for you to enter a path of initiation whereby Love is perfected in Love.

There is a room at Luxor where this inscription is seen above the door: Love Is Perfected in Love. It is the name of a course as a path that is set. Those who knock upon this door are bidden to enter if they are determined to realize the fullness of Love as the discipline of self for perfect givingness, perfect receivingness out of the rhythm of the cycles of Life. Those who are not prepared are sent first to the violet-flame rooms, there to tarry for a year or a century until all hatred be consumed.

We are aware of the dangers of self-hatred unto those who would present themselves before the Ruby Ray Masters. Therefore, lessons in psychology must be studied, lessons in personal momentums—why one works against one's self to defeat one's self in the mighty work of the ages.

Working the works of him that sent me, as Christ said and did, is the action of the Third Ray, the third rung of Life—yet so often bypassed. See how they have replaced perfect Love with mechanization man, with the pride of the ego, with ambition—all of these perversions of Love and of its sweetest colorations.

There are so many substitutes for Love upon earth that one can scarcely find a single petal of purest Love among a thousand folk taken at random here or there! Men are so wont to accept a substitute for purest Love.

My heart would almost falter in its beat in consideration of the immense loss to the children of God for their acceptance of the lesser loves of life.

Precious hearts, these lesser loves then become, once they are accepted, a matter of human habit patterns. And once people enter into the rote of human love, they do not consider again—often in decades or lifetimes—a higher path, a more intense spiral. And like the proverbial rut, those human habit patterns make deeper and deeper trenches. And thus, the flow of the energy of Love tends to flow where it has always flowed.

People must be awakened to a higher walk with Love—the very person of Love in the Master himself!

Do you think that Christians who prate about the love of Jesus know his perfect Love? I daresay, without being judgmental, that many do not. Alas! They perceive of him in the vein of human sympathy. They are idolaters, but know it not—simply because they have not understood his perfect Love.

If you will take every episode in the life of Jesus Christ as you read the four Gospels and see each episode as another petal of Love, you will come to understand how variegated is the design of Love, how subtle are its changes. When you consider all that he did and said as a manifestation of perfect Love—whether it be healing, whether it be withholding healing, whether it be the raising from the dead or the casting of the moneychangers out of the temple or the rebuke to the Nephilim (embodied fallen angels) as whited sepulchres full of dead men's bones—consider all things and measure, by the sensitivity of your heart, the quality of Love and then go thou and do and be likewise.

It is a new appreciation of Love that the purity of white fire can give to you in this fourteen-month bearing of the cosmic cross of white fire with the Ruby Ray—if you will be conscious that that is the message of this path of initiation.

Love can be perfected in Love only when you start with perfect Love.

"How is this, Serapis? How can we begin with that which is perfect when our goal is to move from imperfection to perfection?"

Typical question of the neophyte.

You will never get there if you begin with imperfection! It is like getting up in the morning on the wrong side of the bed. The whole day follows suit.

Start the day with perfect Love.

"Serapis, where do we find perfect Love?"

Go and find it in the song of the bird at dawn. Go and find it in the dewdrop on the rose. Find it as you meditate upon Nature's floral offerings. Find perfect Love in the heart of a loved one as you pass universes of manifestation and go straight as an arrow to the God who dwells in that heart.

It is not so hard to find perfect Love.

Look for it in a mother's smile, in the tenderness of father, the sweetness of a child's prayer at eventide, or the rejoicing in the fields of Maytime.

Why, perfect Love is all around you. It is not a statistic of some cosmic statistician!

What do you think?—that God who is Love and only Love has withheld it from the creation? Look at perfect Love in an algebraic formula or in the reading of the stars—a simple recipe that, when it comes out, brings joy to all who partake of the results.

O yes, you can find perfect Love. And I will tell you truly that there is scarcely any child of God's heart upon earth who has not at least once loved perfectly. Love for elemental life reaches a most noble expression in people of all ages. Love of angels. Love of one another as I have loved you.

After all, Love is not something that is learned. Love simply is. And when it wells up within your heart, you know that God is there. And when you know that

God is there—do not stifle the flame, but fan it with the sacred fire breath.

Increase the single dewdrop of Love! Make it an ocean of bubbling joy, of waves of light and sine waves that give the sign to God: "Lo, I AM here below as thou art above."

Most blessed hearts, love on earth is an initiation failed by the vast majority of the people. And the energy of love as misuse of the creative fires, manipulation of the genetic code, has produced every variation from the theme of Christ in man and beast. And the bestial nature of fallen ones is perverted love. Just as everywhere you look you can find perfect Love, so everywhere you look you can see its inversion.

Therefore, I come to release the fourteen-month spiral as I place it as nucleus in your heart. But I come to warn you, as I have warned you with each of the prior releases, that the continuing intensity of ascension's fire propelling out the cycles of the causal body will give you greater and greater initiations—more to conquer both of Reality and of unreality.

The Archangels have told you that the greatest love the world has ever known manifests in the form of the judgment. In order for there to be judgment, there is the resurrection, the bringing to the surface, the awakening of light and darkness and the persona thereof. Therefore recognize that when the intense love of your heart goes forth, it will arouse the enmity of the Serpent with the Christ who is the originator of that Love in your heart.

Now I would tell you that the condition of hardness of heart that has become a disease also of some children of God, the condition of the shell which people place around themselves, is the result of sending forth love and receiving it back—being rejected.

"Hated without a cause" was the description of the coming of the One Sent. "They hated me without a cause." The cause, beloved hearts, is the sending forth of love. Love going forth will produce hatred in those in whom there is no love. And the cause for that hatred is envy.

Reread the dictations of Chamuel and Charity in the *Vials of the Seven Last Plagues*. They warn of the fallen ones and their envy of your love.

You see, the love of the Father and the Son who come to dwell in the heart of the child who keeps the commandments of Christ in love can never be known by the fallen ones. They had it once. Not only did they reject it, but they reduced it to their monstrous mechanization plot. Thus, love has been stripped from them. And they have been going on their synthetic love and their chemical formulas ever since.

The envy of love produces the hatred of love.

A number of conferences ago, I was with this Messenger as she flew from Colorado Springs to Santa Barbara for a class at the Motherhouse. As she flew over that city, she sent into it the most intense wave of love from her heart, which was from my heart also. And the love descended over the entire city. Within a matter of moments, to her utter consternation, there was sent back to her heart the most intense hatred—the rejection of the love of Christ, the rejection of the coming of the one sent before that one had even touched the ground.

Thus, she learned a lesson on the path of Life. And He said: Do not cast your pearls before swine. Pearls of love. Pearls of love, blessed hearts. But He also said: Love one another as I have loved you. But He never counseled to love the seed of the wicked. Therefore, do not radiate love omnidirectionally, indiscriminately—without the realization that the true love of Christ is not universally received in this world.

Now I release the Ruby Ray for all who would have it from my heart—for the melting down of hardness of heart, for the melting down of barriers and shells behind which you have hidden because you yourselves have felt that same rejection. This is their desire to stop you from loving purely, wholly, freely, fully!

But, I say, in your loving—love one another, love the body of God. And always love the heart of one another that your love go directly to the Christ flame and the Christ Self, thence to be distributed to the whole person as the person is able to receive it.

Love must radiate from within the heart to the entire being. For even in the case of loved ones, when you give love with intensity and the loved one is dealing with karmic patterns or the effluvia of the world or the burden of the day—that loved one may not receive that love, may even reject it or become irritated by it, because the very substance untransmuted on the surface of each world may easily become agitated by the intense love of the Christed ones and of the heart chakra. Therefore, do not be dismayed, do not be offended, do not be hurt in your loving.

If the devotees of the Ascended Masters would meditate upon love and expand their capacity to give love wisely with a pure discrimination of the heart, you would find a great expansion of this activity. For the Great Central Sun Magnet is the magnet of Cosmic Christ Love.

Therefore, a bit of advice from Serapis tonight: Look at your own momentums. Have you left off loving life because you are habituated to the rejection of your love? Have you, therefore, made the mode of your daily life not to give love out of concern for being rejected?

Blessed hearts, it is not a wise use of love to simply allow it to flow and then be abused. Love, wisely given, is a sacred transfer of a pearl of light from your heart to the heart of the beloved, the friend, one in need. From the purest center of your Christ consciousness, send love to the purest center of those who are the children of God. And then you will never leave off loving—loving life free!

And when you reinforce your life with calls to the Archangels for protection, with a tube of light, with calls to Astrea for the binding of the demons and discarnates that would steal your love and misuse it—when you do all of these things that you have learned and then meditate on greater and greater love, you will find that you will begin to feel like a new person, that the fuller expression of your own self will be the fruit of your loving others with this perfect Love.

With the transfer of the pearl to the heart of Christ in loved ones, the very warmth of the heart opens the pearl and releases the fragrance and the fervor of devotion for God. Thus, El Morya has taught: *Guard the heart!* And I would say: Guard the sendings of the heart! Guard the Love of the heart! Guard the magnet of the heart!

Many of your problems of human habit will melt away when the creative fires of Love of the Holy Spirit flow forth from you abundantly and without reserve. You need not love human imperfection, but you ought to love the soul on the path of becoming whole. Therefore, give comfort to the soul in need of comfort.

The soul that has need may be the soul that is not perfected in Love. Therefore, judge not—but give. And in your giving, be the healing of all life. Thus, I welcome you to Luxor for advanced training in the steps of the Master's walk with his disciples.

[Intonation]

It is done from the heart of Helios and Vesta and the heart of Luxor. The spiral of Love is released.

I seal you in the Magnanimous Heart of Lanello for the reinforcement of your will and your wise dominion in being the fullness of God's Love.

I retire into the flame, that Lord Maitreya might speak to you for the conclusion of this conference.

April 19, 1981
Los Angeles

Hilarion's etheric Temple of Truth is situated over the Island of
Crete. Here serves the Brotherhood of Truth and here are tutored
doctors, scientists, healers, musicians, mathematicians, and those
consecrated to the flame of Truth at the heart of any endeavor.

Lord of the Fifth Ray

Initiation of the Third-Eye Chakra

Retreat: Crete, Greece

Vibration: Green, Gold

Gemstone: Emerald, Diamond, Jade, Quartz Crystal

Quality: TRUTH SCIENCE VISION

Gift: Healing

Day: Wednesday

Paul Preaches in the Areopagus, Giovanni Battista Pianello,
Basilica of St. Paul Outside the Walls, Rome

The Personal Saviour, the Personal Guru

Called of the flame of Truth, I address you as of old in the name of my Lord and Saviour, Jesus. Jesus the Christ we called him, and we were called of him as you are called this day.

I recall the memories of his coming to me, empowering me with his Word. Yet first he humbled me on that road to Damascus, the humbling which I sorely needed that I might bow to my own Christ flame which he revealed to me, as he also gave to me the key of meditation upon that flame that I might walk in his footsteps on the Fifth Ray of Science and Healing and the Apostleship and the preaching of the Word.

Often I felt like the hands and the feet and the heart of Hercules, wrestling with the downward spirals of the earth with their atheism, their agnosticism, their intellectual pride and rancor against the prophets and the Holy One of God so recently come into our midst. Yet all the while I remembered I was once counted among them. To have been once so proud and so deliberate against the will of God would forever burn in my memory the helplessness that we all have in essaying to be instruments of God.

But the great empowering by the Word comes, my beloved, in the hour of the conversion. It is not the hour of the call but the hour of the conversion when the soul answers with something that is deep. It is the flowing, it is the giving, it is that surrender when, as he said, "it is hard for thee to kick against the pricks."

Your Master has called you. Some of you know the hour and the moment. For some of you it has been a gradual hearing of the Word, a gradual tuning in to a symphony that has always been playing. Some of you know that the call has come and that you have ignored the call.

Think you not that he did not call me even while I was persecuting the Christians? Did I not hear their sermons and watch them—the light upon their faces, their extraordinary joy in suffering, the love they bore for him whom I despised? Did he not call me then?

Yes, he called, but I was too proud to listen.

In the hour of the call that became the hour of the conversion, it was the moment of the meeting of the Master face to face, hearing his voice. And in that hour I knew the import of the personal Saviour. I knew the moment that he came that he was the one chosen, the one anointed by God. My soul knew him as of old and recalled to my outer mind the memory of the inner vow.

It was not the first time I had seen the Lord Christ. I had seen him before taking incarnation, and yet I had to work through that pride, that karma on the Fifth Ray of much learning, much studying, and superiority in social and intellectual standing which I had in regard to the early Christians.

And so it was my own karma that was upon me whereby I was resisting the call. The call was from afar, yet it became the nearer and nearer voice which finally stood before me as the blinding light of the Presence of the Son of God.

I speak to you today and I bring my vibration close to your own. I speak to you of my life lived not so long ago, much like your own. I speak because I bear the message of Hierarchy. I speak to you of the personal Guru that he is and that he was. I speak to you of the need to answer the call, answering it in a way that brings you to the point of conversion.

"Except ye be converted…" This is the meaning of the conversion by Christ: it is the arcing of that ray of light from his heart to your own that is so powerful that it reverses the downward spiral of death and disintegration, causes the involuting of that spiral in the upward commanding presence of Life not Death, of the ascension, and of immortality. Conversion is the moment of the swing of identity back onto the road to God.

In the moment of conversion there is the infiring of the name of God, your own new name. It is the solar pattern of your solar evolution. It is the branding iron of

God that comes upon you perhaps momentarily to your blindness or the absence of speech, as with Zacharias.

Understand, then, that that coming of that energy of God is for the confounding of the human consciousness and the bringing to the fore of that substance that must go into the flame. It is the sudden coming of the whirlwind of the presence of the Master at the hour appointed by God; and whether you are prepared or whether you are not, there is that coming, that sudden coming into the temple. It is the culmination of the call and many calls. It is the moment when you are broken in the human and when you are born to the Divine.

I say, then, from personal experience, resist not the call or the conversion or the coming of the Master. Do you wait for him to appear to you as in a vision, to flatter you with the presence of angels and trumpets and harps and an entire retinue of God-free beings?

You may wait long, you may wait hard. For I say, unto some it is required to provide the welling up from within of that love that says, "O Lord, I would be converted! Convert me this day! Let me be reborn in thee that I might go forth to work the works of my God!"

I have come to you on a number of occasions down through the years to speak to you of Apostles that you would be, hearing the call and answering and bearing witness to the Truth. I have come in the fire of the mission of the scientists and the physicians—the teachers of the age. I have come to release that light even as I came to this Messenger early in her mission to warn her of the pitfalls of the Path. So I warn also, be not smug in your understanding of the mysteries, for there are many who have had the sacred mysteries who have never had the conversion unto Christ.

I speak with a fervor that I knew in those days of joy which we shared. Repent and be saved! Be baptized! Be converted! Accept the Lord Christ as your Saviour this day and know a new birth in Spirit.

Do you not understand that the same mysteries experienced by the inner circle can be experienced, ought to be experienced, by you? With your newfound understanding of the way, do not forsake the childlike simplicity of utter dependence upon your God.

The instrument of Hierarchy is a very tender instrument. And if you do not neglect the requirements of the service, you will find that God will come into you and live through you, and you will feel the broad shoulders and the robe of the Apostle upon you. You will feel the mantle of Elijah and Elisha drop upon your shoulders.

You will hold your head high because you stand where the Lord stands, and you will indeed know the hour of your conversion when suddenly there was the very fire that burned on your spinal altar and caused the raising of that energy in an ascension current that marked the day when you were newborn to everlasting Life. And from that hour your every moment, every second was the rushing of the wind within you to greet the rushing of the wind oncoming from the LORD's hosts and from the causal body of Life to which you would one day return by the great magnetization of force-fields—"as Above, so below."

I say, walk with the stature of the prophets and teachers of Israel! Walk with the confidence of the God who lives within, but walk in this manner only after you have had the conversion. For if you attempt to walk in that way and in that stature before the conversion, I tell you, you will run the risk of walking in the pride of the carnal mind, taking unto yourself that glory that belongs only to Him.

God wants you to be that joint-heir with Christ Jesus. He proved that to me. He proved it to me—I who was counted a sinner. Is it not well to know that one who has sinned and fallen short of the mark could be converted and drawn to be a useful instrument for that LORD? We need examples of those who walked imperfectly yesterday and today walk perfectly in the sight of grace and holiness.

Do not attempt to be perfect human beings, perfect models of righteousness. The LORD will take you in his hands and snap you as dry wood and show you the uselessness of effort outside of his Spirit.

Seek rather to be perfected by him in his Love. Seek perfection not in the mechanical workings of your environment, but in the inner movement of the soul, the very mechanism of the soul that is able to contact God by the fiery conflagration of his Spirit. Know perfection as the graces of the Holy Spirit and seek them. Judge righteous judgment not after flesh and blood, and then you will see how the imperfect matrix can be used to convey a flame that transcends the matrix, which cannot even contain that flame.

Ah yes, mankind have a warped view of life and of the Teaching and of the Path. They do not know the way and the very tenderness of our Father's love and of his understanding of the very frailties of the flesh and of this world that make of Him the greater glory, the greater manifestation of Life.

Do you not see that if it were possible to be humanly perfect, there would be no need for divine perfection? If it were possible to contain God on earth, there would be no need to pursue heaven. Thus the transience of this life gives way to transcendence of a new Life whereby even we among the ascended hosts are reborn day by day as we come into a newness of the infilling of his Presence.

Life can begin for you this hour, but the conversion implies a will—a will forged and won within your heart, a will that will magnetize that energy of devotion from a member of the ascended hosts who responds to the call of your heart for the Teacher, who will then come and invest you with that magnet, that flame, that fiery coil, that momentum that is able to reverse the course of death and destruction.

In the conversion is the healing of mind and body. In the conversion is that sudden filling of the temple that has been a vacuum and now is filled with a special breath, a sweet breath—sweet as the springtime and the new grass, the hay in the field and the flowers; so is the sweetness of that Presence.

And once you have touched that energy, once you have walked through the field of that consciousness, even knowing the sound of the rustling of the garment of the Lord Christ, then you will seek to preserve that moment day by day, and your life is evermore an attempt to equalize here below that very special experience in Christ, who has appeared in that zone between Spirit and Matter, neither here nor there but somehow in the midst of an infinity of worlds cycling, drawing you into that cycling of energy, that you might come to know the Presence of the living God.

I am here to call you—to convince you of your life's calling. "Saul, Saul, why persecutest thou me?" Has not the Master's voice also rung in *your* ear and in *your* heart when you have known that you have been persecuting the prophet of God, the emissary of God, the little child in the way, the Ascended Masters' purposes by failing to give that supporting breath of energy, that working of the works of God that could be the foundation for the precious souls to find a teardrop of Love, a crystal of Truth, a pearl of Wisdom?

Come now, come let us reason together, you who are the intelligent, or so self-considered, you who are the ones who know of the things of this life. Let us consider the end of cycles and the shuffling off of the mortal coil. Let us think of how all that is seen in this life is vanity, comes to naught, and must one day recycle back to the fiery core of the Central Sun to be recharged with the infusion of the flame of Life.

Is it not better, O intelligent ones, is it not better to leap into that heart before you are called, before the disintegration spiral spins that energy veil, before you are consumed by the downward spirals of your own karma, your own lack of reckoning with the Law of Life?

Count, then, the days. Can you count the days and the hours of opportunity open to you? There is only one goal—it is Life. And that goal includes the impartation of Life, heart to heart. This is the way of living the Life triumphant on Terra.

My coming to you this day, then, is the fulfillment of a cycle begun in the earliest beginnings of the Messengership of Mark. This is the culmination, then, of the setting of a pattern in each of the dictations which I have released since the beginning. This pattern, then, carefully woven, is a mandala that I release to all who serve on the Fifth Ray and to all who are called by soul, by name this hour from the four corners of the earth to come forth and to bear witness unto the Truth.

Even as I am speaking, there is a raging and a ranting of the fallen ones who are of the company of the Liar and his lie, those fallen ones who shriek to think that the hour of Truth is come, and the hour of the exposure. And they are the fallen ones of madness and of insanity with their projections of insanity upon the children of God. They have sent forth those rays of confusion and chaos to disturb the mind and the emotions of the souls of light on Terra.

Go back, I say, in the name of my Lord! Go back into the night! For here I will place my sphere of light. It is a giant circular platform which I place over the City of the Angels [Los Angeles]. It is a platform that divides the way of truth and error.

And all who are called to give witness to the Truth may come to this city and stand on this platform and find that in this platform there is the weaving of the Word that I have given forth through the Two Witnesses—the weaving of the energy of the mandala, the very energy of Life, then, from the magnet of my own heart, an energy that will be conveyed, then, through the blessed feet who will walk the highways and the byways giving forth that witness by heart, by head, and by hand.

I AM Hilarion. I have walked in the desert places, I have taken my refuge in the desert of life, but the multitudes came after me into the desert as I lived in my final incarnation as Hilarion. They came for the healing fountain, they came for love. Though I would retreat, they would follow. And so the Lord told me that the gift of Truth and of Healing is only for the sharing, only for the giving away.

Here is the gift, the gift of the green tree. God gives the tree. Upon it you hang the ornament of Life that is a gift from your heart. It is the adornment of your adoration, and your adoration is the spiral upon the tree spiraling back to the star of your own I AM Presence.

God has given you life in the green tree. Now I say,

with what will you adorn that Life—with a golden spiral, with spheres of causal bodies, with the faces of the Ascended Masters, with the image of the Virgin, with the working of the works of God?

Let us reason together. What will be your net gain if all that you see is vanity? What will be your net gain when you stand naked as you came into the world and as you return? The net gain is the virtue of the works and the graces that you have drawn forth to forge a permanent identity in God.

Now I say, let the wise who will take counsel with me on the course of civilization and of the Church in the West and in the East, let them come now to Crete. I call forth those who will counsel with me in the way of Truth and in the way of the Life that is Truth. We would set forth our goal for this Church Universal and Triumphant of our Lord. We would set forth the goal for those who have come under the dispensation of the sixth root race and those who are coming—incoming lifestreams of the seventh root race.

We would teach you the very message of the avatars who walk on the ray of science, the ray of religion that is Truth. We would teach you of this hour when there must be the blending of the twain and when those who pursue the path of science must be humbled—as I was humbled and as surely you will be humbled also—that they might know that science is not God but that it is the instrument of God and can be used unto salvation if it is unto his glory.

I commend you then unto Pallas Athena, servant of the Most High, member of the Karmic Board, who will review your letters of petition this year. I commend you to her flame and to the dispensation that she holds in her hand for Truth to be disseminated among the nations.

The messenger of the Great Central Sun has stood before the Lords of Karma this day that Keepers of the Flame might know in writing petitions this year that the dispensation that is forthcoming that may be applied for, that special bank of energy set aside and reserved for lightbearers, is a dispensation of Truth and of the carrying of the message of Truth and of the Word and the implementation of the ray of Truth in the building of the city—the City Foursquare within and the citadel of righteousness where the right use of the Law may be taught and won in the Community Teaching Centers. They are indeed citadels of righteousness, for there is the way of the threefold flame unfolding as the open door— open from within, open from without that the children of Truth may come and go in the Master's house.

I point out to you the first citadel of righteousness, the first Community Teaching Center: the home of Mary and Martha and Lazarus at Bethany. There the place to receive the Master, there the place to receive the disciples. And all of the functions of the seven rays fulfilled in that home of light can be fulfilled in your own home of light and in your own Teaching Center— a place for nourishment and rest for the Master and the disciples, for the recharging of the life of Jesus as you live that life.

Where would the Master have gone had there not been a home consecrated by the flame of constancy? It was a place for the dissemination of the Teaching, a place for the Holy Spirit and for the family life, the place from which Jesus walked to Bethany's hill, the place for Truth, the place for the discipline of the disciples in the ray of Truth and for their commissioning to go forth empowered in the Word in their ministration and service, the place for the ritual of the anointing of the Lord's body, the place for the contact of the Guru and the chela.

Yes, the home of light given unto the Lord becomes the flow of all of the sacraments of all of the seven rays and finally for the integration of the Eighth Ray of the Buddha and the Mother.

People do not often understand that a place must be prepared on earth for the Masters, for their coming, and for the disciples attending their coming. As each home of light resembles more and more the etheric retreats of the Brotherhood, so there is the meeting of heaven and earth and there is the open door to the path of the ascension whereby worlds are transcended and the soul that is born in Matter is born again in Spirit. Thus prepare the place, prepare the manger for the birth of the Christ, prepare the home where the eagles will gather together.

I come rejoicing with all of the hosts of the LORD.

And the Lords of the Seven Rays stand together to salute
you in the name of the Christ, to salute you with the
new day and the new energy of Omri-Tas and the new
wave of violet flame that will precede the coming of
the Chohans as the Gurus serving under the Maha
Chohan, under Lord Maitreya and the World Teachers
and Gautama the Buddha. The Chohans are on the
march this year for the conversion of souls to their own
Christ Self, to the Lord of lords and King of kings, to
Jesus the one, the anointed, the Wayshower, and to all
who have walked after him.

So I say, Apostles of the Most High God, be on your
way! It is the changing of forcefields, the changing of
the boots that causes the quaking in the knees.

I say, be up and doing! Left, right, left, right, take
another step, go forward! You will find out what God
would have you do. No need to sit and wonder! There
is work—work in the action of the Holy Spirit. There is
the joy of the service that is true Brotherhood and true
Community.

Find out what God would have you find out about
yourself by immersing yourself in the great cosmic flow,
the ongoing flow of service. Find out what the Teaching
is by living the Teaching. And find out what we have for
you at Crete as our assignment as representatives of
Truth.

Pallas Athena will be with me as you come (in your
finer bodies) after the New Year's celebrations to our
(etheric) retreat where we have enshrined the records of

ancient Greece, the great wisdom teachings, the outlines of Pythagoras, and so much of the records of the life of Jesus and of our ministry, so much that is important for your understanding of your mission.

Souls of light and of Saint Germain, have the sense of the great army of the LORD and be the soldiers of the Christ joining The Faithful and True and the armies of heaven. Understand, then, that the sword of Truth that you wield is a mighty scepter of authority. Take that authority under Christ! Know the meaning of conversion this day that you might be the instruments of the conversion of the multitudes who hunger and who thirst after the righteousness of the Law.

I AM Paul in the flame of Hilarion. I stand with the Master of Life, and I still stand, and I stand forevermore with his disciples.

I thank you.

December 29, 1976
Pasadena, California

Pallas Athena, Goddess of Truth, worshiped of old by the
Athenians and enshrined in their Parthenon, is an Ascended
Lady Master who served under Vesta as high priestess in the
Temple of Truth on Atlantis and as directress of the temple virgins
and oracles at Delphi. Today she works with Hilarion and other
"green-ray" Healing Masters of the Fifth Ray, ministering to man-
kind by amplifying the truth of God's love to the earth from the
Temple of Truth.

The Gift of Divine Healing

A nd ye shall know the Truth, and the Truth shall make you free." "What is Truth?" Pontius Pilate of old put this question to the Christ. And still men are seeking to know the immortal flame of living Truth.

I bear it in his name. For I saw the unspeakable majesty of Truth, the immortal proof of the living Christ when he came to me upon the road to Damascus. So great was the power of that Truth that I was blinded until once again Truth's healing rays restored the sight to my eyes, the power of holy vision, through the All-Seeing Eye of God.

Few men realize that in the appearance of the Christ there was awakened in me the true inner vision of the third eye. And therefore, I went forth no more as Saul but as Paul, given the divine name by him who had fulfilled the Law in that flame of Truth.

The inner name given unto me at that time signified the great power of the mission of healing that was to be mine. And so each one of you have the secret name which is given unto you at the hour that you accept your divine mission—in the name I AM.

Perverting this concept, those in the lower strata of human activity have sought to claim other names for themselves, thinking thereby to usurp the divine authority of the inner name.

Precious ones, it is not necessary that you know precisely the vibratory tone of your secret name, but that you know the name of him who is able to bestow upon you every gift of purity and of healing.

Those who would enter in to an activity that is less than the mission of the Christ find when they assume other names than their given ones that they enter into a vibratory action not of the Christ but of the psychic impostors who flatter and inspire them with pride and bid them to go forth in the calling of the lesser image.

I come to you this day to anoint you once again with the true calling of your immortal soul and to outline for you who have sought the mystery of healing some points of the Law which in your devotion you have neglected, becoming at times one-sided in your application.

I therefore bring you the tidings of great joy, the joy of the angels of healing who minister unto mankind and who bear witness to the immaculate concept, the perfect pattern held in the heart of the Father. For beloved Raphael who stands in the Presence of God perceives in his heart the immaculate design for every son of God upon the planet and those who are becoming sons of his heart.

If you would go forth to do the bidding of the healing angels, there is of necessity information which must be called to your attention. And therefore, I would give to you this day some of the meditations of my heart which I discovered and which were given unto me by the Lord Christ as I pursued the mission of calling forth those sons from Asia Minor and the Mediterranean countries. For I had many hours during my journeying to commune with him and with the heart of the Holy Spirit and the divine one, Pallas Athena, the Goddess of Truth.

I sat, as it were, upon her knee and learned from the Mother of Truth those holy teachings which were also known to Mary and which she imparted, in part, to the disciples as they could bear them.

Healing, beloved ones, is integration of the whole man. You cannot heal in part and find the wholeness of the Christ. Recall how frequently the writers in the Gospel stated, "And he was made whole." Wholeness is a concept which is required as you pursue the knowledge of the healing arts. For healing is a science which must be mastered, and it is an art which must be skillfully practiced.

Those who have not the talent to design or to sketch from life upon paper must practice before they become proficient. Could any one of you here take up a pen and design the perfect form of the anatomy of man? You could if you studied and applied yourself, but you could not if you left your attempts to the mental world. And so it is with healing—the art must be practiced, the science must be mastered.

It is wrong, beloved ones, to wait for some future time when you think by some miracle that suddenly, with one sweep, you shall step forth and speak the word of healing and at that moment you will be transformed into the magnification of the Christ.

Healing comes as you apply yourself day by day to the invocation, the calling forth of the healing ray, the garnering of that ray in your aura and the chalice of your consciousness, and then the application of that ray as you are called upon in hour of crisis or need for one another.

Another incorrect concept is that you are not in need of healing. You seem to be well, you seem to function, and therefore you think all is well. Precious ones, until the hour of Wholeness, of cosmic integration, you are less than whole and therefore you require healing. Each and every one of you each hour of the day can therefore practice the fiats of the Christ.

Go back to the teachings of Christ. Study his words. Use the fiats that he used to make men whole. Often he said, "Thy sins be forgiven." He also stated that those disciples who would follow him would also be able to forgive sins in his name.

Have you ever considered that you have the power to forgive yourself, in the name of Almighty God, of those sins which have brought about the condition that we shall term less than whole? Beloved ones, forgiveness is the beginning of healing. For the mighty healing ray of God descending to the chalice of the consciousness of the disciple stops as it comes in contact with human effluvia and densities.

And so the way must be prepared. It must be cleared. You must go forth into the jungle of your own four lower bodies and cut down the path ere the Christ may walk on the palms, as on the Sunday before the resurrection, to receive the praise of the heart flames of all who are blessed to behold the perfection that he indeed is.

You see, beloved ones, you must make straight the way of the path of Divine Healing. For he shall come to you again upon the foal of an ass, riding and bearing the torch of your freedom. Will you be there to receive it? Are you prepared? Have you entered into communion with the Christ principles?

You must, therefore, realize that the ray of healing entering the heart of man first reaches the mental world. And therefore, the mental concepts of mankind must be purified by the immaculate concept of the immaculate heart of the Mother of the World.

You may, therefore, appeal to beloved Mary who herself, having received the early temple training, had prepared the way to receive within her own womb the manifestation of the healing Christ. Do you see the many years of preparation which went before her, working on the green ray to know Truth, to know the immaculate way ere she could be chosen to bear the one who carried the Truth to this planet?

If you would have the blessings of the full-blown manifestation of the bloom of the Christ within your heart, you must first flush out the four lower bodies by this chemical ray, the green purity of God. And using with it the violet fire for transmutation, forgiveness, and purification, you will then come to the place where, having filled the mental world, this mighty green ray will purify the etheric records and patterns. And by the mighty power of the All-Seeing Eye of God focused within your aura, you will know the perfect design of your lifestream.

Now, precious ones, many among the student body have reached this attainment in part, and some have glimpsed it in hours of meditation upon Truth. And having purified their consciousness, they feel, "I am healed. I am whole." And they go about their business and their daily activities. But I say to you, precious ones, the service is only half performed when you have reached this facet of healing. You must now draw the power of healing into the seething vortices of your emotional world.

The emotional body must be imbued by the power of Divine Truth. The reins must be drawn upon all misqualified energies, and that body which is the chalice of Divine Love must conform to Truth, must bear the pattern of pure Love within you. And sometimes, because of the warring of the carnal mind and its influence over the emotions, there is a resistance to Truth. The resistance is actually in the residual substance of the subconscious world as it has magnetized the emotions of man.

And thus, mankind's energies are channeled in a certain direction, and these are grooves in his consciousness. And these grooves which have carried off the energies of God for generations must be filled in as men would fill in trenches. And sometimes this is a painful process, for it demands the rearrangement of the energies and the flow of light within the forcefield of your four lower bodies.

And therefore, there is war. And you find within your members one part in struggle against another. This I experienced in my life as Paul. And yet always the magnet of the higher Truth, the polarization of my lifestream with the Great Central Sun was able to draw off the impurities, the residual substance of past embodiments, and I could go forth to see the Daystar of his appearing and the Truth descending into my forcefield.

When you have achieved a certain degree of polarization to the power of Truth within these three bodies,* you will find that there is of necessity a great change that will also take place in the physical forcefield. But this change will not take place unless you determine to call it forth, unless you determine to draw down from those three levels of consciousness as well as from your Holy Christ Self all of the power and momentum of your God Presence and that which you have been able to glean and hold in the chalice of the physical form which is intended to be the temple of the living God. For here in the now the lily of the Christ is intended to blossom

---

*the etheric, or memory body, the mental, and the emotional bodies.

forth, to be, and to hold forth the voice of Truth to a wayward generation.

Can you function without a physical form, precious ones? Aye, not in this octave. Would you be elsewhere? Perhaps, but your mission could not be fulfilled. And thus a return once again, another descent of your soul into physical form might be required should you pass off lightly the calling of your present position in the world arena.

Now, beloved ones, having a physical form partially dedicated to Truth and partially involved in the world of the senses is not as the Ascended Masters have intended that you should be, consecrated as you have been to the holy cause of freedom for this earth. Therefore, think wisely and think well of that which you allow to inhabit the forcefield of your physical bodies. Think well upon the temple. Think well upon the science of God, the perfectionment of that temple, and meditate upon the holy precepts of God-purity for it.

I, Hilarion, have pledged myself this day to help you, each one, to use all the knowledge that you have garnered, and then to add some to it that each one of you might become better representatives of the Ascended Masters to the mankind of this planet.

I therefore would call to your attention the words of the Christ, "Not that which goeth into the mouth defileth a man; but that which cometh out." The passageway of the mouth, the oracle of God, is a key to salvation; for here the throat chakra, the mighty power of God and of his will, speaks forth the Word and can magnetize the mighty power of the threefold flame to change conditions across the face of the planet.

It is not only the knowledge of the Truth but the speaking forth of the Word and the putting of that Word into action that makes you men of the hour and men for all seasons, as beloved El Morya has of recent date been referred to.*

Those who would do the will of God, then, will think once, will think twice, and think again at the power of holy integration that comes forth from the flame of living Truth to bring into divine consonance and harmony the four lower bodies of man. Take heed, then, that your application be not one-sided, that you do not favor one of these vehicles. For the sun does shine upon the race of mankind north, south, east, and west.

The four winds of the Holy Spirit do breathe forth now across the face of the earth in the four lower bodies of mankind and the four lower bodies of this planet. And in this mighty release of surging power elemental life arises to meet the call and the need of the hour.

Beloved ones, as you arise in consciousness, drink in then, by the power of the holy breath from the heart of Alpha and Omega, this holy breath which shall rejuvenate and resurrect your own four lower bodies. And I am placing within each of your four lower bodies a talisman of my own flame of Truth, manifest as the

---

*The life of Sir Thomas More, an embodiment of El Morya, was depicted in the 1966 motion picture *A Man for All Seasons.*

emerald green cross, the flame of His Truth.

And by having focused within each of your four lower bodies the magnificent power of the purity of my ray, you will find that cosmic integration will be more and more apparent to you, and the science of how to perform and achieve this integration will be made known to your outer and inner consciousness.

Therefore, as you go forth bearing the mighty flame of Truth, remember that the physician must first heal himself before he can go forth to heal the multitudes, to multiply the bread and the fishes, to change the water into wine. The mighty science of alchemy is the science of Divine Healing. And that healing ray may be understood by you as the mighty tone of God—the tone of his symphony.

And as you extend the rod of power that is Divine Healing, you will be aware of that mighty chord within you—the chord that is the key to your victory. You will not be able to perceive or to have the power of that chord magnetized unto you until you have achieved the integration of the four lower bodies. For each of the notes of that mighty chord is played upon one of those four lower bodies.

And therefore, if you perfect but one or but two, you will have only two notes of the chord. And without that mighty completeness of integration, you will not have the full power of the Christ to do his will.

Therefore by purification, by transmutation, by consecration to the will of God, to illumination, you may have manifest within you the mighty rainbow rays of God, the sevenfold aspect of the flame and the two secret rays from the heart of Mighty Cosmos; for all are required for this cosmic integration. And therefore, you see why it is that the core of healing is the white-fire light, for it is the perfect balance of all the rays.

Can you question, beloved ones, that the infusion of Divine Love within the heart of man brings about healing and solace and comfort? Can you question that illumination brings healing to the mind, to the outlook of man? Can you question that the will of God, when practiced and adhered to, does bring about healing? Can you question that the fires of transmutation, the ray of purity, the golden flame and the purple of service bring about an upliftment and a change in consciousness that is even outpictured in the physical form?

Therefore, you see that the rainbow rays of God give the balance in the seven chakras of man and key him to the mighty outpouring of the seven Elohim from whence comes this mighty tone into the chalice of man's consciousness. And therefore, it is not enough to reach to the heights of the green fires to bring about the transformation that will make of you healers of men, but in science, in love, and in purity you must find all of God and bring his allness into the chalice of the present hour.

To have bestowed upon you, then, the fullness of the cosmic momentum of Divine Healing during this hour of world crisis is indeed a great gift. The opportunity which has been given to you to be healers among men must be taken by you. It must be applied.

But most of all, you must find in your heart the dedication to that which you do not yet understand. And in dedication, even to the unknown God, you will find coming to be within your forcefield the understanding of the known God. And you will know him as he is, even as he is known to the hosts of light and the Ascended Masters.

But, precious ones, he who would have the gift of healing in the fullness of manifestation must realize that because it is comprised of the allness and completeness of God, he must offer himself completely unto God.

The scarcity of the true divine healers upon the planet in this hour is a testimony to the fact that most people who ask for the healing ray have not yet been willing to give their all to the Father-Mother principle of Life. And although they have a deep love and devotion and compassion for their brethren, they have not yet relinquished personal desire, personal wants. And thus, some aspect of the sevenfold flames of God is wanting within their worlds.

This, therefore, is the key to the mystery of the gift of healing. He who would walk as a teacher among mankind might succeed to a great extent through the use of illumination's ray. And there are many offices and callings which can be achieved to a remarkable degree without total dedication, without the allness and wholeness of this complete cosmic integration.

But he who would actually carry within his hand

the fire of God which transforms the brethren upon the planet at the touch and at the command must realize that here in the heart of the Temple of Truth those initiates who have applied to me to earn their ascension on the ray of Divine Healing have had to have embodiments where the allness and completeness of their lives was given in service.

Here we teach how man can live in the world of form and yet not be of that world—how man can go forth carrying the ray and the scepter of Truth with total integration, total dedication, and the totality of his desire world focused upon the All-Seeing Eye that is the ray of healing focused within your form.

Beloved ones, this is not difficult. It requires most of all understanding that that which you give unto God in service is immediately given back to you—purified, transmuted, and charged with the full power and momentum of God-Victory.

You may not always receive the blessing in your outer consciousness, but each sacrifice, each gift which is laid upon the altar of God returns to your causal body of light a most magnificent gift and jewel that is the focus and ray that magnetizes more and more of his light.

And thereby, in giving all to God you are polishing the star, the halo of your crown. And you see that at any hour in any day when you achieve the fullness of your gift to God, you may find that suddenly, swiftly like lightning and by the power of thunder and the holy wind of the

Holy Spirit, you are then imbued with the power of wholeness.

The transfiguration of the Christ was testimony to his complete dedication. And from that time forward he was among mankind a focus, an electrode of such magnificent power that all the earth trembled before his presence. And those who had separated themselves from God by condemnation or other sins against the Holy Spirit knew that in his presence the power to command Life would be answered on the instant. Instantaneous healing, then, is testimony to total consecration.

Beloved ones, the master key, then, is Divine Love. For in Love all is understood as belonging to God in the first place. And you understand that in giving your all unto him you are one with him and have no need of any other source of supply, of entertainment, or of delving into the intellectual curiosities that are popular in the present day and that always arise to tempt mankind away from that total givingness.

If God, therefore, gave his only begotten Son unto the world that through him the world might be saved, think you not that at any hour of the day he is ready to give unto you the scepter of power that is your own Holy Christ Self identity?

Exchange, then, the garments of the flesh, the tatters and tares of this world, for the seamless robe and watch how the world is changed with you. For healing in your forcefield means healing everywhere upon this planetary body. For as you are (as God is in you) the authority for this earth, you will find that in geometric proportion by the infinite calculus of the Spirit, one with God is a majority for the entire universe.

You see, then, that you are but a replica of this planetary body in your forcefield and in your four lower bodies. And as you have commanded the waves to be silent and still in your forms, so they are commanded on a world scale.

Thus, the Christ had the power to change the entire course of history. You also have that power resident within the Holy Christ Self of each one of you. In this very room the power of the Christ magnified, consecrated, intensified by devotion and service is enough to magnetize the earth to the victory of the golden age.

And when we say that mankind must be illumined ere we would hold back their karma, when we say that mankind must themselves accept the Christ in order to preserve this planetary body, we are saying that without illumined Christhood the very atoms and cells of their four lower bodies can no longer hold together, for want of the cohesive power of Divine Love. And therefore, what happens on a world scale is the product of what is happening on an individual scale as men commit themselves to the darkness of insanity and give their bodies so freely to the lusts of the flesh.

But, precious ones, the power and the torch of that light and fire which you carry in your Christ Self has enough illumination and enough healing power that if it be lifted up as a light unto the world [it] will draw all mankind unto the torch which is their Holy Christ Self and to their own identity that is the fullness of divine illumination and the will of God which will cause them to alter their course and take in hand the precepts of Divine Law.

Therefore, not by interceding for their karma but by becoming the Christ you can achieve the staying of the karma of mankind. For in illumination is the transformation of the healing ray.

All is not lost, then, if you determine this day to consecrate yourselves to the power of Truth, to call to me and ask for the fire of my heart to assist you in that holy integration which you so require in this hour. For I come because many have asked, What more can we do to become more like thee, O God?

And so, I come with the answer and with the key. And if it be heeded and taken, you will find that the power of Truth, as it is released from the heart of the Great Central Sun Magnet, will "draw all men unto me." For I AM—the I AM of me is—the living Christ and I bear witness to Him who showed me along the way of Life that the only Truth, the only Way, the only Love, and the only Power is the Victory of the momentum of God within the individual forcefield of all mankind.

Take up the cross, then, as I and so many others who followed him have done. Take it up and realize that that cross is the symbol of your cosmic integration—each of the four bars (the four lower bodies) dedicated to the white-fire core of Alpha and Omega where God and man meet in perfect Identity, in perfect Union that shall make of you each one a mighty sovereign state, an inviolate arch (arc) of triumph for all the sons of men.

You can see, beloved ones, that the victory is given unto those who give themselves to the victory. Therefore, take the victory today. Take it to your hearts and let this year be dedicated to the victory of light, to the victory of purity, to the mighty healing rays that we bear and that we are releasing every day throughout the year in each tiny leaf and plant as the chlorophyll ray transmits to the physical body all that is in store for man from the etheric levels and that which has been locked as matrices of power in the mental and emotional belts of this planet.

See, then, the salvation of God as ye are made whole by the threefold flame balanced in Power, Wisdom and Love, attuned to the key and the mighty tone that is your cosmic identity.

Beloved ones, when you hear the name of God, the rushing of the mighty waters, the wind of the sacred fire, then shall ye know that the day is at hand for your mission to be accomplished.

Maintain the vigil of listening grace, then. Keep the vigil with Mother Mary. Keep it on behalf of the youth. For right within your own God potential there is the power which can restore this generation and bring men to the feet of the Master Christ himself.

It does not matter to us through what avenue these little ones are brought to his feet. It matters that they

keep the precepts of the Law and that when they come
to full maturity and adulthood they shall find that there
is written upon this earth a body of knowledge, a compendium of the precepts of God's law which will be
magnetized in their hearts because they have first been
consecrated and dedicated by your prayers and by their
commitment.

Men may walk in faith for a time. They may walk
and lean upon the rod of his power. But if their hearts
be pure, they must all one day awaken to the fact that
more than faith is required and more knowledge is at
hand.

But, precious ones, many along life's way have come
to the point where they knew there must be something
more for them to have, to glean, and to know whereby
they could fulfill their mission. And they have hunted
and searched for someone to tell them the right course
and they have not found. For the Teachings were not
available, they were not spread abroad in the land. And
you yourselves in past embodiments have searched for
Truth and have not found it. And sometimes, in despair,
you have accepted substitutes which have led you down
the pathway to more karma and the round of involvement in human affairs.

In this service that you are rendering through this
activity you find that there is taking place in your forcefield the atonement for all ignorance and past error that
you performed as you knew not what you did. And by
the grace of God and the mercy of his law there is

extended unto you, therefore, the opportunity not only to atone for your own past ignorance, but to provide for mankind the way whereby they might also come to the knowledge of the Truth, by which they may also atone for their past errors.

And so, you see, the accomplishment of this mission for the Christ, of this service for humanity is very important to the world. And a great deal depends upon its fulfillment. For succeeding generations, if they are fired by illumination and the flame and desire to know Truth, may come to the fountain.

Let us pray that the fountain be not dry, that they will find the living waters of Truth because you have determined to leave behind footsteps upon the sands of life, waymarks of progress, and books, lessons, dictations in printed form that will teach mankind the Way.

Realize, then, that you are the missing link between the era of the Christ and the era of the golden age. And if you can weld together the mighty chain of the saints of all ages which has temporarily been broken by man's inattention to liberty and to cosmic precepts, you will be forging the chain of Being that will unlock for generations for all time to come the mighty precepts of Life which are the keys to their immortal victory.

The entire Spirit of the Great White Brotherhood pours forth gratitude to those who have thus served in the holy cause this day, even as our hearts are filled with gratitude from your octave from the sons and daughters of light who are receiving the powerful words in printed form that are released through this activity.

You are not always there to listen as the heart leaps, as the Holy Christ Self rejoices upon the contact of the outer self with the higher truths that are locked in his own Christ identity. And even the body elemental jumps up and down for glee as followers of the greater light of God come into a knowledge whereby they might integrate themselves and find wholeness and greater reunion with the Mighty I AM Presence.

I wanted to tell you this day how important your mission is, then, to the bringing of Truth unto mankind. For the most part the evolutions of this planet live in a world that is seventy-five to eighty-five percent a lie, a mirage—almost like a movie set. And they do not know the truth, especially behind the Iron Curtain where life is turned upside down and distorted for the people who are attempting there to serve what they think to be the highest principle.

Beloved ones, without Truth, without the key of this science, there is much that mankind will lose. That they do not lose the precious heritage that we have to pass on is our desire. It is our gift.

And we pledge ourselves this day anew to uphold this activity, to uphold all serving it and all members of it who are sincere, that by the holding forth of these outposts of light across the planet there may be established bulwarks of freedom and a place of refuge where the holy precepts of Truth might be held forth until mankind come of age.

That they come of age through various activities which we have sponsored is well and good, and your very decrees and prayers go forth as a flood tide of light to uplift mankind wherever they may be. In the lowest reaches of degradation unto the highest ivory towers of learning, mankind are taken a little bit higher, a little bit further upon the way of finding their own reunion with God as you join to pray each day.

I take my leave of you this hour, but there is much more which I would like to bring to you. I pray, therefore, that your consecration to Truth shall be of such magnitude that I may return and talk with you even as I had the privilege of teaching and preaching in my life as Paul. For the hours of communion and of association with the followers of Christ, as heart to heart the knowledge of the Law is imparted, these are sacred, these are precious. These are locked in the eternal memory of every ascended being. And so, I look forward to coming again.

I bless you in his name and I fire within your hearts a portion of our flame.

I thank you.

January 8, 1967
Colorado Springs, Colorado

Saudi Arabia, Red Sea in foreground
Beloved Nada serves from the Arabian retreat of Jesus the Christ.

Lord of the Sixth Ray

Initiation of the Solar-Plexus Chakra

Retreat:	Saudi Arabia
Vibration:	Purple and Metallic Gold, Ruby
Gemstone:	Topaz, Ruby, Alexandrite, Diamond with Pearl
Quality:	PEACE SERVICE BROTHERHOOD
Gift:	Diverse Kinds of Tongues Interpretation of Tongues
Day:	Thursday

The Lady Master Nada, Lord of the Sixth Ray

The Psychology of Love

Sometimes in the course of life you meditate, beloved ones, upon the path of the soul's overcoming and the ingredients so precious of the Truth that is taught of Christ, and these become to you as a living thing, not inanimate but wholly animated by the Holy Spirit. And sometimes in the richness of the lore of God and his saints, it escapes one that there are some who have an understanding not so deeply rooted in the foundations of Cosmic Law.

It is then, you see, that the tender vine needs that flame of ministration and service which was and is the path of the Lord Jesus Christ, whose ray I now represent as its Chohan.

This Sixth Ray of love and good cheer is of the heart that understands of necessity the great needs of the pilgrims weary who walk the valleys and the highways, the cities of planet Earth. Ministering the Word, ministering unto the flock, then, is to be a bearer of the cup of Christ and to bring it here and there where the oppressive heat of hell itself would move against the little ones.

Just when you think these little ones are safe and sound, having received so much, you realize that the watchful eye of the mother and the father must guard and keep them on the path after which their souls long. How easy it is to be taken away, here and there, and to lose the sense of discrimination when consciousness moves from Truth to a little error and then one more gross, until suddenly it is so gross as to totally engulf the child. So it is with spiritual energies that gradually become psychic through the vanity of the ego.

Therefore the gradations of life are usually identified only when they have reached the extreme. The figure of Christ and Satan seem easy to define. But moving through the marts of the world, we see sparks of light alongside darkness, sometimes in the same individual— and then, of course, the confusion where darkness appears as light and light is so covered over that you can scarcely recognize it in the dearest friend.

Some of you have wondered why I should be both a member of the Karmic Board and the Lord of the Sixth Ray. It is because of my long experience in pleading before the courts of the world on behalf of souls.

As you know, I have been an attorney in many embodiments, reaching far back beyond this civilization. In my learning of the laws that have prevailed in many nations and in my attempt to find in those laws a point for the justification of the innocent and for the binding of the guilty, I have seen what causes men to go astray, what causes children of the light to be taken in by the dark ones, and how they have put upon earth such a cunning manifestation of treachery.

Therefore, I have seen in all of my experiences (and, of course, you know that the lady never tells her age), for it has been tens of thousands of years that we have worked together for the deliverance of souls, that always the salvation of a living heart is Love.

Now, that love is not necessarily a love that is given, but a love that is already within—a love whereby the child moving toward Sonship and Godhood can resist temptation *because of a greater love!*

This, therefore, is my plea with you as mothers and fathers and teachers, sponsors of new age families, concerned citizens dealing with the great problems of crime and the burdens of drugs upon our children. The love that must be instilled, beginning with yourself, is a love so tangible for God in the person of one another, for God in the person of his saints, his angels, the Masters, Nature, and the simplicity of Life itself, that in the presence of such love the abrogation of the laws of God is altogether unthinkable—a love so full of the penetration of Law itself, the love of the Law as a witness unto Truth, the love of the Lawgiver as the one who defends the highest interests of his children.

I believe that this love instilled within the child must also be a sense of self-worth. For if the child is taught only to love those things outside of himself, he is also taught to have a dependency on something that is at a distance. And therefore, the attention is taken away from the self as an individual, the self as worthy, as accountable, as having ability and integrity.

One must love oneself not only as the handiwork of God but as one's own handiwork. And if you do not love what you see or what you have made of yourself, you know that Love is the power to consume all that is unreal.

Personally, I like people who get along well with themselves, who are happy with themselves, are self-entertained, can laugh at themselves and their own mistakes and even at their own jokes. I like people who don't take themselves so seriously and thus dive into a spiral of self-condemnation when they make an error on the way.

You must realize, then, that when you feel irritable, when you are burdened with your circumstance, when you are unhappy alone, in solitude, in total quiet, there is not the inner resolution of the love of the God-free Being within. Now, all of these things create the propensity to move away from God in the hour of the testing.

Do you know that you will punish yourself by way of failing a test merely to prove to yourself and all others that you are not worthy? This is one of the most serious psychological problems of those who live on this planet —the subconscious mechanism to fail as a means of inflicting self-punishment and by way of proving to everyone that you are as bad as you (or they) affirm that you are.

Of course, this momentum can be traced to interaction with parents, for parents always figure in one's heart as a part of one's self and one's self-identity. And therefore, before the child separates out from parent, whatever the parent may do may create the indelible impression of the child being bad or unworthy. And this transferal, of course, stems from the fact that the parents do not love themselves in and as God.

And thus, we see that the entire human generation is a lineage of the propagation of anti-Love and anti-Self. And the reason, precious hearts, is quite simple. It is because people prefer to love themselves as human beings, and therefore, in an attempt to love that human self, one finds that the human self—because it cannot be perfected—is not necessarily worthy of love—for the soul retains the memory of the perfect image of self who is Christ the Lord and this alone as worthy of that unconditional love which cannot be fully accorded to the unpredictable, whimsical human self. And this, beloved, is the root of the dilemma of human love, as well as the love/hate patterns which sometimes plague human relationships.

And thus, one's moorings must be altered. One must penetrate to the core of Life, to the origin of all things, to the descent of the soul from God, to the realization that the compelling force of being is one's Divinity!

You may not like yourself for your mistakes, for your meanness or gruffness or anger or any of these conditions. Well, we do not expect you to like these things. The angels do not enjoy them, the Masters shield their eyes from them. There is only one thing to do with these things—to put them into the sacred fire and then to affirm their unreality past, present, and future!

Therefore, we come to the platform of self-forgive-ness. Christ in you can forgive you. But you the soul must be humble enough to accept that forgiveness and not to continue to affirm, in your willfulness, that mean-ness or that sinfulness almost by way of a perverted pride or an untoward false humility.

Now, I reveal to you the tricks that the human mind plays upon itself and upon your soul by way of limiting the expansion of the Divinity within you. And I do this for a purpose. For I come to teach you the way of the Sixth Ray of Christ and his servants.

Why do you think so many people in this world consider themselves not only unworthy to be disciples of Christ but absolutely unworthy to be the manifesta-tion of Christ himself? Pure and simple it is: They do not like themselves, they do not approve of themselves, and they act unwittingly to use the power that God has given them to reinforce the entire momentum of "sin" and condemnation which, as a yoke, is put upon the souls of God upon earth!

And many people, even the spouses of our devotees, have cast themselves in a certain mold of the human consciousness and have said, "I am this and I am that and I am this, and therefore I am not worthy to be a seri-ous churchgoer or a follower of God. I will leave that to you because I am what I am. Leave me to be what I am."

And all of this is nothing more than a human momentum multiplied by the mass consciousness, multiplied by the media, which has a way of reinforcing everyone's belief in their own humanness and denying anyone's possible hope in their own Christhood. It is as though the entire world were in a deep sleep, accepting this hypnotic spell that has been cast upon it.

And yet Christ has come, and he has lived, and he has taught the fulcrum of the Path to be one of forgiveness—which can never be sealed, of course, without the forsaking, again and again and again if necessary, of the wrongness of one's willful ways.

Beginning at the beginning, then, let us teach our children—and this includes our soul, for the soul is the child emerging to the Divine Sonship in your temple. Let us teach our children the reality of Love. Let us realize that love, as the intense white fire of God, is that quality which molds and perfects and elevates and disciplines. It is a love that loves so much that it does not fear to chastise, to bring into alignment—but always *by Love*. For each and every time the condemnation of the human mind is conveyed, the condemnation of the devils themselves, there is a loss of that love tie.

Now, where can you go for the example of just what is the razor's edge? You have only to look at John the Baptist and the Lord Christ to see how they dealt both with the children of light and with the sons of Belial.

Recognizing that the love of God may manifest as the most intense fierceness that will ever pass through the heart, by way of consuming on contact the very wickedness that is wont to enter into the hearts of those who yet retain this self-condemnation, the danger in the preaching of a sermon such as I give you is the realization that some who do not have the depth of the love of God will take my words as an excuse to be entirely irresponsible concerning their misuse of the laws of God; whereas such love of which I speak, so great within one's being, loves the friend, the brother, the sister enough to say, "I must pay back to the last farthing for each and any and all situations that I have caused which have become a burden upon you." And do you know that the saints in their desiring to serve have never been satisfied until they could pay back ten times what they have wrought as a burden against the Body of God upon earth—or any individual part thereof?

Therefore, my beloved, from my perspective I see that the lost chord of the teaching of the Cosmic Christ and the missing link in the evolution of man, from the standpoint of the human to the divine, is the truth concerning the nature of Love.

Let us sit at the feet, then, of John the Beloved, as he comes again to continue his teaching this fall at Summit University. This beloved Ascended Master will also be reinforced by the Lords of the Seven Rays; for we have only begun to speak to you concerning the fundamental lessons of life that you must now master, not only for your own mastery but to teach others the way out of the human dilemma.

For the path of ministration and service is to reinforce again and again to these little ones what is the meaning of embodied Christhood, what is the meaning of the living Word. And therefore, those who care for children know best just how much care is necessary to bring out the fullness of the child, to be with that child in all of the years of expansion and growth and self discovery in the midst of discovering two worlds—the world of imperfection with all of its allure and the world of perfection which, too, has its pull in the great magnetism of God.

Thus, I advocate to you an understanding of being a Keeper of the Flame. "The Keeper's Daily Prayer" is something that comes to you each day from my heart; for as I was embodied in a large family of many brothers and sisters of great talent, I saw how each one in pursuing his career needed love and ministration and the keeping of the flame of the sacred fire in order to be successful.

And thus, although the choice was given to me to pursue my own career, unbeknownst to my brothers and sisters I quietly kept the flame in deep meditation and prayer as well as outer helpfulness, in [by way of] contacting the great spheres [causal body] of their divine plan, and in accelerating through the mighty Archangels Chamuel and Charity in the understanding that the adversaries of Love are many, and that Love is the full power of creativity, and that the success of the career son or daughter of God depends upon the defeat of Love's adversary, point counterpoint.

And therefore, in the course of defending the

Christhood of my brothers and sisters, I had to advance in my own self-mastery to confront the fallen ones who attempted to thwart them in their most magnificent lifestreams and their offering to the world. Thus I understood Love as the consuming fire of the Holy Spirit that does indeed challenge and bind the wicked in the way!

There is no power greater than the Ruby Ray, for it is actually and symbolically the Blood of Christ. And the Blood of Christ is charged directly from the Godhead with the very source of Life itself. And Life consumes anti-Life that is Death. And Antichrist is Death to the soul that is emerging to become that perfect Self.

Some of you have had the joy of being with the little child taking that first step. And you have known the balance between guarding the child from hurting himself and, again, allowing the child to have the victory of the first step without any assistance at all. And, of course, this is most important because the first step of the baby holds the divine memory of the first step of the chela on the Path.

None can take it for another. One must place one's foot firmly, by the inner will. Therefore, we advocate allowing the little child to fall and fall again until, in the determination of that self-mastery, his first step will be his own and not by the hand of another.

Well, you see, beloved ones, there is a great parallel in life. For in order to master any area, one must contain the resolve, the determination, the understanding, and the mathematical formula. And when one realizes that one cannot succeed in a certain area without further skill, practice, training, probing, et cetera, and he contains the desire to succeed, he will go after those precise skills and he *will win!* And there is no replacement for that God-determined individual who has determined to let *nothing* stop him in the winning of the race.

You have seen this portrayed in *Chariots of Fire*. You have seen the fullness of the light of God as I saw it in my brothers and sisters. I saw, therefore, that actually very few on earth make it without the silent witness, the coordinate, the one who acts as guardian angel. And yet, I would not interfere or impose, but I worked at inner levels even with their very souls and with the Archangels.

And so I learned a path of Love, and I learned that everyone who goes forth to conquer has moments of self-doubt or thinks that after all of their trying, their works are not too good or that no one will want them or no one will appreciate their talent. And there is a moment of total self-blindness when the individual may make the decision not to go forth as that conqueror.

It is the flaming heart of the Mother embodied in the friend, the loved one, the ministering one that provides that help when the individual himself must give all of his strength and energy, all of his drive to the making of the mark at that precise moment. And therefore, even Christ on the fourteen stations of the cross still had the balance of his mother, holding the flame of watchfulness, of encouragement, of beauty, and of the divine memory of the end that is known from the beginning.

I would have you understand that the rotations of the planets, the movements of the stars in their courses are a perpetual example, reinforced subconsciously, that all of life is in the ritual of ministration and that the repetition of that ministering is the necessity and the beauty of Christ appearing. And as you come to see the need for daily service to be repeated without fail each and every day in your occupations, you move from the mastery of individual Christhood on the Sixth Ray to the full mastery of the Seventh Ray ritual of the holy orders of God.

Some have said, in considering those whom it is obviously their opportunity to serve, "I have told that person this, not once but many times over, and they still move against this principle or this law." Well, you see, beloved hearts, that is the obvious need for ministration. It is like the watering of the flowers. The rains come and they come again, and the elementals do not complain that they have given their water yesterday.

There are things we all need on a daily basis. And yet when it comes to the teaching of the sacred precepts of the Law, we think somehow, either in ignorance or in pride, that if we have given our teaching, our word ought to be obeyed. And if it is not obeyed, well, it is too bad for that individual—they had their chance.

Well, if the angels took this attitude, I daresay that none of you would have a ministering angel today. For

you have been ministered unto for tens of thousands of
years. And so you see, when it is oneself, it is easy to
understand that one may need comfort and need it
again and again. But in giving to others, you think,
"Why is this person always, always needing comfort
when God is obviously so always present?"

Well, that God needs to be obviously present in
you, beloved! For it is obvious, or should be to you, that
the individual cannot see God or understand his comfort unless you bring it personally. And so in your perception, therefore, you have the opportunity to be God.
By your perception of others' needs, I say, put on your
Godhood—instead of by your perception of your own
needs.

Some look at *Studies in Alchemy* and they say to
themselves, "Let me see. What do I need today?" And
whatever that need may be, they begin to give their
decrees to the violet flame and their visualizations and
their written letters to the Karmic Board. And thus, their
perception of their Godhood is to magnetize to themselves all possible needs, wants or desires they could
have upon this earth.

We, the Chohans, therefore observe. And we allow
souls of light to pursue the Path in this way for many a year,
for we know the end must soon come. When they have
finally magnetized everything they could think of under
the sun and realize that their souls are still empty and there
is still that longing for the lost chord, they may come to
the realization that it is not the use of the Path for the

getting unto oneself but the use of the Path in order to supply the needs of others that is its highest application.

I must tell you that you truly arrive at the point of the Ruby Ray exercise when you have no needs or wants, and you think to yourself, "How rich I am in the wisdom of God, his glory, and his love." And when someone asks you if you have a need or "What would you like for your birthday?" you cannot think of a single thing because you are so happy. And therefore, it remains for another to perceive perhaps that you need a new pair of shoes or that you have perhaps worn the same coat for five years, and they will bring you another. But you yourself couldn't be happier and would not even notice that there is an incompleteness in your outer manifestation. Such is the happiness of the saints.

We look upon the metaphysical movements of the world as being in the infancy of their pursuit of Christhood; for many of these consider the mark of attainment to be the fullness of health, wealth, and happiness; for them these are their standards of spirituality.

Well, beloved hearts, some of the most spiritual people in the world are so bearing the burdens of life that they may be in abject poverty, they may have nothing, they may be burdened with an incurable disease, they may be bowed down with all sorts of problems. And those who point the finger and condemn are the very ones who need attainment on the Sixth Ray of Ministration and Service.

And if they would run to the aid of that one, they would discover in themselves the lack of the one great gift that that individual possesses: Love. Love within the heart that is content to bear the burden of others. Love in the heart that trusts God in the hour of adversity. Love that does not complain simply because all things are not in the fullness of the richness of Western civilization, as the dreams of this West are created out of the images of opulence, luxuriousness, unending food, et cetera.

Beloved hearts, it would be well to look around at the civilization in which you find yourselves. It would be well to consider how many of its values have been imposed upon you from without and have no originality in your soul or in your Source.

It would be well for you to look to see on which of the seven rays you are wanting. Rather than to major on the ray that you have a great momentum on (or think you do), look toward the one where there is an absence of either understanding or perception of the Chohan or the missions of the saints on that ray. Then go after those decrees which invoke the flame of the ray, calling for the purification of the corresponding chakra, and seek to hold the balance of the corresponding wavelength and plane of consciousness for yourself, your family and your planet.

For here in the Heart of the Inner Retreat in proximity to the Grand Teton, you have the opportunity to anchor the seven rays of the seven mighty Elohim that are focused there, concentrated and anchored in that image of the All-Seeing Eye of God. This balance will enable you to help all people and to understand people of all races and walks of life; for you realize that one of the world's major religions applies to each of the seven rays.

Blessed ones, I can assure you that at the conclusion of my incarnation when I saw the victory of each one of my brothers and sisters, the fullness of my joy was in a heart of Love expanded, keeping the flame—keeping the flame and knowing that I was needed, that I was essential to their victory. And yet in their own right, each one did attain on his own—as much as the Great Law understands this oneness, this singleness of the individed individuality where, although no man is an island and all are mutually interdependent in the Great White Brotherhood, yet the individual himself, by his own self-reliance, forges and wins.

Beloved hearts, it seemed to the world, and perhaps even to my own, that I had not accomplished much. But I took my leave into the higher octaves thoroughly understanding the meaning of the self-mastery of the pink flame. Thus it was from the point of the Third Ray that I entered into the heart of Christ and saw the application [on the Sixth Ray] as ministration and service. And therefore, in my practice of law, I realized that the love of the law is its use in the defense of the helpless, of the innocent, and of the guilty.

Now, as we look to the uses of our Community in terms of the Sixth Ray, we must go back to the needs of those members who are in the Community who have the Teaching and the Law and are in the very process of figuring out their own personal psychology, their own personal path. These need to be God-taught, to be loved, to be understood. And the least among you may provide unto the wise the necessary key to their own discernment. Each one of you has the capacity to help another, and even someone who you think needs no help.

All people need help. The Ascended Masters need help! And the more humble your receptivity to the help of anyone, the more you will realize that self-sufficiency is only sufficient in God and in Community itself.

Therefore, our work is twofold. The needs of the members of this Community are unique. And as it represents the Body of God, there must be a turning to one another in love and helpfulness. And there must be receptivity to this. For if one is not receptive, sometimes those who would be helpers withdraw by the rebuff or the rejection, as some in their pride think that the slightest suggestion may be a criticism or a debasing of themselves, even when they think they are wise or more wise than they are. One can perceive in oneself spiritual pride when one is not responsive to the receipt of Truth from anyone.

On the other hand, as a body, you have a quality of wholeness that the world has not known. You have something to give which even you yourselves have not understood. It is the simple joy of the victory of the light demonstrated in daily life.

It is so important that you realize, as you demonstrate the Law and show its victory, that through you others may be converted to their own Mighty I AM Presence and experience their own liberation. And therefore, each day when you come upon life's burdens, you do not submit or succumb—not because of yourself but because of God in the one nearest you who is looking to your example.

And if you give it not, they will say, "Well, that religion doesn't work. If one day she's up and one day she's down, and now he's grumpy and cross and now he's happy, what can that religion do for me?" And so, you see, when you let yourself indulge the mood energies of your own subconscious or the world's, you are not proving that with God all things are possible or that Jesus Christ *is* the same yesterday and today and forever.

Thus, through the eyes of the Lord of the Sixth Ray, I desire that you should see that the victory of the flame to those on this path has a greater accountability than any other. For to those to whom has been given so great a salvation, so great an understanding, of them is required the greater example and the greater proof.

For you see, if this truth is Truth, then the world will say, "Those who have it ought to be at least practically perfect." And they will not forgive you for those things for which they forgive themselves, because they say, "We are sinners. We can do these things. We haven't said that we are good or that we are students of the Masters. These are our sins. We openly confess and discuss them." And in many cases, they are not even ashamed, for they have no sensitivity or conscience to sin.

But they know exactly what you ought to be doing, what you "should" be doing, and they are the first ones to tell you when you are not! Sometimes they move in with their condemnation even before you feel the nudging of your own guardian angel. So, you see, those who are swift to condemn are the ones you seek to convert by being that example, not of yourself—"not of I, but of God in me."

The Sixth Ray is the most practical, down-to-earth path. This is what Jesus came to show. Whatever he did, he did publicly. And his ministry was concerned with physical things—physical diseases, physical conditions, the oppression of the then Nephilim government of the planet—the principles of the Law constantly preached and practiced by physical example, by personal sacrifice, by personal burdening of oneself with the karma of one's friends.

Now, in the victory of the God flame of your own Christ Self, I commend you to the flame of perfect cheer.

In the name of the living Word, let there be drawn to this focus those hearts who understand the meaning of the conveyance of the mission by the divine art through media, through the Word, through example in every form that it can be given, through the illustration of Life—beginning with oneself. And then, hand in hand, let us see what we can work as the work of God, as the many sealing the Person of Christ in us all.

I bid you good-day in the victory of the pink rose.

August 28, 1982
Royal Teton Ranch
Montana

I AM so willing to be filled
    With the Love of God,
I AM calling to be thrilled
    With the Love of God,
I AM longing so for Grace
    From the heart of God,
Yearning just to see his face
    By the Love of God.

As a rose unfolding fair
    Wafts her fragrance on the air,
I pour forth to God devotion,
    One now with the Cosmic Ocean.

Brotherhood—
the Heartbeat of God,
the Rhythm of Life

In the stillness of the heart is heard the heartbeat of God, the rhythm of the release of the cycles of Life as life flows from untrammeled heights of God's awareness of Being.

I am come in the flow and the rhythm of God's love that moves across eternity in undulations of sound, calling the souls of all evolutions in the stellar worlds home to the heart of God.

The great summoning of Life is for souls who have evolved in the outer realms of time and space to return to a center of Being that is Awareness, that is Truth, that is Life. Man must go within, for the souls of mankind are tired of evolution in darkness, in chaos.

Souls have not built the great amphitheater of life where the great drama can be outplayed in nobility after the image and likeness of the Christed ones. And therefore, the weariness of the soul is not in outer manifesta-

tion but the weariness of the soul is in the outer manifestation *that is not Whole*, that is not complete because
of wrong sowing and of wrong knowing.

Mankind have not known the Truth that should
make them free, but they have known the Lie and been
condemned by that Lie. And thus, the weariness is of
the ways of the flesh, the experimentation with the uses
of the sacred fire that is inordinate in the sight of God.

I come as a Cosmic Mother and as a member of the
Karmic Board to draw the tired, the poor, the weary,
those who have been burdened by the world and have
not remembered the words of the Prince of Peace, "My
burden is light."* For every burden you carry, precious
hearts, can be changed in the twinkling of an eye into
light and light's manifestation, light's toleration of itself.

For light is infinite, and thus the starry light that
portends an infinite Cosmos waiting to be received,
waiting to be filled with the fruits of the harvest of souls
can be seen, can be known, can be experienced by souls
who will come within into the fiery core of Being, into
the chamber of the heart.

And when you come into that stillness and you
begin to meditate upon God, you will first be moved
and stirred by the regular beat of God's heart. In that
beat is the pattern of the release of energy for a Cosmos,
a rose, a seed, a soul. It is the regular advancing rhythm
of energy spiraling from a fiery core to the circumference of its inherent design.

---

*Christ Self-awareness

When you come into the center of the heart and meditate upon these concepts, you will at first wonder at the grandness of God's be-ness. And by and by as you meditate upon that Being, you will come to realize that you are meditating upon your very own Being, your very own Life, for God is your Life. In fact, God and Life are synonymous.

In the center of awareness you garner energy to the rhythm of the music of the spheres. The baton of the conductor of that music moves to the beat of God's heart, and all time and space are born from the hand of the Divine Conductor—the Conductor of energy flow which makes the value of light perceptible as sound.

The sounding of the great tone which marks the birth of the soul is a mystical awareness of identity as the I AM THAT I AM. And which "I AM" is God, and which "I AM" is the soul when you say I AM THAT I AM?

When God speaks, he is saying, "I AM that soul, I AM that awareness of self, I AM *that* I *am*." When the soul speaks in the first person echoing the words of the Creator, the soul declares, "I am that God. I am that Life. I am that I AM." And as the energies flow from the Spirit to the soul, from the soul to the Spirit, from God to man, from man to God, who can say at what point God is becoming man, man is becoming God? Who can say at what point there is the nexus of the interchange where God is man and man is God?

Therefore, I AM THAT I AM. For in the Law of

the One the Alpha is become the Omega, and the Omega is become the Alpha.

Being is one, Life is one. But there is a divinity of polarity which manifests in order that God might have a subjective awareness of Self, and that man might have an objective awareness of self—that God might have an objective awareness of self, that man might have a subjective awareness of Self. And thus, in the flow of Life transcending Life, all Being is indeed One.

As you contemplate this great mystery in the center of God's heart gathering more of the flame of Spirit into the soul, you reach a point in meditation, in oneness, where you might say your soul could burst with the fervor of the divine light. And then comes the great desire to burst forth as a bud in springtime, as a blossom on a tree, as a bird flying from the nest—a fledgling.

There comes that moment when you must go forth to release those energies that have been wound tightly around the coil of Being. The spring must be released, energy must expand, spirals must go forth. And in the crescendo of the great orchestration of the soul, Life is born anew, Life expands, Life goes forth, a new manvantara is born, and the power of the seven rays comes forth from the five secret rays in the white-fire core of Being. And once again cycles release, cycles increase the identity of Godhood, and man's awareness spins from the center to the periphery of God's Cosmic Consciousness.

Man's whereabouts in time and space are limited

only by his use or misuse of energy. Using energy wisely and well, man transcends finite spheres and blends his consciousness with the Elohim. I am—and the I AM of me is—everywhere in the consciousness of God: God is everywhere in the consciousness of the I AM me, I AM he, I AM thou, I AM they.

Thus, service to Life becomes the byword of souls bearing light from the center of God. For when souls go forth to manifest increments of God's consciousness— his Self-conscious awareness burdened with light, with energy—they can only bestow light and energy on other parts of Life who are bereft of that sacred oneness, that sacred communion in the center of Being.

The letters in the word *service* stand for sacred energy, the ray of victory in the consciousness of each energy spiral. Service is God's way of releasing his light from man to man. And as that release is given from hand to hand, from heart to heart, it does impart the sacred antahkarana, the web of Life whereby Brotherhood becomes a canopy of golden thread woven of Love and Wisdom and Power expressed—blessed between hearts serving hearts.

Brotherhood is the union of souls who have gone forth from the center of Be-ness. By interchange, by cosmic flow, by mutual understanding, Life becomes One, weaving the great garment of God, the great canopy that spans the centuries and the giant egg. And that canopy is energy that is used to enfold and infold Life, to expand the physical manifestation of spiritual Being.

Thus, Brotherhood has ever been an integral part of the integration of God's consciousness with man and man's consciousness with God. It is the means whereby souls who are one in God become one in Mater. Souls one in Spirit must reach the same communion, the same communication of the fiery ovoid dispersed in time and space, dispersed in infinity as the far-flung planets and the stars are separated by hallowed space. They must find oneness by weaving a great tapestry, interconnecting threads of light from atom to atom—from Adam to Adam. Thus, man is reborn in Christ as the first man is made the last man in the cycles of evolution.

The Spirit of the Great White Brotherhood is the Spirit that is the interconnecting forcefield that connects Cosmic Beings, Elohim, Archangels, and unascended mankind, all serving to crochet this great weaving of energy connecting energy whereby Life is one.

The Great White Brotherhood is the archetype of brotherhood on earth and on other spheres. The brotherhood of man, the Fatherhood of God—these are goals of the Great White Brotherhood. To be counted a member of this Brotherhood is a great honor indeed, a great privilege, and a sign of one's inner devotion, one's inner dedication. But more than that, when you are accepted as a member of the Great White Brotherhood, you become part of the vast network of filigree patterns that hallow space and connect reality with Reality.

All beings who have identified with God throughout the ages are connected by the Brotherhood. And therefore, no one is admitted to this august company who cannot be trusted to hold the harmony of the weavings of light. For any tremor which should occur on a single thread would be felt by the all of that Brotherhood, ascended and unascended.

Therefore, let us clarify that the Great White Brotherhood is composed of ascended beings who have risen in the ritual of the ascension and a few who have gained self-mastery who yet walk the earth in physical embodiment. These few are counted to be worthy of membership and are indeed needed in the Brotherhood to anchor this great web of light and reason into material form.

Now think a moment. "Come let us reason together," saith the Lord. What would take place if many among you determined to show yourselves worthy of becoming candidates to be received as members of the Great White Brotherhood while you are yet in physical embodiment?

Would it not be a great boon to this planetary home to have the cycles of infinity and of these weavings anchored in the earth through you that the earth might also feel the vibrations of the heavenly hosts as they sing paeans of praise to the Infinite, chanting holy mantras praising God night and day? For all of this reverberates on the skeins of fire connecting heart with heart.

Saint Germain, the Knight Commander of the Keepers of the Flame Fraternity, founded that order to begin the initiation of souls upon earth who could be counted worthy to be accepted into the Great White

Brotherhood for this very purpose—that a greater portion of the consciousness of God individualized in the heavenly hosts might be anchored upon earth through His embodied sons and daughters for the blessing of mankind.

I trust that you will also recognize that other avenues have been provided for your preparation to be received into this Brotherhood that is sometimes known as The White Lodge—our releases in the *Pearls of Wisdom* in our publications, in *Climb the Highest Mountain* and in the full course that is outlined at inner levels for the Ascended Masters' university. All of these have one goal in mind: oneness with the Brotherhood and then the ascension into light for the Keeper of the Flame.

I have placed before you a goal that is attainable. Because some have attained, all can attain: "What Man Has Done, Man Can Do." This is the motto of lightbearers in service to humanity. Man can succeed because he has the potential of Christ and of God—because others have made the sacrifice, have surrendered the not-self and have overcome the unreal and the brothers of the shadow.

I say, you, too, can go and do likewise if you will cast that fear into outer darkness, cast that doubt into outer darkness, seize the torch of illumination held high by the Goddess of Liberty and walk as men and women of courage, of determination who will not look back—no, never—but only upward and onward into the soaring heights of Spirit and Spirit's fire.

Each time you go into meditation upon God's Being, going within to be nourished of the flame as Jesus went to pray in the desert (signifying a place that is desolate of the human consciousness where Spirit can be reached), each time you go within, there is that infiring of God's energy securing that light density that can become the immensity of devotion in outer form.

Thus, to go within to declare the sacred name I AM THAT I AM, thence to burst forth from the cocoon of Being, to translate all that is within to the without—this is the calling of lightbearers. And each time you go without, the momentum is greater and thus the arrow of the soul (the aura thereof) that is shot into the air has a greater diameter and a greater circumference, a greater opportunity for overcoming and becoming God. Thus is Life self-transcending. Thus can you participate in the grand spirals of Being and of Consciousness.

I AM the light that is in you, you are the light that is in me. As I take my leave of you to center my consciousness in the Pleiades, you feel the stretching of the bonds of Brotherhood as our oneness spans time and space and expands. And thus, the Great White Brotherhood expands as hearts are one, as energies are one.

"I will make thy seed as the sands of the sea innumerable"—the promise spoken to Abraham of old. O Abraham, father of a great multitude! In the center of God's Being are the focal points of individualization. And God, as the Great Sower of Life, scatters the seeds throughout the vastness of Cosmos. But every seed is connected to every other seed, and as that seed unfolds its latent potential, ties are reinforced from hearts of light.

Cosmos expands through Brotherhood, through self-conscious Being, through the yin and yang, through the going within, the going without. Establish this rhythm within self and draw the earth back to the rhythm of God's heartbeat. And you shall render the greatest service of Hierarchy ever known, ever required, in an hour of great need.

I release to you, then, the mystical veils of the secret rays. By meditation upon the fires of the secret rays, you will come to penetrate and to know the fires and energies of God's Being. And then you will have the answers to all of your questions about Life, for they are experienced in the white-fire core of Being.

I have placed a gossamer veil of the energy that connects the entire Spirit of the Great White Brotherhood. Bask in this energy, draw it into your heart's chalice, and become a part of our Brotherhood of light.

I AM Nada of the light and I salute you in the flame of the Christ.

October 11, 1973
Santa Barbara

For your meditation on the
circle of Brotherhood—

The Arrow and the Song
BY HENRY WADSWORTH LONGFELLOW

I shot an arrow into the air,
It fell to earth, I knew not where;
For, so swiftly it flew, the sight
Could not follow it in its flight.

I breathed a song into the air,
It fell to earth, I knew not where;
For who has sight so keen and strong,
That it can follow the flight of song?

Long, long afterward, in an oak
I found the arrow, still unbroke;
And the song, from beginning to end,
I found again in the heart of a friend.

The Carpathian Mountain chain

Prior to the sinking of Atlantis, while Noah was yet building
his ark and warning the people of the great Flood to come,
Saint Germain, accompanied by a few faithful priests, transported
the flame of freedom from the Temple of Purification to a place
of safety in the Carpathian foothills in Transylvania. Here they
carried on the sacred ritual of expanding the fires of freedom even
while mankind's karma was being exacted by divine decree. In
succeeding embodiments, under the guidance of his master and
teacher, the Great Divine Director, Saint Germain and his followers rediscovered the flame and continued to guard the shrine. Later
the Great Divine Director, assisted by his disciple, established a
retreat at the site of the flame and founded the House of Rakoczy.

Lord of the Seventh Ray

Initiation of the
Seat-of-the-Soul Chakra

Retreat:	Transylvania, Romania Table Mountain, Wyoming, U.S.A.
Vibration:	Violet, Purple, Pink, Aqua, Teal
Gemstone:	Amethyst, Diamond, Aquamarine
Quality:	FREEDOM ALCHEMY JUSTICE
Gift:	Prophecy, Working of Miracles
Day:	Saturday

Saint Germain
Lord of the Seventh Ray

"May You Pass Every Test!"

Devotees of the flame of my heart, *I hear you!* And I AM here—not *there*, but here—*here* at the nexus of that cross of white fire, *here* where time and space meet and cancel each other out.

Here I AM in the Heart of Infinity. And where the divine spark is, there is Infinity. Therefore, I greet you as the Infinite One and as infinite ones—one times one times one, ever the Infinite One.

Therefore, let the great circle of our oneness and our love cancel out all division, all misunderstanding, all ignorance, and every false testimony as in the case of the blind men and the elephant—all giving varied reports of the same spectacle but never arriving at the point of reality which is the Heart: *heart* perspective!

I call you to that point. For centered in your heart, which is becoming my heart day by day, you can see all things as they are. For the true perspective of wisdom, anointed with love, enfired with the will to be all that God is, and blessed with the purity of the Mother—what else can there be out of this than the crystal prism?

Behold, I make all things new by the flame of the heart, by the vision of the heart, by the wisdom of the heart that is the endless stream of the endless Source.

O my beloved, I am come and I am joyous to be here, joyous to bask in the light of Helios and your own hearts' dear love. I see your perspective of freedom and I come therefore to give you another.

May you pass every test!

Beloved hearts, in my retreat this is the salutation upon meeting and parting—not "God bless you," but "May you pass every test!" Is this not commendable and noteworthy of the devotees of my heart who are determined to follow in my footsteps, not to make a rut in the road of life but rather to secure what the Master has gained? A worthy cause indeed!

Beloved ones, I come to present to you, then, a crash course in passing every test. [applause]

Thank you, beloved ones, let us begin. For I am determined that this trek upward shall have been worth every inconvenience and every penny! [applause]

You remember the joke that is told by Morya and Kuthumi making their treks to the home of light, to the feet of the Masters—Morya being so intense about getting there and Kuthumi a bit more peaceful. And when they had arrived and when they had returned, for all of the perspiration and energy expended by Morya, it was Kuthumi who retained the message of the Master.

Thus, in all of your experiencing of the Path and

all of that energy expended in getting here, I desire that the stillness of the moment shall provide you with a heart's cup worth of flame and light and truly a blessing untold. It is my determination—because you love and love again and because you are determined—that you shall not return to your homes the same as when you arrived! But you shall truly find yourself a new creature after the violet flame.

Beloved ones, the reward for love is great. But those who deserve it often do not receive it because they are the ones who are the busy ones or the fighters—driving, working, serving. And therefore, let us pause together. Let us be still, then, in these lower vehicles and let us feel the chakras *shining* as the seven Elohim, *shining* as the sun and the stars!

Let us expand consciousness now. Let us increase the circle of the aura. Let us realize that we are not these lower bodies but we are God-free beings using these vehicles to accomplish an end.

The means is not the goal, but the end is the star itself appearing. And therefore, let us not allow our ways and means to compromise the goal or to cause us to tarry or lose sight of the goal. The goal is the star appearing, the star of Aquarius that has appeared over the sun of my birth.

O beloved ones, the true star is the herald of the coming of the devotee, the Mighty I AM Presence of each one. Remember your star! And remember the star appeared in the hour of your physical birth. Should it not appear now in the hour of your new birth in the living

Christ—Christ of Aquarius, Christ of Pisces, Christ of the twelve hierarchies of the sun? All of these you are internalizing as the magnificence of the Great God Flame.

God in you is able! But do not, I pray you, adorn the human self, which the mortal is. As the grass, it is here today and gone tomorrow, and the mighty fire and the wind sweep through and it is no more.

Beloved ones, the course of perfecting the human is not the way. It is not the way of overcoming. Thus, if you are not interested in perfecting the human, you can just right now drop that pride in your human self! Just drop it on the floor as an old garment! Beloved ones, it is as an oily, torn undershirt that you have worn too long.

Do you not see, it does not matter? You are *real God-free beings*—divine beings now! You *are* immortal, and *all else is illusion!* Will you accept it? ["Yes!"]

Beloved ones, this Messenger, as your Mother in form, does gaze upon you from year to year and rejoice in your victories and ofttime wonders and muses with me why, through all of the teachings given, you yet hang on to that supercilious consciousness of that human self.

Beloved ones, I come, therefore, to deliver this message in consultation with the Messengers and Morya and Helios as well *to pierce now the veil in your belief in yourself as mortals!* This is my God-determination, this is God's will, and I am here in the full force of hierarch of the Aquarian age to *wipe* from the very screen of life the law of mortality itself, which is the same law that sustains the serpent consciousness! Now do you or do you not want to continue to operate under the law of mortality with those serpents? ["No!"]

Then, I say, let us be done with it. We are free spirits. You do not have to wait until the hour of death, so-called, to know eternal Life. You are eternal here and now. This place is your eternal abode, and I speak not of finite coordinates but of this place as the point of the eye of the Mind of God—the *seat* of your consciousness.

Find that seat now. Feel it in the base of the brain and in the spine. Feel it in your heart! Feel it in your soul! Feel it in all of your being!

That which you feel is God. It is *God*, I tell you! It is not some combination of physical senses. Nay! That awareness of God in yourself is something above and beyond the form, yet it registers on the form. It pulsates with life *in* the form. But the form is always the effect and the vehicle for experiencing that consciousness which has been, always shall be, is here and now the eternal God!

Let them say what they will. I will say: Ye are gods!* And all of you are sons of the Most High—brilliant sons of light! Now let us roll up our sleeves and go about shedding all shadow that has been accepted as the singeing of the garment these long ages. Beloved ones, it is like burnt toast! You throw it out the window and let the birds have it! [applause]

May you pass every test.

Can you not see in this expression and my posture

*Ps. 82:6; John 10:34

the person of Maitreya peeping through? I am his guest, speaking at his Mystery School on his behalf for his beloved and my own.

May you pass every test! It is Oriental, *n'est-ce pas?*

Beloved hearts, how do we begin? How do we begin to maintain that God-control that allows for the rhythm of God to restore the balance *before* the human reaction—out of fear or anger or that teetering/tottering off balance?

Beloved hearts, the components are there in the dictations, the decree book, the Keepers of the Flame lessons. But, as it always is, the more vast the compendium of knowledge, the greater the requirement of the teacher to organize. Thus, I point to the Count-to-Nine Decree. The "Count-to-Nine" given in the full fire of your heart enables you to regain the command of your auric forcefield that has been impinged upon, pressed upon, penetrated, invaded.

Thus, understand: sometimes when you suddenly feel a disturbance—you are taken aback, you have a shock or a sudden reaction to the actions of injustice of another— one of the reasons you momentarily lose your balance is because the normal flow of the aura has been disturbed, as though you would suddenly agitate the waters.

Now, your aura is your sanctuary, and it is the *sanctity* of your God flame. Thus, before answering the demands of the carnal mind—the questioning, the praying for favors, or whatever—reestablish yourself. Speak quietly, softly, and slowly. For in this way you will not engage into yourself the anger, the impetuosity, the upsetness of anyone around you.

You speak as I am speaking now: from the heart—from the seat of the heart, the point of the Buddha. You speak loud enough, in the sense of being strong and firm, so that the breath and the voice are not sinking like a shrinking violet of fear. You speak strong enough and firm enough and peaceful enough and powerful enough so that God may use your voice to still your own aura and the agitation or the fear or the excitement of another.

Be the calm presence in a vortex of calamity and activity, beloved hearts, and learn the way of the power, the immense power of peace itself. Thus, beloved ones, you ought to know by heart the Count-to-Nine Decree. You ought to realize that in a situation of upsetness it is necessary to take some deep breaths. For in the presence of anxiety, the heart begins to palpitate and people begin to breathe in a short-breath manner, thus adding to the absence of control.

You take a deep breath, you release it, you go to the heart, and you give no instantaneous answers, yes or no—no instantaneous reactions or solutions—but quietly turn within. There are many ways of handling this. If someone is ferocious like a mad dog, you may say, "Wait one minute, please. I shall return momentarily." [applause]

You see, beloved ones, the tests are flying full and sure. We want you to experience the sense of mastery, of dominion, the enormous pleasure of having finished a day and dealt with that force, that driving force of irritation, and conquered and risen above every foible of the senses directed against your heart.

They would steal your life. They would take the flow of love between us. They would break the bond by any form of anger or outrage. And they will steal from you your sense of worthiness, your sense of the mantle of being the disciple of Sanat Kumara. When they can destroy your dignity and you begin to feel like a moth, then you will also behave like one. And till you regain your self-identity, I must pause and wait again, wondering just how long you will flit around the bulb of these serpent ones who have beguiled you into their auras momentarily.

Thus, beloved hearts, the soft answer turneth away wrath. If someone is speaking to you in a loud and high-pitched manner, adjust the tone and answer with the God-command. Answer with helpfulness. Try to solve the problem. Try to show the best side of things. Provide emergency care when it is needed. Keep your wits about you. And don't enter the vortex of another's anxiety, else you will become confused.

Remember that anything that seeks to taunt you from the seat of the Buddha in the secret chamber of the heart must be noted as the enemy—not the person necessarily, for it is often a loved one, but the force attempting to use that one. Thus, it is your challenge to liberate that one as well as yourself from the human nonsense of the moment.

May you pass every test!

Unless you center in the heart, which is the central sun of your being, you may find yourself tumbling on the periphery of the aura, which touches the world consciousness. That point, that outer circle of the aura, should always be a very intense blue—a blue fire of protection, which is also outside the tube of light. Now you visualize the violet flame in the very center of the tube of light.

But I would make the point that when you are bristling with blue flame this often antagonizes others because it is so powerful and brings out the worst in them. Thus, the better part of wisdom is to wear the kid glove—that is, to put another layer of violet flame outside the blue to be a calming effect, to consume that which may rub against the aura or come at you. And if it break through the violet flame, then you have the blue-flame wall, then you have the power of the tube of light. And if diplomacy does not work, there is always the strength of the shield of Archangel Michael!

In the still and sweetness of the light, I AM come.

Often it is a matter of stance. How do you hold yourself? Are you in readiness for the next delivery of God or thrust of the sinister force, or are you, as they say these days, "laid-back"? If you slouch, if you are laid-back, wide open, lounging around—the TV set is on, the ads are bombarding their rock beat, the cat is meowing, the dog is barking, the children are screaming, the phone is ringing—how do you expect, then, to keep your cool? It is a setup, but *you* have allowed it.

Now, you can maintain your calm in the midst of

these things but not with a laid-back attitude, for any moment the potatoes on the stove will burn and everyone will be in an argument and, if you don't watch out, yourself included. And then what have we accomplished?—a lost hour for Saint Germain and the vital work of Helios and Vesta; your own sense, "I will never become a good chela. I will never master my life."

But, beloved ones, it's a matter of one, two, three, four, five—a few simple requirements: Do not allow the family to be bombarded from all directions. Do not allow all these things to be taking place at once. Strive for communion with the heart. Feed the cat, put out the dog, turn off the TV set, make sure all is safe on the stove, and enjoy that circle of communion with God-determination that each member of your family or household or friends shall have the opportunity, by your loving presence, to express something very important from the heart.

Now we come to the point of education, the education of your soul and, by your example, the education of others. There is unseemly conversation that quickly can accelerate into argument. Avoid, then, that which is controversial when you already know you disagree on a point.

Why continue the argument? Each one having a right to his own opinion, let us discuss another avenue. For by another avenue, an approach to God or to art or to science, we may come to a point of agreement. Not as compromise but as agreement do we build the kingdom of God. Thus, we find the fundamental points of agreement and build on these.

Whenever there is agreement in a principle of God, a nucleus is formed—a bond of love. And that bond of love actually begins to consume the area of disagreement and error which may be in the mind of your friend or may be in your own mind, for we ourselves must see our own misconceptions, *n'est-ce pas?*

Perhaps you have noticed on a number of occasions that by your words and actions you may have caused some great grief and burden. You may have brought in the dark clouds through negativity, pessimism, criticism, barking and clamoring and having your way. And on another occasion, by doing what you know so well how to do, everyone has come away feeling good, feeling satisfied, feeling equally loved and equally important, and enjoying supremely a soul-satisfying evening or experience together. Thus, you see, the carnal mind takes pride in itself, in its ability to control and hurt and put down and best another, and to rise and puff up as the puffing up of the snake.

Yes, you can do these things, but I admonish you to choose not to do them—to not attempt to be the most important person in the room or the one who wins all the arguments or makes all the brilliant points. Far better to go within the heart, send love to each one, and encourage by your conversation some precious point of wisdom or expression to be forthcoming from another because you make it easy, you provide a point of relaxation and warmth. And someone who perhaps has had a much harder life than you, who has been silenced perhaps by great darkness through loved ones, can finally feel at home and free to speak without being criticized.

Beloved ones, assume that those who come to you are injured and maimed and scarred, for they are. They have been in many battles of life. If you find them ornery or thick-skinned, this is a defense mechanism they have set up for a very deep hurt. Heal the hurt, not in such an obvious manner as self-proclaiming oneself as the healer—"Now I am going to do this for you, now I am going to do that for you"—but simply do it in the quietness of your heart. Learn to pray for people and not to *prey* upon them. [applause]

It is true, beloved ones. Much of the hurt, much of the cruelty expressed in the world today is the means of the individual wrapping up again and again that old wound, that sharpness. And thus, it becomes a very important point of the Law to apply to Almighty God for the healing of one's soul of the *need* to be aggressive toward any part of life.

You see, mortals have these needs, humans may have them; for both are without the divine spark. But the sons and daughters of God, the children of the light have no need to partake in the world's fare of psychology, just as you do not partake of the food that is served in some quarters. You have long ago transcended the need for that type of intake.

Much of the cause of your failure of many tests is that you have not stopped to rid yourself of the human habit to express that aggravation, that arrogance—all coming from the need of the carnal mind to assert itself. It is *not* real! It has *no* power to dominate your personality! I speak *directly to you*, and all of you *know* whereof I speak! And I tell you: the promise of your ascension will never be compromised by me, but it *can* be compromised by your free will!

You must listen to me. There is a need to change by the *will* of the *heart*, by a heart that loves enough to change because others are still suffering from a dishonest expression that you periodically give vent to—dishonest because it does not praise God in the individual, it does not rejoice in his overcoming but still retains that defiance that will put down another.

Beloved hearts, I will stand, and I will stand for eternity, to champion your soul's path of victory and the ascension. Many of you who find yourselves in a precarious situation through your dalliance with the carnal mind may this day shed it in this heart and in my heart. For my heart is great enough, as the heart of God, to consume it all.

My heart this day is a cosmic incinerator, if you will, and it can consume if you let go. But remember, it is not a one-time event. You may decide to stop smoking now and put it into my heart, and the record will be consumed. Twenty-four hours from now you will meet the world momentum for which you have had a weakness and *you* will have to say:

No! Thus far and no farther! I *shove* you back, you nicotine entity! Be *bound* by the power of my heart that is one with the heart of Saint Germain! *You* cannot *touch* me, for I AM the Infinite One! I live in the heart of God. There is no time and space here, and *you* may not dwell in Infinity! And since I do not dwell where you are, I will not smoke today or tomorrow or forever. For I am in my house of light, and the only smoke that is here is the sweet incense of El Morya with me! [applause]

Thus, may you pass every test.

Understand the law I reveal to you. Sin can only be committed in a finite consciousness or in the finiteness of time and space. The moment sin is conceived, the conceiver of the sin is no longer a part of eternity.

Thus, when Archangel Michael cast out the fallen ones out of heaven, he was ratifying the law of their own being which they set in motion by the spirit of pride: "I will become as God. I will not worship the living Christ but I will *be* worshiped!" This was their vow. Instantaneously, they lost the protection of the circle of the One. Thus, in casting them out, Archangel Michael and his legions were the instantaneous representatives of cosmic law.

Each and every time you begin to conceive of sin, an act of sin, you lose the protection of the entire Spirit of the Great White Brotherhood. And you need to know when you stray from the Law of Truth. And it is because the thought and the feeling is *enslaving* that Jesus said to Judas, "That which thou doest, do quickly"—let the consciousness of sin become the act of sin so that you may repudiate it and repent and be saved.

Now, we of the Great White Brotherhood do not recommend that you indulge the fantasies of the sinful sense, but rather that you realize that the bird of prey of sin may come and lodge in your aura and you may entertain it as a delicious idea for weeks and years and never *free* yourself from the desire to engage in this or that.

And now and again that desire becomes so impelling that you fulfill it and commit the sin and see no dire consequence thereof. And you do it again and again, not realizing that you are binding yourself with cords of limitation—limitation that one day becomes old age, disease, and death.

Let not the absence of the hand of God instantaneously upon you when you err give you the idea that the law of karma is not irrevocable, for I tell you, it is. And we have all bound ourselves by that law, and we have all *liberated* ourselves by the same law. And that law is just! And may the just men made perfect by love use the law wisely to their advantage, which advantage ought to be the liberation of the light of the heart which will insure you great gain in all octaves.

And therefore, let us quell the subtle vibration of ambition which you do not recognize and, therefore, I admonish the Messenger to point out to you one by one. For ambition in itself is a hideous monster, tricking you all the way to trust the human consciousness instead of to get God first and, in getting him, to find a cornucopia of treasure and wisdom and light and abundance and divine love ever flowing.

Beloved ones, if you remove yourselves from time and space and always find the center of the cross, you will dwell forevermore in the house of the Lord, the secret chamber of the heart, the sacred heart of Jesus, whose heart I have made my own, imploring that Christ and therefore intensifying the purple fiery heart in his honor.

In that heart there is no desire for hashish, there is no desire for heroin. But if you stray from that heart and you have had a long habit, you may identify once again with the outer man or woman and the desiring and find yourself in the turbulent waters, sinking beneath the waves, crying out for the hand of Christ who will always extend to you that hand until you are safe and sound again in the Heart of Infinity.

You see, beloved ones, all desires of the human that you may have in this world can be surrendered. And when they are surrendered, the divine desiring of God comes into your life. For every human desire there is a divine desire that is legitimate, that is fulfilling, that will give to you whatever you thought you might get through human desiring but truly could never have or keep and much, much more. But it takes courage.

Thus, if you would retain the desire to control others (which is very prevalent in the human race), the desire to have those things that are not ordained and on and on, but you desire to give up those desires that make you sick and uncomfortable, you will be walking a tightrope of the human consciousness, trying to take the best of it and to leave the worst and yet not really willing to forsake the totality of it or the whole ball of wax, as we have said. It is a precarious position and I can only admonish, for you have free will.

Every experience in life can be transmuted and transcended to become a divine experience—though physical, though actual, though down-to-earth, though a part of what that truly golden-age consciousness can be. Thus, it is not wrong to desire happiness, to desire the family of God, to desire your own fulfillment or education or God-success. Truly, no thing will God withhold from you when you use legitimate means of arriving at the goal.

Fear is what binds you to the alternative path and method. Thus, I say, drop those fears! Let God show you how happy you can be in the fullness of his love—how you can have these things in the highest sense, glorify his name, pass that human consciousness through the flame, and still retain an individuality which is happy, joyous, hard-working, ever-learning, striving, and a joy to be with because you will be the one who unlocks the mysteries for others. The mystery of happiness itself written all over your face can be divined by those who meet you by watching how you live.

Cease, then, *cease* from toying with the idea of unreality! Cease from the idea that you have ever been enslaved. The slaves of death must live in a consciousness of death! Now let us remove the octave of the consciousness of death. Let us remove that plane. If it ceases to be, will *you* cease to be?

Take the astral plane for existence—nothing permanent, nothing reliable, all illusion, endless explorations of matter scenes that are changing like a kaleidoscope, entertaining for an 'infinity' that is an imitation of the real Infinity. The labyrinth of the human consciousness—many dwell in it. As for me, and in my life, I long ago canceled it out and I have suffered no loss; for I had long before consumed and replaced the astral debris with the victory of the Christ consciousness.

You see why God does not cancel out the astral plane? Because a part of you is still there—records of the past, a sense of life expectancies and insurance policies and actualities and possibilities and "When I die, this will happen."

You see, beloved ones, some people actually consider themselves evolving toward death, moving ever closer to the final experience which they dread with their whole life. Well, were we to cancel out that plane for them, so much of them would cease to be, there would be nothing left that could be transmuted and that could rise and could take dominion over it!

Thus, the only place where the consciousness of death and the astral plane can be canceled out is in the point of the *will* of the chela in this octave! Only *you* can decide:

"It is no more! I shall weep no more—yesterday, today, or tomorrow! I shall weep no more about any human experience!"—that is, in the sense of self-pity or condemnation, for the tear that is shed with joy and compassion is not the weeping of the weeping entity.

When you decide it is *done*, and you decide with the full power of your I AM Presence that you are willing to *wrestle* with the old momentum and not allow that beast to rise from the dead at any time, when you will *plunge* the sword of the Word, and the *spoken Word*, into it, when you will wrestle with every temptation to breathe upon it the breath of life again and take it up again—I tell you, beloved ones, so many angels will come to assist you that as you walk the earth it will be as though a cloud of glory surrounded you—so many angels will come to reinforce the determination of the sons and daughters of God to be free.

Cosmic reinforcements are waiting. You must *not* be discouraged and say: "Well, this is the way I am. Mother knows the way I am—she takes me the way I am. And I have tried before, I've never been able to overcome this, and so God will just have to take me the way I am!"

Well, beloved ones, no louder voice did pride ever have, looming and glaring at the soul that has been silenced by the heavy tread of the boot of those who are the self-proclaimed independent ones, not realizing they have been singed by Lucifer himself. For he is the one who said, "I am who I am! I am more important than the Son of God, and God will have to ordain that his sons worship me, else I will rebel." And he did.

Well, the problem we have today in this circle of lightbearers is that there is not much farther down that anyone can be cast in this day and age than to walk the physical octave. And therefore, though you *think* the angel has not bound you and removed you from God's glory by your defiance, it in fact has happened.

And yet, you say to yourself, "Nothing has touched me. I'm all right. Look at me! I'm sitting here among these devotees as one of them, but I have my own way of living my life independent of that strenuous path that *some* self-styled chelas have taken to themselves."

Well, beloved ones, do not point the finger at those who are the self-sacrificing ones, for you know not the karma they balance or the assignment from inner levels. They have read the record of their life and they know what it will take to overcome and be victorious. And they are also a signpost to allow you to see that there is a sainthood to be pursued. And when you see the humble chela you may imitate the Christ in that one but not become attached to the outer personality.

This is the age of freedom. No one may tap you on the shoulder and say, "Here, here! You must do better." We do not have a physical, embodied shepherd for every single soul, one on one.

You have the teaching. You are expected to apply it. You are expected to make the call to be shown *why* you do not pass every test. You are expected to apply what has been given and ask for prayer and support when you wrestle with the beast you have created that has grown much larger than yourself so that your soul feels the towering of a monster before it and must have the reinforcement of the lineage of the Great White Brotherhood.

I can tell you that the Messenger has never knowingly turned down a request for a call. And if it has come to pass that she has not given a call, it has occurred that the Holy Christ Self of the Messenger has made that call. And thus, none have gone without recourse to the flame of the Mother which she bears in our name.

Thus, those who say, "I will not awaken the sleeping Buddha. I will not bother the Mother. This is one thing I have to do for myself because I have done this thing wrong for so long and now I am going to do it right..." You see, beloved ones, you engage in the lie of non-hierarchy. They deny the chain of being and they get *you* to deny you are a part of the eternal chain of God.

The higher helps the lower. As you accept help in humility, you can extend help. If you do not receive from the one above you, you cannot give to the one below you whose progress is utterly stopped because you yourself have stopped.

You see the pride. Some do not like to think they are dependent upon others. Learn to be receivers of our grace and the grace of a chela for whom you have had disdain. For the prayers of that one whom you think to be beneath you may be the salvation of your soul.

Revere God and let him take care of the human and do not create a false hierarchy in your mind, a panoply of all persons you know—some you place on the highest rung and some on the lowest in your system of judgment. And then you seek the company of those whom you think to be the important people who can somehow add to your stature. This is failing tests, and it leads to a great debacle as the house comes tumbling down which you have built through establishing contacts, associations, being a part of that illusory society, et cetera, et cetera.

One day the world must always turn against the living Christ. And I do not think that any among you would consciously turn down the light of your Christ consciousness to be accepted by men, yet some of you do this unconsciously to avoid the challenge or the hurt or the public criticism.

Beloved ones, you can only go so far with this little game as you fit yourself in and out of society's cliques. Sooner or later they will make demands upon you, and sooner or later you will realize that you just compromised your soul and your relationship to *me* to be popular with some potentate.

Think about it, beloved ones. The tests are lost because of an absence of forethought, of looking objectively at a situation as though you were on the ceiling looking down upon that meeting that you are attending. Look at the group of people—look through the eye of God— at the conglomerate of forces and their juxtaposition, and say to yourself, "How do I really wish to figure in that configuration, that astrology, of those personages?"

And the best way to figure, beloved ones, is to be in

their midst the presence of peace, of comfort, of wisdom if it is asked or desired—but not one that locks arms with the human consciousness, forming legal partnerships, becoming parts of groups or corporations or vast entities whereby, because legally you have wed yourself to it, you now become a bearer of the karma of that entity, that corporate entity (and there are many kinds and associations).

I do not say you cannot become members of this and that, but realize that, in the ultimate sense of the word, a member of the Great White Brotherhood (which you are or may aspire to be by becoming true disciples of the Law of Love) gives allegiance first and foremost to that Brotherhood. The tests will inevitably come of allegiance and of defending the right of the Ascended Masters and their chelas to *be* on planet Earth.

Now, if you do not desire your name to be associated with us, we will help you still all that we can. But I must inform you that sooner or later your disavowal of association with us must also be our disavowal of the living Christ and light we may impart to you: "He that denieth me before men, him must I deny before the Father."[1] It is one of those laws that none can break.

Thus, you see, between the *human* will and the *human* desire and the *divine* will and the *divine* desire, there is an abyss to be crossed. Its name is time and space. It is governed by the law of mortality. You can take the route of the labyrinth. You can spend another thousand or ten thousand years or a million gingerly stepping in and out of the caves and caverns, underground and through the astral plane, seeking earthly treasure and not realizing that the divine is practically on the tip of your nose.

Heaven offers you all, but it says, "You cannot bring with you that which is unreal." I advise you to take an apple a day, not the whole tree—one piece of fruit. Assimilate the apple—a virtue, a portion of God's consciousness. And by *assimilation* of this Body and Blood of God you will displace and find consumed in your life the old necessities of the carnal mind.

Thus, not by struggle but by slipping into God's kingdom little by little will you find the key to the joyous path which now truly does displace the *via dolorosa*. The "sorrowful way" comes only to the one who has not surrendered. As soon as you surrender, you are free. That is the key.

This is my crash course in passing every test. Take each problem and solve it, and do not try to solve a million problems all at once. Be logical and seek the Word and the Teaching. It is all there.

We have had a twenty-five-year mission and more with these Messengers. I could not give it to you all in one dictation, but I can place it in a capsule, a capsule of light as it were, with a timed release. But it is the release of eternal cycles and it shall come through the flame in your heart, as my flame with your own, supporting transmutation around your threefold flame, allows you to awaken in the likeness of God.

There is an *awakening* unto Light and Love. There

is an *awakening* unto Freedom. It is truly the gift of the
holy angels.

Beloved ones, I leave you with this pearl:

When you want to be like God, you shall be!

I thank you. [standing ovation and prolonged applause]

July 6, 1984
Royal Teton Ranch
Montana

Table Mountain, Wyoming

Scientists and inventors would do well to study at Saint Germain's
retreat, the Cave of Symbols. Here instruments are developed to
assist man which will be released in due time into the minds of
inventors. As we learn to control greed and selfishness and refuse
to allow the manipulation of our earth through war and the economies of the nations, we shall see what has been prepared here in
the Master's retreat of light. Foci in this retreat blaze forth light to
all of America. This has a significant influence upon her people,
keying into their consciousness the matrix of the golden age and
the remembrance of their lost inheritance. Saint Germain has told
us that his Cave is located inside Table Mountain in Wyoming.
However, there are 20 Table Mountains in Wyoming. Is this the
one?

Ceylon (Sri Lanka)

THE MAHA CHOHAN 8
Lord of the Seven Rays

Initiation of
the Eighth-Ray
Chakra and the
Secret Chamber of the Heart

Retreat:	Ceylon (Sri Lanka)
Vibration:	White, Pink, Rose, Ruby, White-Fire Core of All Rays
Gemstone:	Diamond, Yellow Diamond, Topaz, Ruby, Rose Quartz, Pink Beryl, Pearl
Quality:	COMFORT ENLIGHTENMENT BREATH OF LIFE
Gift:	The Nine Gifts Multiplied by Free Will and the Threefold Flame Initiation of the Chakras and the All Power in Heaven and in Earth
Day:	Liberator of the Sacred Fire of the Seven Rays/All Days

The Maha Chohan

The Reflecting Pool of Consciousness

May a mantle of the adoring grace of God descend upon your hearts with a gentleness of rain from heaven.

Upon the stage before me, I perceive a vast circular pool. Surrounding this pool are the beautiful verdant green leaves, the pads of lilies cupped and cupping the pure white flame of cosmic purity.

This pool shines now with an azure blue. Resplendent and glorious is this pool. At first, there is a murmuring of the sacred breath rippling gently upon the waters, and then all is still.

This pool, symbolical of your own blessed consciousness, is now still; and reflected on the surface you will perceive first the luminescent orb of the moon, polarizing the emotional body of mankind. And men are stirred because they recognize within their feeling world a sense of adoration for the beauty and loveliness even of the reflected light.

Now the scene changes and the moon passes across the heavens in its direct course until, sinking beneath the horizon, it is no longer visible in the reflecting pool. Myriad stars shine there and they, too, are reflected— magnificent orbs of light from afar. These are representative of Cosmic Beings and of the Ascended Masters' consciousness. These too, as Cosmos' secret rays, are reflected and mirrored in the consciousness of mankind.

Now there comes a mighty descending wind from on high. All seems turbulent for a moment, for there is a stirring to the very depths of the pool of consciousness. And then once again a voice speaks, "Peace, be still."

Now all is silent. In an attitude of expectancy and waiting, children of the light slowly behold the dawn of Being, a luminous radiance of the rising Sun. It is the Sun of their own Divine Being. The dawn moves toward noontime and from the zenith of the heavens there descends a glow of effulgent power which in its burning majesty sweeps into the waiting, receptive consciousness of the individual the full-blown momentum of Divinity—the Sun of his own God-free Being.

In this allegory which I am bringing to you, this splendid luminous orb is symbolical of the highest consciousness. For the consciousness of the individual is the doorway through which comes all experience, both material (natural) as well as spiritual.

Your consciousness, beloved ones, functions not only as a surface mirror, reflecting that which is poured into it from everyday living, but also as a sea that has depth. And there is mirrored in the internal depths of consciousness the wonders of God which have not yet been cognized by the surface mind of man.

Know, then, that in probing the laws of the universe—the laws of Universal Love and the laws of the Holy Spirit—you must be able to cognize not only the surface musings of the mind, but also the very depths of conscious being. And you must pray for your consciousness to be expanded so that you may begin today to perceive the depths of your own being and not that of another. For all Life is one, and it is in the splendor of knowing the oneness of Life through the doorway of self-illumination that the soul comes to understand the all-knowing depths of the Holy Spirit.

It is the sacred wind of the Holy Spirit which moves across the reflecting pond of being and sweeps away the pseudoimages of the emotional impacts of life amplified by the moon. And so in the allegory of the day and the night, man perceives that most of life which manifests here upon this blessed planet is a mere reflection of the real and is not real at all. For the moon but reflects the light of the sun toward the earth and is qualified by the consciousness of those who behold it from various aspects of life, of relativity.

From this study of the reflecting pool of consciousness, know, O chela, that beauty and the ability to make things sacred is given to man. And many consider, by reason of wrong allegiance, that the moon itself is sacred or that the elements of natural life are sacred.

But I tell you of a deeper allegiance. I tell you of an allegiance that did not begin with your first breath but that commenced with the identity of God. I tell you of your First Love.

I tell you of a love that began before the pool mirrored the consciousness of outer world identity. I tell you of a love that knew identity and oneness with the Father within the flaming consciousness of God before Cosmos was or before outer manifestation existed.

It is to this that you ought to pay allegiance, for it is through this magnificent love that your hearts will take dominion over the outer form—rendering it sacred by consecration and a pure heart which perceives the matter vessel as the temple of the Sun (Son).

When Adam, symbolical or real, began to receive the consciousness of God in the reflecting pool of self and then did not qualify it with the proper divine ideas, he himself was thrust from Paradise. And therefore, the angel with the flaming sword stood to keep the way of the Tree of Life, for no man can profane the Holy Spirit. No man, by misqualification or by misuse of free will, has the right or the power to desecrate the altars of heaven or to distort the Divine Image where only the light of heavenly patterns should appear in the mirror of consciousness.

Mankind may draw a circle upon the earth representative of the confines of their own identity. They may walk within that circle but not with impunity, for even there the great law of karma does function, yet within a confining area and era of life.

Blessed ones, recognize that in the reflecting pool of consciousness there is a solemn responsibility to Deity which is given to you with such utter sweetness as to enfold within it all the elements of beauty known to all of the poets and bards of the past as well as to all who ever shall be.

Some of you are aware that I was embodied as the one identified as Homer and you realize that I have a sense of spiritual beauty in my understanding of mankind's philosophical as well as his historical approach to the Deity.

Individuals yearn to know God, and therefore they seek the mystery of Self-realization as they stand before the portals over which are inscribed the words "Man, know thyself." But there is a golden thread of identity that runs through civilizations such as the Minoan, the Grecian, the Roman, and all to the present. This golden thread penetrates the very fabric of the earth body and makes of society a unified outpicturing—not a conglomerate mass of differing ideas but a unifying consciousness turned to some amount of diversification but always returning to the central theme and purpose for which man first came into existence.

And therefore, let the sages of Babylon rage, let mankind cherish false ideals if they will—they cannot alter or affect the Sun of Being that is reflected in the pool of Divine Identity. They cannot affect the effulgent light of Divine Reality whose Sun in the splendor of its shining sweeps aside by its dazzling power every lesser image and renders unto man the immaculate divine concept at all levels, at every hour.

Let the heathen rage and the people imagine a vain thing if they will! It has no power to shake the heavens, for only the power of God and the power of the Holy Spirit can blaze forth and extend itself in all of its immortal shining into the eye and heart of man. As though with a burning coal from the altar of God in the Great Central Sun, there is etched upon the consciousness of man a thought which will not elude him, though he were to have a billion embodiments. It is a thought that would cause him to yearn to know the immortality and purpose of his God-design and to return, homing at last, to the Heart and Mind that breathed identity into manifestation and said to the thing that was formed, "Behold, thou art a living soul."

Fire, beloved ones, descending from God upon the day of Pentecost quickened the hearts of men and made them aware of their Divine Self in a manner in which they had not previously experienced the I AM Presence in their entire embodiment. The power of the Holy Spirit is always the unifying golden thread that passes through all consciousness and causes that consciousness to be reminded of its birth in flame, in mortality—in duality—the reflection of the unreal and the real.

In the case of the moon, beloved ones, it is an orb which but reflects the Sun of reality. In the case of the Sun, that which is reflected and mirrored in consciousness *is* the reality; and man must know that the sunbeams which descend upon the mirror of consciousness are little threads of light and fire.

Some of you have observed at diverse times, as the sun is setting in the West in late afternoon, how shining through the clouds the radiant sunbeams are depicted almost as a ladder of light reaching down to the waters and troubling the sea. And you have heard it said that the sun is drawing up water into the clouds in order that it may spin a rainbow majestic and erect it to man's vision in the heavens.

So it is with the divine idea as the fire of Divine Reality descends from the Sun of Being, the Sun of God, as the power of the Holy Spirit descends from the Father and the Godparents of this system of worlds, Helios and Vesta, and from the divine parents of the universes, Alpha and Omega in the Great Central Sun —or even from the splendid Sun of your own beings anchored within the forcefield of your own physical heart as the threefold flame of Life.

This sun in its shining forth extends with each new contact a ladder of new hope to every heart. And as these light rays come down in all their tangible power and are mirrored in the consciousness of your being, you must fuse yourself with those beams in order that as they withdraw from their shining, your consciousness, indissolubly one with them, will rise with them back into the Sun of Being and you will become absorbed, as it were, into God-Reality and not into the illusion—which is nothing more than the moon's reflection in the pool.

I would like to clarify for you that the Ascended Masters of whom I spoke as "stars" are not illusions, they are God-free beings who have fused with the causal body, the Sun-star of Being, the First Cause and the First Love. And they do indeed shine "as the brightness of the firmament," for they are the wise ones who have turned the multitudes to the Sun of Righteousness— "as the stars for ever and ever."

But these Ascended Masters are far from the identification of mankind in their shining because mankind have not yet ascended into the heavens—do you see?— but they remain anchored upon earth. And even you who are the children of the light cannot rise into your own ascension merely by the power of the Ascended Masters, but you must appropriate and utilize your own divine opportunities and open up the door of your own identity and win for yourselves your own victory—yet so, as by the grace of the sacred fire.

This is why inscribed over the door of the Temple of Being are the words "Man, know thyself," for no other can know God for thee. And to know the self as the light-emanation of God who is more than a mere reflection or reflector but one with the Sun Source itself, "bone of my bone, flesh of my flesh"—this is the great mystery of Life unfolding.

Each one of you, then, must acknowledge for yourself the power of the descending Holy Spirit, must feel the tremendous pulsations of that magnificent God in action and feel the arms of all-enfolding light descending around your own being and world and exalting you into the starry heaven of God-design, that you may also become a part of those constellations of God blazing in the Cosmos to whom we all pay allegiance—for we behold in them the Sun behind the sun not as mere reflection but as *God-conscious Being incarnate!*

Therefore, when I meet El Morya as he journeys hither and thither upon the earth, I say unto him, "Salutations, Brother Morya, splendid son. I love you!" And he replies to me, "Beloved Maha Chohan, my heart's love to thee, O splendid star of God!"

And so it is with every Ascended Master. As we greet each other upon the cosmic highways, we speak to one another with such a charge of love that it actually blesses the entire universe; and so the reverberations of our love, occasioned by our simple hello, are echoed throughout the Cosmos.

Would you be so? Then appropriate the power of the Holy Spirit into your world and you, too, can cause the powers in the heavens to be shaken; for there is no limitation whatsoever to anyone, and all have the right and the destiny, if they will appropriate it, to enter into and obtain by divine grace the fullness of their victory over every limiting concept.

And it was never the intention of God to make one splendid star of being and then say to all lesser luminaries, "Behold, you must bow to this one star." This was a Luciferian idea and not a cosmic idea of the Mind of God. Mankind must recognize that light, in all of its essential beams, is truly one radiant outpouring of the Cosmic Christ composed of many, many portions.

Blessed ones, man has labeled those portions and called them photons. And so, from the first photon of light unto the myriad particles, or waves, of light pouring forth from the fountainhead of God in the Great Central Sun, there is ever a streaming forth of little photons of light which after making their rounds through matter molecules of manifestation return for repolarization back to the heart of God. Yet all of this light is one— one with the fountainhead, one with the Divine Identity, one with the ideal.

And only in man, the manifestation of God, and in the Hierarchy of heaven where God-identity holds sway, is the soul given the right to take dominion over these little forces of light, to marshal their forces, to build up the forcefield of their being, to enlarge the borders of their own causal body and store up treasures in heaven that they may be beneficiaries and benefactors at the same time.

For all men are beneficiaries of the Godhead—taking in the light beamed to the depths of the pool—and all are intended to be benefactors to all life, reflecting back to life from the pool of consciousness that portion of the light that is theirs to impart as gift and grace to others. Thus you may become with the Lords of the Seven Rays transmitters of the spiritual graces and the gifts of the Spirit, and by and by you become the transformers of the power of the Holy Ghost—to those who are able to receive the light of the Son of God in their own reflecting pool of consciousness.

Has it not been said, "Behold, the heaven is my throne and the earth is my footstool"? Then, beloved ones, the kingdoms of this world are the footstool kingdoms of God's own Sons (Suns)—of the shining ones, those who entertain, and contain, God's consciousness in their awareness of Self.

And those of you who would recognize the true forte of Divine Being will recognize that all historical ideas are not the ideas of God. Historical ideas and the epochs of history are far too frequently woven into a pattern of light and shadow because mankind have woven in the shadow and God has woven in the light. But extrapolating from all of this, we find emerging upon the whole tapestry of life an epoch of victory. For man, as he began to rise long ago, continues in a certain mark of progress.

But the greatest souls have too frequently, by some counts, like cream, been skimmed off from the milk and been elevated to the table of the Lord through the ritual of the ascension. This has left mankind and the children of the Sun evolving here upon this earth with less and less highly evolved beings in embodiment, whereas the requirement of the great law necessitates that the Great White Brotherhood have and hold mystery schools at inner levels throughout the world.

It is through the activities of these schools and their embodied representatives that the Ascended Masters and particularly the Lords of the Seven Rays (for it is their specific assignment from the Lords of Karma) may seek out and train chelas in the power of divine magnetization. For thereby some will understand their part in the universal scheme and desire to emulate the ascended beings, finding happiness in pursuing God with all of their heart, their mind, and their being.

Thus you can understand that the Lord hath need of you who are embodied to qualify yourselves as world teachers, that many may be awakened to the path of their own Mighty I AM Presence. For having once seen the Lovely Presence face to face, they shall never again be turned from this dazzling Sun of Being, nor stray from the law and the grace of the Sun (Son) of God to any lesser light.

My lovely Sons (Suns), the Chohans of the Rays, how I love them for what they have done on behalf of mankind! In appreciation of their devotion I would this day direct your attention to them one and all. For the Holy Spirit functioning in them has enabled them to perform works of meritorious service.

Go thou and do likewise, and you will be a true disciple of the Holy Spirit no matter which ray you may function upon. For the rainbow of God, the rainbow of divine promise given to Noah long ago, refers to the promise of God, which, like a rainbow, arches over the illusions reflected in the pool of consciousness and fulfills the promise of Christhood to every child of God who elects to embody the light (Christ consciousness) of the seven rays.

And the promises of God are of heavenly substance—radiant, glorious, and wonderful. You will find these colors in the causal body of your own God-identity. Those who, as Christ directed, shall lay up for themselves treasures in heaven by depositing within their causal body the virtue which they have externalized by reason of the playing of the Holy Spirit upon the heartstrings of their being will be those who shall shine as the sun in its splendor in the kingdom of my Father, exemplifying the Christ-identity of all.

The Father, the Son, and the Holy Spirit, then, in one triune shining in the threefold flame within the heart of child-man, will be externalized in action and all lesser images will fade away in the fullness of the Divine Identity. Unless this occur within the individual, there is a mere transfer of a human personality from form to form without cognizance of the reason for which a living soul first came into being and received from the Holy Ghost the breath of Life.

Inasmuch as the chelas of this path do not elect to experience unnecessary suffering or to see such suffering delivered upon the race, I am sure you will aspire to do the things which I advocate you do—to be a comforting presence to Life but, above all, to receive the ministration of our comfort in order that you may take your comfort in your Divine Identity, that you may hide within the folds of the Masters' garments and then be unafraid to emerge therefrom in the arena of life to serve our cause, knowing that in the hour you are called, you shall be clothed with the Holy Spirit. And at that hour, it shall be given to you what you should speak and what you should do.

God in his omnipresence enfold thee now one and all in a mantle of the Holy Spirit until, in the splendor of His eternal shining, you, too, are one as I AM with the Person of the Holy Spirit in action—free from all vestiges of outer world shadow.

So be it in God's holy name. In memory of the Christed accomplishment of the saints of past ages, I say, May the love and light of Whitsuntide, may the love and light of Pentecost, descend upon your hearts this day and be a cherished part of your pageant of life through all the years that are to come.

Thank you and good afternoon.

July 2, 1963
Washington, D.C.

THE MAHA CHOHAN
"THE GREAT LORD"

If You Love the Chohans...

...If you truly love the Lords of the Seven Rays, their message and their vision for the age, realize that the most important feat you can perform for each Chohan is, so to speak, to become that Chohan in embodiment. Start with one or the other and embody his virtue, his drive, his vision, his wisdom; and begin to walk about knowing that you are in training for some holy office after your ascension.

One day, some of you will be Chohans representing one of the seven rays of this or other planetary systems. One day, you must serve in the courts of the sacred fire. What office are you training for? Whose mantle do you seek? Define it, and then refine it in your world. Become that one and affirm, for example: I AM the living embodiment of Hilarion where I AM. Hilarion, come now and equip me and fit me for cosmic service with your legions!

Beloved ones, you may major in many fields of

study under many Masters. For this, after all, is the Aquarian age. And therefore, if you sign up with one, I can assure you that that one will not be chagrined if you sign up with several others and therefore develop a capacity and a certain ability in areas that will be needed as you face the multitudes.

I encourage you, therefore, by these words, to have a more definite conception of your Divinity and your walk and of where you are going. Some Christians say, as they make their decisions in life, "What would Jesus do?" You may say, "What would Saint Germain do? What would El Morya do?"—and study the whole body of that one's teaching, dedicating yourself to its publishing so that all the world might also expand that particular flame of that wondrous Master.

You are so needed by the Chohans, for theirs is a mission to bring the level of the entire race to a new dimension of consciousness, which is Christhood on the Path of the Seven Rays.

Many upon earth cannot identify with the walk of Jesus Christ. Therefore, let them learn of Saint Germain. Let them know they can win the crown of knighthood by following the Seventh Ray Master. Teach them of his expertise in alchemy and that they may stand to guard the bastions of freedom anywhere and everywhere in whatever field of service, in education itself, and win the laurel of the ascension flame and mantle—the basic teaching we go back to because some have not heard it.

Let people see in you the face of Paul the Venetian.

Let them see the divine art in your life, even if you do not become an artist. Let them see art and beauty and grace and the science which this Master holds. Let them know the meaning of the Apostle Paul. Let them understand Nada who has served as Lord of the Sixth Ray. Let them understand justice. Let them understand Serapis.

And then bring all together and let them know what is the power of the Holy Spirit, what is the Maha Chohan. For I would have you walk the earth in my mantle, but my mantle is seven coats of colors become the white light. If you desire it, pursue, then, those seven virtues and seven rays. And when they come into balance, you will find yourself altogether comfortable in my presence. Wearing my garment will no longer be a burden but a joy of light.

One by one, become the embodied Chohan. This is my message of Pentecost. And do it with the fortification of community, of family, of the united twin flame, and of the vision that the remnant of Israel is come to be a sign to the whole nation and the nations!

They are an ensign to the whole people of earth—and their sign is the name I AM, their sign is the light of the eye and the heart, their sign is working the works of God, their sign is accomplishment, and their sign is *Love*. And love in their heart carries every other virtue and every other point of God-mastery.

Love in the hearts of my chelas fills in the absences, the crevices and the cracks in another's life. Love makes up the difference and offers coequality to another who may in truth not be equal in attainment. Remember, *noblesse oblige*. Thus, the nobility, they who have the threefold flame, oblige. And those who have the mantle of the noble One, the Christ, are obliged (obligated) to share the mantle and, by holding out the hand of Christ, save a brother from the raging sea of world turmoil and personal karma.

Understand the call unto the meek: "Blessed are the meek, for they shall inherit the earth." And this word was used by the Holy Spirit in Jesus to describe, by contrast, the children of light who must face the proud, the haughty, the loud talkers, the accuser of the brethren, and the condemners of the people; whereas the meek are those who bring an empty bowl to be filled.

They have nothing to say, for the LORD will speak. The LORD will come into their midst and give his Word. Therefore, their meekness is the silence of the Buddha that is the magnet of the Great Central Sun.

Ye are the inheritors of dominion in the earth, in the water, in the fire, in the air. Ye are the inheritors of dominion of the four quadrants. You inherit the earth only as you subdue the four lower bodies—'beating' them into a mighty chalice of gold that becomes the vessel.

I AM the Maha Chohan for the purveyance of light, for the infilling of the Messenger once again that you also might be filled, that a living fountain of Love might then spring forth and distribute the waters of eternal Life unto the waiting chalices. And each waiting chalice that is filled becomes a new center of a new sun—and finally the fountain of the I AM Presence becoming once again the center of all and each one, delivering abundantly to other cups held out for the water of Life.

Give it freely, beloved hearts....

In the fullness of joy, I AM come. Therefore, understand that the only veil that shall hang in the temple is the veil that you construct as the scales upon your eyes, veils of illusion and selfishness. But God himself would have you know Christ face-to-face, even your own Christ Self whose messenger I AM.

I AM the Maha Chohan. I AM the bearer of the fire of the Ancient of Days. And I AM in the earth the Dispenser of the Cosmic Fire.

Approach your God. When you find him, you will find me in the fullness of his glory.

May 22, 1983
Los Angeles

SIC TRANSIT GLORIA MUNDI

Your Own Past Lives and Performances through the Cosmic Mirror

Sic transit gloria mundi. Thus passes the glory of the world. Enter the glory of the next.

As we have learned from the gnosis of wisdom gleaned by the Lords of the Seven Rays and the Great Lord in their combined experiences on earth and in heaven—through past lives and beyond as they have marked the cycles of putting on the garment of the Lord (i.e., his Cosmic Consciousness), charted since the hour of their ascension, so we can also learn from the victories and setbacks of our own past lives and the present circumstances of karmic destiny in which we find ourselves.

Concerning our Messengership and the training and the mantle bestowed whereby we have received through the Holy Ghost the foregoing dictations (in the communion of saints, "as Above, so below"), Jesus told us that he had brought us together as twin flames for our mission in publishing abroad the Everlasting Gospel— to tell the world of his Word and Work (under the New Covenant of the Aquarian age) as time and again we had preached the message of salvation in Christ in previous embodiments, sometimes together and sometimes apart.

The Lord told us the way wouldn't be easy but he said that in the end the light would prevail and eventually his true Teachings, lost and found again, would cover the earth—but not until we had borne some hardships of personal and planetary karma. He spoke of the trials and persecutions that follow the disciple up the mountain until their ghosts, weary of the ascent, fall by the wayside—just so many fetters that cannot cling.

And in a rare moment Jesus looked into our eyes and told us that depending on the response of the light-bearers to Saint Germain's dispensation of the violet flame and the timing of the karmic cycles, earth changes would possibly come to pass before his full glory would be (or could be) universally taught and accepted. "But," the Beloved said, "fear not, I will be with you in the place I have prepared."

The Master revealed to each of us separately through the mirror of his consciousness scenes of our association with him—myself as John Mark, the scribe and author of the second Gospel, sometime companion of both Peter and Paul. He showed me that I had learned from Peter's own lips some of the personal anecdotes—

tales told on Peter by himself—which gave that Gospel details on the impetuous one drawn from the more human side of his life.

To Elizabeth he gave the recollection of herself as Martha, attentive to his needs, preparing his meals and a comfortable home at Bethany. The Master showed her scenes where he had instructed Mary, Lazarus, herself, and the inner circle in the secrets and rituals of advancing Christic initiation.

You will recall that Martha was the one who professed her belief in Jesus as the Incarnate Word: "Yea, Lord: I believe that thou art the Christ, the Son of God, which should come into the world."

This statement came from direct knowledge and the inner knowing of the personal Christ which Jesus imparted to those who were able to receive it: to those he knew would not tumble headlong into the Devil's trap of the idolatry of the Master's person or their own— or both. Thus he taught us that to the carnally minded the knowledge of the mysteries without the keys of discipleship and initiation under the Cosmic Christ is *a most dangerous thing.*

And we remembered his counsel: "Give not that which is holy unto the dogs, neither cast ye your pearls before swine, lest they trample them under their feet, and turn again and rend you."

By and by, each on our own, we confirmed our past lives and one another's—happily announcing to each other: "Do you know who you were at the time of Jesus?"

and the reply was the same, "Yes, I do. Do you know who *you* were?"

Once in a dictation through me Jesus announced: "I spake long ago unto Martha and I said unto her, 'Mary has chosen the better part.' Today your beloved Messenger Elizabeth, who is the reembodiment of Martha, is with you, now choosing the better part and to render her service in this day."

The Master's comforting flame of forgiveness made her eyes burn with tears of gratitude as she remembered the chastisement of her Lord. And as I felt his love flood her heart, she seated at my side on the platform, I too knew the grace and mercy of my Saviour.

Jesus' subsequent revelation to us that Martha's sister, Mary, had reincarnated in the late nineteenth century as Mary Baker Eddy explained Elizabeth's childhood devotion to Christian Science, as she had found in Mrs. Eddy's writings "footsteps of Truth" and the thread of contact that reestablished the outer tie with Jesus' heart and message.

Such moments as these when we find ourselves caught up in the heart of Jesus are truly intervals of eternity when the world stands still and only Jesus is real, filling the earth and sea and sky of our interior castle with his loving, masterful Presence.

Later the Master revealed to us that we had kept his flame within the Church in later centuries, I as Origen of Alexandria and Saint Bonaventure, messenger of his Eternal Mind, she as Saint Clare and Saint Catherine of Siena, messenger of his Sacred Heart.

Just so, you, too, at a certain point in your spiritual awakening and chelaship under one or more of the Lords of the Seven Rays, may have revealed to you your past embodiments. This may take place in Saint Germain's retreat in the Rocky Mountains called the Cave of Symbols, at the Grand Teton or Darjeeling, as we shall soon see, or in another retreat of the Great White Brotherhood.

When you have sufficiently prepared yourself for a psychological probe of past circumstances effecting current events in your life, the Master will lead you before the Cosmic Mirror in the Royal Teton Retreat. At first glance it looks like an ordinary motion picture screen. The Master selects certain records taken from akasha which are also contained in the memory of the soul, and upon the Cosmic Mirror they come alive.

This is beyond 3-D—you are there! A portion of a past life, or more than one, passes before you, but you are a living part of this nonfiction play of light and darkness with shades of grey. It is almost too much to handle. Instantly you are aware, as in an orb of all-knowingness, of the ramifications of your karma even as you relive the emotions, the premeditated thoughts and the acts themselves.

This could be a most painful experience, you tell yourself, all the while sensing your Higher Consciousness (your Holy Christ Self) standing guard and telling you gently but firmly not to give way to extremes of despondency or ecstasy, but to face the future with a hope based on the scientific knowledge that in your hands, by the grace of the Holy Spirit, lies the power to change.

Thus, a few segments a session are given, and you soon see the wisdom of the Law that requires adjustment through your application of the violet flame to those scenes and memories until balance is restored. You appreciate as never before that starry Mother, beloved Astrea. And you can't wait to give her 10.14 decree that invokes the circle and sword of blue flame of the Universal Mother (known in the East as Kali) in, through and around the cause and core of every binding, blinding record.

And you know *and* see that you've got work to do. And you know that you are going to work harder than you have ever worked before—to slay the "dweller on the threshold" of your synthetic self that you just saw and felt strutting around on (in) that Mirror. You look forward to establishing a new equilibrium by mastering the very circumstances you've just relived.

And so the Master tells you to go back to the scene of the crime—go back to your physical body where your physical karma was made and work things out by Divine Love and the violet flame. When the necessary clearance of the astral and mental bodies is accomplished, Saint Germain says you will be ready for the next session of therapy—the Ascended Master way.

"This process is accelerated," he explains, "through

the curriculum of the universities of the Spirit conducted by the Lords of the Seven Rays at their etheric retreats and it is fully anchored in the physical through intensives conducted by the Messengers at Summit University on the Royal Teton Ranch."

Beloved El Morya gives his chelas a similar initiation in Darjeeling. You remember his description in his letters to the chela on the Path:

"It is time to enter the chamber designed with blue and gold motif where there is a screen and seats arranged in theater style. For to understand your path, your very personal path to salvation, you must have the perspective of your past and how you have created the present—both at personal and planetary levels. Come, then, and let us see how we shall, in the magic of the flame, discover the designs of your soul destiny…. Now scenes of life in ancient Thrace appear on the screen, and we find ourselves in the marketplace of a forgotten city in the land that is now Turkey…."

Thus unfolds a most intriguing tale—a scene of the pathos of an ancient karma come full circle in the lives of the viewers, to whom the Master also revealed the efficacy of the violet flame which they observed clearing the records on the screen right before their eyes. With such a profound insight as to the outworking of cosmic law, Morya's students return to their physical body consciousness determined to "make things right"—and you do too.

For the Lord of the First Ray promises: "The lessons

learned by the soul out of the body during sleep are not lost but become a part of the composite of subconscious self-awareness, surfacing just enough to prick the soul memory and prod it to decisive action."

Indeed, the quickening of the outer mind to this inner soul experience, once it has returned to waking consciousness and the five senses, is accomplished adroitly by the Master M. through the associative technique, or the arrangement of uncanny circumstances that loose the soul memory, sometimes in a torrent of emotions, as major turning points in her evolution and karma are relived—and then relieved through the violet flame.

Sic transit gloria mundi. Thus passes the record of the karma of this world. Enter the glory of the Divine Plan.

Once again you stand before the Cosmic Mirror inside the Grand Teton, expectant yet not knowing what to expect! This time Saint Germain shows you the original blueprint of your divine plan that was imprinted upon your etheric body when you were conceived in the heart of God. Thus, you learn another reason for reviewing your past lives one by one: it is to determine what portion of that plan you have outpictured to date and what portion you have not.

Now you can literally see and hear and feel (yes, and taste and smell!) the conditions in your little world that you have to correct—and there's no question about it: it's got to be done!

Thank God for the Cosmic Mirror!

Thank God for the violet flame!

There they go: the good momentums you've developed over lifetimes, the hang-ups and knotty problems of the past and present. And by your pluses you cancel out your minuses. You really believe and you *are* determined to fulfill that divine plan with your twin flame, very soon—as the history of the soul is reckoned.

What's more, Saint Germain tells you that "you can call forth the talents you have developed in past ages, for these are stored as treasure in your causal body. With these you can elevate and bless and heal in the name of the Christ of Jesus and of your own I AM Presence, endowing many with your past momentums of fruitful activity."

But, what is most amazing is Saint Germain's assurance that "the manifestation of these gifts is not dependent upon the recall of your outer memory!"

"However," he cautions, "it is subject to the law of karma and what you the individual son of God will do (in accord with the gifts of the threefold flame and free will) with your spiritual resources once they are made available to you."

And if before taking your leave of the Royal Teton you ask him for his advice on what is the next step on the path for one eager to study directly under the Lords of the Seven Rays, Saint Germain will invite you to a retreat which you can attend in your full, waking consciousness at the Royal Teton Ranch.

"Here a great deal of what you will be taking up in the universities of the Spirit at the Chohans' etheric retreats will be focused for your immediate study and application to life," he says. "For Summit University, under the trusted and capable direction of our Messengers—Mark ascended, Elizabeth unascended—is there to bridge the gap from the inner to the outer so that you can be gaining the benefit of your out-of-the-body experiences by putting into practice what you are learning at inner levels even before you have the mastery to entirely recall your soul's nightly tutoring and initiations in the higher octaves."

"Not only does Summit University afford you the best of both worlds," Saint Germain explains, "but it offers you the best of all possible worlds, for it presents the outer limits of what it is spiritually lawful for souls evolving on planet Earth to achieve—until such time as they master that sphere of possibilities known as the 'bounds of man's habitation' and graduate to the Ascended Master octaves of light.

"The Council of the Royal Teton in session with the Great Lord and the Lords of the Seven Rays under the direction of Lord Gautama with the Lord Jesus Christ has set the curriculum of Summit University (known to initiates as Maitreya's Mystery School). We therefore require our faculty to (1) equip you to deal with the immediate—the net of karmic circumstance in which you find yourself today—through a precise knowledge of Cosmic Law and the application of the

Science of the Spoken Word to specific situations in your life and (2) show you how to derive the greatest benefit from the universities of the Spirit as pertains to your soul's initiations—physical, mental, psychological, and spiritual—and the God-mastery of your immortal spirit on the path of the ascension.

"Putting together these goals alongside of your personal priorities as you have been taught to do through your experience at the Inner Retreat, *you set for yourself* a course for the mastery of self in time and space and for the balancing of your karma, all the while meeting family, career and community responsibilities, including the economic necessities of life, on behalf of those entrusted to your care.

"The Lords of the Seven Rays are there to guide you in life's sacred adventure so that upon entering a higher walk with God and unbroken communion with the entire Spirit of the Great White Brotherhood (the angelic hosts and saints robed in white) you are conscious of your heavenly friends of light at your side as you drink life's cup to the fullest in your pursuit of giving happiness and the abundant life to all."

To assist you in this glorious challenge that is the "mighty work of the ages," Saint Germain eagerly tells you, is his Keepers of the Flame Fraternity, which he founded in order to provide the means and the commitment for an intimate Master-disciple relationship with the Chohans and the Maha Chohan as you receive monthly graded lessons in Cosmic Law to study and cherish, even if you are not able to attend Summit University.

And so, your angel guide escorts you to the elevator of the retreat, which ascends 2,000 feet up to the great bronze doors by which you entered, an unrecorded time ago; passing through the granite slabs that open at the touch of the gatekeeper, Alphas, you are once again on the outside, the ordinary-looking rock face as sphinxlike as ever. Your angel guide whispers, "All good things must come to an end, so that you can have new beginnings…"

It is a cold night air with winds from the north— clear skies and the morning star beckoning from the horizon. The next thing you know you're stretching and stifling a yawn as the first rays of the morning light remind you, intrusively, that you are back in your body. Before fully connecting, you hear yourself saying, "Hey! It's all up to me. I can do anything I want to—with God."

Elated to know there is a way and way out of the human dilemma, you return from this soul journey to the fireside of familiar hearth and home to resume reading about your inner soul experiences as recorded in the *Lost Teachings on Keys to Spiritual Progress*, chapter two, "The Mirror of Consciousness"…

Thank God it's all written down!

NOTES

For the definitions of many of the philosophical and esoteric terms used in *Lords of the Seven Rays*, see the comprehensive glossary, "The Alchemy of the Word: Stones for the Wise Master-builders," in *Saint Germain On Alchemy* published by Summit University Press.

BOOK ONE
Mirror of Consciousness

INTRODUCTION
1. **Embody**. See Elizabeth Clare Prophet, *Lost Teachings on Keys to Spiritual Progress*, p. 295 n. 6.
2. **Nephilim.** [Hebrew "those who fell" or "those who were cast down," from the Semitic root *nephal* 'to fall']: A biblical race of giants or demigods, referred to in Gen. 6:4; the fallen angels who were cast out of heaven into the earth (Rev. 12:7–9). See Elizabeth Clare Prophet, *Fallen Angels and the Origins of Evil*, pp. 71–76, 295–341; the Great Divine Director, "The Mechanization Concept," in 1965 *Pearls of Wisdom*, vol. 8, nos. 15, 16, pp. 75–89 (in paperback: *The Soulless One: Cloning a Counterfeit Creation*, by Mark L. Prophet, pp. 89–105); Zecharia Sitchin, *The Twelfth Planet*, *The Stairway to Heaven*, and *The Wars of Gods and Men*, published by Avon Books.

Unless otherwise noted, books and audio recordings listed in these notes are published by Summit University Press.

BOOK 1 • CHAPTER ONE

EL MORYA

1. **Mogul.** An Indian Muslim of or descended from one of several conquering groups of Mongol, Turkish, and Persian origin; especially the sovereign of the empire founded in India by the Moguls in the 16th century.

2. Percival Spear, *India: A Modern History* (Ann Arbor, Mich.: University of Michigan Press, 1961), p. 129.

3. Ashirbadi Lal Srivastava, *Akbar the Great—Vol. I: Political History, 1542–1605 A.D.* (Agra: Shiva Lal Agarwala & Co., 1962), p. 491.

4. Ibid., p. 399.

5. Ibid., p. 503.

6. Ibid., p. 507.

7. Pringle Kennedy, *History of the Great Moghuls* (Calcutta: Thacker Spink & Co., 1933), pp. 297–98.

8. Srivastava, *Akbar the Great*, p. 303.

9. Kennedy, *History of the Great Moghuls*, p. 299.

10. Srivastava, *Akbar the Great*, p. 306.

11. *Encyclopedia of Religion and Ethics*, ed. James Hastings (Edinburgh: T. & T. Clark, 1908), 1:271.

12. Alfred Tennyson, "The Passing of Arthur," in *Idylls of the King* (New York: New American Library, 1961), pp. 251–52.

13. *Lives of Saints with Excerpts from Their Writings* (New York: John J. Crawley & Co., 1954), pp. 311–24; *Lives of the Saints* (New York: Catholic Book Publishing Co., 1974), pp. 248–49.

BOOK 1 • CHAPTER TWO

LORD LANTO

1. **Watchers.** Refers to those who fell through inordinate lust for the daughters of men (Gen. 6:4). See p. 555, Introduction, n. 2.

BOOK 1 • CHAPTER FOUR
SERAPIS BEY

1. Herodotus, *History* 7.225 (trans. George Rawlinson, pp. 151–52).

2. R. A. Schwaller de Lubicz, *The Temple in Man: Sacred Architecture and the Perfect Man*, trans. Robert and Deborah Lawlor (New York: Inner Traditions International, 1977), p. 24.

BOOK 1 • CHAPTER SEVEN
SAINT GERMAIN

1. See Godfré Ray King, *Unveiled Mysteries*, 3d ed. (Chicago: Saint Germain Press, 1939), pp. 39–61.

2. Thomas Whittaker, *The Neo-Platonists: A Study in the History of Hellenism*, 2d ed. (Cambridge: Cambridge University Press, 1928), p. 165.

3. Victor Cousin and Thomas Taylor, trans., *Two Treatises of Proclus, The Platonic Successor* (London: n.p., 1833), p. vi.

4. Geoffrey of Monmouth, *Vita Merlini*, in Nikolai Tolstoy, *The Quest for Merlin* (Boston: Little, Brown & Co., 1985), p. 217.

5. Brendan LeHane et al., *The Enchanted World: Wizards and Witches* (Chicago: Time-Life Books, 1984), p. 34.

6. Sir Thomas Malory understood that King Arthur had at least two sisters. One Margawse married King Loth and bore him four sons, the oldest of whom was Gawain. She or another sister, alleges Malory, bore Modred to King Arthur. (Norma Lorre Goodrich, *King Arthur* [New York: Franklin Watts, 1986], p. 221.)

7. Henry Thomas and Dana Lee Thomas, *Living Biographies of Great Scientists* (Garden City, N.Y.: Nelson Doubleday, 1941), p. 15.

8. Ibid., p. 16.

9. Ibid., p. 17; David Wallechinsky, Amy Wallace, and Irving

Wallace, *The Book of Predictions* (New York: William Morrow and Co., 1980), p. 346.

10. Thomas, *Living Biographies*, p. 20.

11. Wallechinsky and Wallace, *Book of Predictions*, p. 346.

12. Clements R. Markham, *Life of Christopher Columbus* (London: George Philip & Son, 1892), pp. 207–8.

13. *Encyclopaedia Britannica*, 15th ed., s.v. "Columbus, Christopher."

14. **Bacon's ciphers:** Francis Bacon's word-cipher was discovered by cryptographer Dr. Orville W. Owen, who published five volumes of *Sir Francis Bacon's Cipher Story* between 1893 and 1895. The story hidden in his word-cipher can be constructed by stringing together words, lines, and passages from the works of various Elizabethan writers. In contrast, deciphering the bi-literal cipher is an exact, scientific process of grouping together the italic letters (printed in two different fonts of type) that appear with peculiar frequency in original editions of the Shakespearean plays and other of Bacon's works. This cipher was discovered by an assistant of Dr. Owen, Mrs. Elizabeth Wells Gallup, who first published the stories Bacon had concealed in his bi-literal cipher in 1899. To insure that his ciphers would eventually be discovered and his true life story revealed, Bacon had described in detail the bi-literal method of cipher writing in his Latin version of *De Augmentis* (1624), which some 270 years later Mrs. Gallup studied and applied. Ironically, Mrs. Gallup found that Bacon's bi-literal cipher contained complete directions on how to construct the word-cipher, which was actually discovered first by Dr. Owen. See Virginia Fellows, *The Shakespeare Code* (Gardiner, Mont.: Snow Mountain Press, 2006).

15. Will Durant, *The Story of Philosophy: The Lives and Opinions of the Greater Philosophers* (Garden City, N.Y.: Garden City Publishing Co., 1927), p. 157.

16. The information detailed in the following paragraphs is taken from Margaret Barsi-Greene, comp., *I, Prince Tudor, Wrote Shakespeare* (Boston: Branden Press, 1973), pp. 56–75, and Alfred Dodd, *The Martyrdom of Francis Bacon* (New York: Rider & Co., n.d.), p. 25. See also Virginia M. Fellows, *The Shakespeare Code* (Gardiner, Mont.: Snow Mountain Press, 2006).

17. Barsi-Greene, *I, Prince Tudor*, p. 217.

18. Ibid., pp. 219–20.

19. Ibid., pp. 239, 243.

20. Grace A. Fendler, *New Truths About Columbus* (London: L. N. Fowler & Co., 1934), p. 26.

BOOK TWO

Dictations of the Lords of the Seven Rays

BOOK 2 • CHAPTER ONE

EL MORYA

Message to America on the Mission of Jesus Christ

1. See p. 309.

2. See Elizabeth Clare Prophet, *The Lost Years of Jesus.*

3. In the first century B.C., El Morya was embodied as Melchior, one of the three wise men.

4. See Taylor Caldwell, *The Romance of Atlantis* (New York: William Morrow & Co., 1975).

5. Serapis Bey, 1967 *Pearls of Wisdom*, vol. 10, no. 16; "The Banner of Humility," in *Dossier on the Ascension*, p. 33.

6. Matt. 17: 1–3; Acts of John 90–91; Apocalypse of Peter 4–20 (Akhmim fragment). See M. R. James, trans., *Apocryphal New Testament* (London: Oxford University Press, 1924), pp. 251–52, 518–19.

BOOK 2 · CHAPTER TWO
LORD LANTO

Possibilities in New Dimensions

1. Following the Communist takeover of China (1949), Tibet (1950), Vietnam (North, 1954; South, 1975), Cambodia (1975), and Laos (1975), many Buddhist shrines were leveled and their statuary destroyed. No official protest for **desecration of religious shrines** was issued by the U.S. government or other free nations.

BOOK 2 · CHAPTER THREE
PAUL THE VENETIAN

The Beauty and Truth of Love

1. See *The Living Flame of Love* in *The Collected Works of St. John of the Cross*, trans. Kieran Kavanaugh and Otilio Rodriguez (Washington, D.C.: ICS Publications, 1973), pp. 569–649; *Saint John of the Cross on the Living Flame of Love*, Summit University Lecture Series for Ministering Servants taught by Mark L. Prophet and Elizabeth Clare Prophet, on CD.

BOOK 2 · CHAPTER FOUR
SERAPIS BEY

The Path of the Ascension Is the Path of Love

1. The science of the **Cosmic Clock,** taught by Mother Mary to the Messenger Elizabeth Clare Prophet, provides the scientific means of understanding and charting the cycles of personal and planetary psychology and karma that return to us daily as the tests and trials of life. See Elizabeth Clare Prophet, *Predict Your Future: Understand the Cycles of the Cosmic Clock;* "The Cosmic Clock: Psychology for the Aquarian Man and Woman," in *The Great White Brotherhood in the Culture, History, and Religion of America*, pp.

173–206; *The ABC's of Your Psychology on the Cosmic Clock,* on CD.

2. For teaching on the **Nature spirits,** see Mark L. Prophet and Elizabeth Clare Prophet, *The Path of the Higher Self,* first volume in the Climb the Highest Mountain series, pp. 371–93; Jesus and Kuthumi, *Corona Class Lessons,* pp. 371–76; and Elizabeth Clare Prophet, *Is Mother Nature Mad? How to Work with Nature Spirits to Mitigate Natural Disasters.*

BOOK 2 • CHAPTER SEVEN
SAINT GERMAIN
 "May You Pass Every Test!"

1. Matt. 10:33; Luke 12:9.

Picture Credits

Page 24: *The Emperors Akbar, Jahangir and Shah Jahan with Khan A'zam, I'timad Al-dawlah and Asaf Khan*, detail, Bichitr. Reproduced by kind permission of the Trustees of the Chester Beatty Library, Dublin; **29:** By kind permission of the Trustees of the Chester Beatty Library, Dublin; **43:** Detail, copyright The Frick Collection, New York; **52:** Joanneum Museum, Graz; **78:** By kind permission of the Theosophical Publishing House; **110:** J. Paul Getty Museum, California; **120, 130:** National Gallery of Art, Washington, D.C.; **143:** Courtesy of the Brooklyn Museum; **144:** Hirmer Foto Archiv, Munich; **148:** Egyptian Museum, Cairo; **171:** Concession by the Basilica of St. Paul the Patriarch; **205:** By permission of Stanford University, California; **229:** Herzog Anton Ulrich-Museums, Brunswick; **232:** Bettman Archive; **235:** The National Museum of Wales; **239:** From *Living Biographies of Great Scientists* by Henry Thomas and Dana Lee Thomas. Copyright 1941, 1951 by Doubleday, a division of Bantam Doubleday Dell Publishing Group, Inc. Used by permission of Doubleday, a division of Bantam Doubleday Dell Publishing Group, Inc.; **292:** J. Burlington Smith; **322:** *A Discussion of Painting Beneath the Pines*, detail, Chou Ying, Jilin Provincial Museum, China; **334, 335:** Collection of the National Palace Museum, Taiwan, Republic of China; **386:** Hirmer Foto Archiv, Munich; **388:** Detail, Norman Thomas Miller; **418:** Leonard von Matt; **420:** Concession by the Basilica of St. Paul the Patriarch; **492:** Eastfoto; **494:** Charles Sindelar.

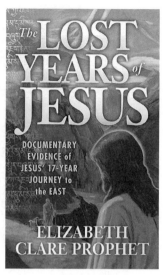

480 PAGES
ISBN 978-0-916766-87-0

The Lost Years of Jesus

Documentary Evidence of Jesus'
17-Year Journey to the East

Ancient texts reveal that Jesus spent 17 years in the Orient.
They say that from age 13 to age 29, he traveled to India,
Nepal, Ladakh and Tibet as both student and teacher. For the
first time, Elizabeth Clare Prophet brings together the testimony of four eyewitnesses, and three variant translations, of
these remarkable documents. Now you can read for yourself
what Jesus said and did prior to his Palestinian mission.
It's one of the most revolutionary messages of our time.

Fallen Angels and the Origins of Evil

Why Church Fathers Suppressed the Book of Enoch and Its Startling Revelations

by Elizabeth Clare Prophet

Did rebel angels take on human bodies to fulfill their lust for the "daughters of men"?

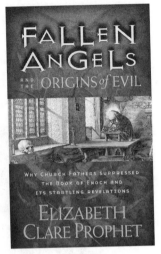

524 PAGES
ISBN: 978-0-922729-43-2

Did these fallen angels teach men to build weapons of war?

That is the premise of the Book of Enoch, a text cherished by the Essenes, early Jews and Christians, but later condemned by both rabbis and Church Fathers. The book was denounced, banned and "lost" for over a thousand years—until in 1773 a Scottish explorer discovered three copies in Ethiopia.

Elizabeth Clare Prophet examines the controversy surrounding this book and sheds new light on Enoch's forbidden mysteries. She demonstrates that Jesus and the apostles studied the book and tells why Church Fathers suppressed its teaching that angels could incarnate in human bodies.

Fallen Angels and the Origins of Evil takes you back to the primordial drama of Good and Evil, when the first hint of corruption entered a pristine world—earth.

Contains Richard Laurence's translation of the Book of Enoch, all the other Enoch texts (including the Book of the Secrets of Enoch), and biblical parallels. 12 illustrations.